Neolithic Mortuary Practices in Greece

Kent D. Fowler

BAR International Series 1314
2004

Published in 2016 by
BAR Publishing, Oxford

BAR International Series 1314

Neolithic Mortuary Practices in Greece

ISBN 9781841716633 paperback
ISBN 9781407327402 e-format
DOI https://doi.org/10.30861/9781841716633
A catalogue record for this book is available from the British Library

BAR Publishing is the trading name of British Archaeological Reports (Oxford) Ltd.
British Archaeological Reports was first incorporated in 1974 to publish the BAR
Series, International and British. In 1992 Hadrian Books Ltd became part of the BAR
group. This volume was originally published by Archaeopress in conjunction with
British Archaeological Reports (Oxford) Ltd / Hadrian Books Ltd, the Series principal
publisher, in 2004. This present volume is published by BAR Publishing, 2016.

BAR

PUBLISHING

BAR titles are available from:

BAR Publishing
122 Banbury Rd, Oxford, OX2 7BP, UK
EMAIL   info@barpublishing.com
PHONE   +44 (0)1865 310431
FAX   +44 (0)1865 316916
www.barpublishing.com

TABLE OF CONTENTS

LIST OF TABLES

LIST OF FIGURES

PREFACE

This book originated as a Master's thesis project aimed at applying the theory and methods developed in the study of mortuary remains by Americanist archaeologists to the earliest farming societies of continental Europe—those of modern-day mainland Greece. Historically, such research has predominantly focused on seeking out the social dimensions of life that influenced mortuary behaviour. After completing that project, which attempted to discern the origins of social ranking during the Neolithic, I began to think about how death is wrapped up in so much more than the social standing of the deceased. Thus, began my search to see how archaeologists may be able to detect the many dimensions of life influencing the disposal of the dead. This book is the result.

I have very many people to thank for their contributions to this project. Haskel Greenfield, Christopher Meiklejohn, and Lea Sterling spend considerable time and effort helping me through earlier drafts of the monograph. Their support has continued since that first effort began to bring the mortuary data of the Neolithic in Greece together. I must also extend special thanks to Tracey Cullen for her help in guiding me through the Franchthi Cave material; Jack Davis and John Cherry who heeded my erratic correspondence for references and guidance; and to Michael Cosmopoulos for first introducing me to the richness of Greek prehistory through his entertaining lectures and the fieldwork I was fortunate enough to participate in under his tutelage.

My family has been a continuous source of support in my pursuit of this study, and forever I am in their debt. My wife, Karen, has graciously put up with years of 'thesis widowhood' through my graduate work, taken care of me throughout the development and writing of this work, listened to all of my musings about these dead people. It is a gross understatement to say that this research would never have been completed without her.

Calgary

12 July, 2004

viii

CHAPTER 1
INTRODUCTION

Life is full of riddles that only the dead can answer.
Ben Okri, *The Famished Road*

This book is about mortuary ritual during the Neolithic in Greece. It is foremost about people's reactions to death and the deceased and the principles that motivate the disposal of the dead. The ways we respond to death are remarkable in their variety. But never is it 'a random reaction; always it is meaningful and expressive' (Huntington and Metcalf 1979: 1). All cultures have a set of prescribed or customary (ritual) behaviour considered acceptable for disposing the dead. As with all ritual practices, mortuary rites involve a series of acts played out in reaction to past, present, and even future worldly events, which are wrapped-up in worldly and other-worldly concerns. The influences on ritual practice are multiple and overlapping. Different physical, circumstantial, social, and philosophical-religious factors condition or influence the form of mortuary ritual (Carr 1995). Most ritualised reactions to death occur in social settings that directly or indirectly reinforce a peoples' philosophy of the universe (cosmology), beliefs about the supernatural (religion), and promote a shared body of social doctrine (ideology) (for definitions see Flannery and Marcus 1993). It is therefore possible to find both social and philosophical-religious functions in a single act of ritual.

For these reasons, I find great heuristic potential in distinguishing between *ritual practices*, or ritual action in the world, from *ritual motivations*, the different physical, circumstantial, social, and philosophical-religious concerns driving the practices. In the study of the past, it is the task of the archaeologist to infer motivations of ritual from the material traces of their practice. I am concerned in this book not only with how archaeologists have and can infer the motivations underlying the practice of mortuary ritual, but also how this knowledge may provide an alternative interpretive framework to understand the organising principles of Neolithic societies in Greece.

Mortuary remains have always been a key data set used to understand European Neolithic lifeways (Champion et al. 1984; Chapman and Randsborg 1981; Whittle 1996). In Greece, however, mortuary remains dating to both the Mesolithic and subsequent Neolithic are rare and infrequent finds (Jacobsen and Cullen 1981). Many burials are isolated finds, and even when several burials can be associated together, intrusive deposits from later periods have often severely damaged the primary context of these remains. In cases when human remains occur in a settlement, a cemetery, or an ossuary, disposal of the dead seems to have been infrequent and unelaborated (Cullen and Talalay 1995).

The quality and quantity of mortuary data from sites in mainland and insular Greece is a result of three main factors. First, the frequency of excavations has varied by region and this has limited the identification of burials to certain intensively studied areas of the mainland and Aegean islands. Second, earlier investigators did not recognise the spatial distinction between areas used for the disposal of the dead and the settlement (or occupation area). In some instances, individual burials or discrete disposal areas (with multiple burials) are spatially segregated from open-air settlements, or are restricted to uninhabited areas of caves. Excavations since the 1970s have purposefully attempted to locate Neolithic disposal areas using numerous methods: survey, by executing test trenches around settlements, initiating salvage excavations of burial areas revealed by modern construction, and more recently by undertaking large-scale excavations of well preserved settlements and outlying areas (e.g., Andreou et al. 1996; Demoule and Perlès 1993; French 1972; Cherry et al. 1988; Gallis 1982, 1989; Pappa and Besios 1999a, 1999b; Sampson 1992, 1993).

Lastly, the size and scale of the Greek Neolithic disposal areas are not only a result of excavation and recovery strategies, but are also a likely reflection of the size of associated settlements and the duration of their habitation. Despite large-scale excavation of several Neolithic burial grounds, it appears that most were small (Jacobsen and Cullen 1981). Even the most conservative rendering of radiocarbon dates from the habitation areas associated with these remains suggests single occupation levels did not extend beyond several centuries (Demoule and Perlès 1993). The occupation of many Neolithic sites represent a palimpsest of redundant, but not consecutive habitation, and many settlements and caves may have only been used seasonally (e.g., Demoule and Perlès 1993; Jacobsen 1984b; Pappa and Besios 1999a, 1999b; Sampson 1992, 1993). Because of different sampling strategies, recovery techniques, and research questions, mortuary data from the Neolithic period in Greece remains geographically uneven and conspicuously under-analysed. Thus, there have arisen many misgivings about this record (Jacobsen and Cullen 1981), and mortuary evidence has received only limited consideration in discussions of culture-history and analyses of the socio-economic issues particular to this record (Demoule and Perlès 1993; Halstead 1999b).

Given these constraints, one may fairly contest any attempt to glean something of Neolithic society in Greece based on mortuary data. I contend, however, that it is possible to say something meaningful about these societies using the remains of their mortuary practices if we are mindful of certain theoretical and methodological necessities and the particular limitations and benefits that accompany this record.

An important concern is that mortuary remains and practices, as with all other kinds of human behaviour, must be considered within the cultural-historical milieu in which they occur. It is not possible to make behavioural interpretations solely on the basis of information from cemeteries or isolated graves without information derived from other aspects of the same culture, such as their settlement preferences, subsistence practices, and technology. Fortunately, recent work in various regions on mainland and insular Greece offer some syntheses of the diverse ways Neolithic peoples exploited the variable environments they encountered (e.g., Halstead 1999b). This makes it possible to consider mortuary practices in a different light than was possible over two decades ago, when Jacobsen and Cullen (1981) offered the first anthropologically informed study of Neolithic mortuary behaviour in Greece.

The most debilitating factor affecting the study of mortuary practices during the Neolithic in Greece is the small number of sites available for analysis. To use these cases as illustrative examples for concrete interpretations of social behaviour and definitive claims about Neolithic society in Greece is dangerous. At present, it is only possible to speak in broad terms about diachronic *trends* or *dispositions* in mortuary practices and motivations. While this may appear overly limiting, the study of existing data is still a worthy exercise. More beneficial, however, is that data is available from sites located in the coastal, riverine, and island contexts preferred by farmers during the Neolithic. While the number of sites is few, this does offer us the opportunity to contrast and compare the mortuary practices of different groups in different areas of mainland and insular Greece that exploited different ecological systems during the Neolithic. Equally beneficial is the quality of data from these sites. Most reports contain good information about the characteristics of the body (treatment, position, orientation, and often age and sex), the grave (architectural traits, orientation, location *vis-à-vis* various landmarks such as settlements), the grave contents (kinds, quantities, and arrangements of artefacts and ecofacts), and the disposal area (local or regional location, spatial organisation, artefact distributions). Overall, the sample size limits our ability to investigate in detail synchronic and diachronic patterns

of mortuary ritual during this period, but there remains potential to utilise existing data to answer certain questions about the past.

In this study, I am concerned with five main issues of debate. The first involves different opinions about the variability in mortuary practices. Previous commentators have made contradictory, and sometimes vexing, statements about mortuary variability during the Neolithic in Greece. While some have argued there are no "obvious differences in ritual or funerary deposits" during the period (Demoule and Perlès 1993:396), detailed studies describe substantive differences in the form of mortuary practices during both the Mesolithic (Cullen 1995) and Neolithic (Jacobsen and Cullen 1981). Mortuary variability is important to understand simply because inferences about the range of social and philosophical-religious behaviour expressed through mortuary ritual derive from a basic understanding of material responses to death (O'Shea 1984). Without a clear demonstration of the variability in mortuary remains across time and space it is not possible to infer the natural or cultural processes that contributed towards it. I argue in the ensuing pages for substantive variability in mortuary practices during this period, which can be linked to differences and changes in settlement, subsistence, and the exploitation of ecological niches.

A second debate also pertains to the mortuary record itself, and this surrounds the physical visibility of the dead. Several authors have observed a characteristic absence of monumental of funerary architecture during the Neolithic in Greece (Demoule and Perlès 1993; Jacobsen and Cullen 1981). This has prompted an argument that there was no obvious physical demarcation of places for disposing the dead or individual graves as seen in the subsequent Early Bronze Age (Cosmopoulos 1991, 1995; Dickenson 1994; Doumas 1977). However, there are many ways to demarcate and designate burial places, not all of which are physical (Talalay 1987, 1993). To investigate this possibility, I examine in detail the spatial, temporal, and depositional history of disposal areas to investigate the metaphorical visibility of the dead; that is, whether Neolithic people viewed the "invisibility" of certain forms of disposal as metaphor for the new incarnation of deceased into the "invisible" realm of the ancestors. The theoretical basis for this, and other arguments, is taken up in Chapter 2.

Stemming from issues of mortuary variability and visibility is a third issue regarding the "complexity" of mortuary ritual. Researchers are of the opinion that mortuary remains give little indication for complex disposal practices (e.g., Demoule and Perlès 1993; Gallis 1982) or elaborate mortuary ritual (e.g., Hourmouziadis 1973; Jacobsen and Cullen 1981) during the Neolithic. I have two main points of contention with this conclusion.

The first is the lack of distinction made between the *process* of disposing the dead and the final *product* resulting from it. It remains an empirical question whether a sophisticated disposal "programme" can result in a rather unsophisticated-looking discard of the deceased. I address this possibility in an attempt to reconstruct the steps and stages visible in the mortuary record. My second objection is theoretical, and I seriously question the tacit connections made between the "complexity" or mortuary ritual and the "complexity" of the societies under study. It is, again, an empirical question whether social directives for these Neolithic peoples fundamentally determined the execution and form of mortuary ritual, since we known so many other factors may also influence attitudes towards and practices of disposing the dead.

Another matter of some debate during the Neolithic in Greece is the nature of community ideology. Ideology is a "body of doctrine, myth, and symbolism of a social movement, institution, class, or group of individuals, often with reference to some political or cultural plan, along with strategies for putting the doctrine into plan" (Flannery and Marcus 1996:355). Ideology is therefore both social and political, and *community ideology* is the political/cultural plan shared by "a social group of any size whose members reside in a specific locality, share government, and have a cultural and historical heritage" (Kottack 1974). Previous thoughts on the nature of community ideology argue for differences in the way ideological plans were put into action. Some contend that the ideological focus was on the village group (i.e., community) and not a network of communities (e.g., Chapman 1989; Hodder 1984, 1990), while others suggest that households excluded the broader community and took on these responsibilities (Demoule and Perlès 1993:385-386). Halstead (1999a) has recently argued for a shift from community to household strategies, if households became increasingly isolated during the course of the Neolithic in Thessaly. Since ritual is a set of practices that manifest the interconnections amongst the principles, values, and beliefs encompassed in cosmology, religion, and ideology, a study of mortuary ritual should yield some indication of the degree of community involvement in the rites accorded the deceased. We may expect fewer indicators of extra-familial participation in the process of disposing the dead if there is little community involvement, and more if many members of the community were involved. In the following chapter, I discuss how archaeologists may detect the role of the household and community in mortuary ritual by looking at the intricacies of disposal programmes, and later examine whether disposal programmes at various places and times during the Neolithic allow us to distinguish the forms and changes in community ideology. I also pay considerable attention

to the increasing amount of evidence for pastoralist, or pastoral-focused (livestock-based subsistence), and agriculturist (cereal and livestock-based subsistence) societies during the Neolithic. By definition, these societies have different ideologies, and I consider whether it is possible to differentiate them in terms of their mortuary practices.

The final issue I wish to address concerns social differentiation. For nearly thirty years, archaeologists have repeatedly stated that there is no demonstrable evidence for socially stratified societies during the Neolithic, and we must instead wait until the twilight of the Neolithic and the beginning of the Early Bronze Age for the emergence of social complexity (Demoule and Perlès 1993:405-407; Pullen 1985:102-105; Renfrew 1972). Not only have such claims raised the question of precedent, but also they have ironically ignored the profound changes in subsistence, settlement, technology, and interaction spheres known during this period. Halstead (e.g., 1984, 1999a) has been a most adamant proponent for the emergence of socially complex societies during the Neolithic, arguing for the rise of an institutional elite in Thessaly during the Late Neolithic. The form of this argument tends to privilege stratification in economic terms, such as competition for status and power through specialisation and the accumulation of wealth, while ignoring forms of stratification based on other criteria, such as political or ritual specialisation (for a recent review of these issues see McIntosh 1999b).

The Neolithic in Greece, I believe, holds an important place in our understanding of human of social organisation during the Holocene. Being the first regions in Europe colonised by immigrant farmers, Greece and the Balkans acted as the proving ground for an agricultural way of life adapted by their descendants and influenced the transition to agriculture across much of Europe. Along the rocky coastlines and active floodplains of Greece, we find the first experiments in the economic phenomenon of the Neolithic. However, the Neolithic was more than a preference for the cultivation of fields and animal husbandry over that of hunting, fishing, and gathering. The spread and adoption of food production not only implies deep transformations in subsistence, but also how people perceived each other and the world around them. If the Neolithic was as much a social and cognitive phenomenon as an economic one (Hodder 1990; Whittle 1996), we should also find in Greece novel principles, values, and beliefs necessary to organise new and emerging communal lifeways. This perspective tends to view the European Neolithic as a long process of socially motivated changes in economic organisation and symbolic life underpinning trends towards sedentism, agricultural intensification, population increases, social inequality, and specialisation. "What mattered," as

Figure 1.1. The study area and location of Neolithic sites with mortuary remains considered in this study. (1) Nea Nikomedia; (2) Plateia Magoula Zarkou; (3) Agia Sophia Magoula; (4) Souphli Magoula; (5) Dimini; (6) Pevkakia; (7) Tharrounia; (8) Kitsos Cave; (9) Kephala; (10) Franchthi Cave; (11) Prosymna; (12) Lerna; (13) Aleopotrypa Cave.

Whittle (1996:370) has commented, "were the values guiding or framing people's activities and relations with each other and the world," not just concerns about competition and conflict over material resources. Mortuary remains provide us with one important and neglected source of data for revisiting thoughts about the mechanisms of social differentiation during the Neolithic, such political and ritual specialisation, and competition, as a fundamental way of distinguishing social individuals within the body politic. I must make it clear that interpretations of the mortuary data in this contribution

do not, in and of themselves, allow broad claims about the character of Neolithic society in Greece, or any detailed understanding of the changes that took place during this period. Instead, these data allow inferences that appear to challenge certain orthodox tenets in each of these five issues. As such, they instigate a revisiting of certain claims and a form a basis for thinking about alternatives. My objective here is not to challenge conventional wisdom of Neolithic society in Europe, but more modestly to explore how a multi-dimensional, multi-scalar approach to the interpretation of

4

TABLE 1.1
CHRONOLOGY OF THE NEOLITHIC IN GREECE

Phase	Age B.C.[a]	Sites Included in Study
Early Neolithic (EN)	6500–5800	Prosymna, Franchthi Cave, Souphli Magoula, Nea
Middle Neolithic (MN)	5800–5300	Nikomedia
Late Neolithic (LN)	5300–4500	Agia Sophia, Dimini, Plateia Magoula Zarkou,
LN 1	5300–4800	Tharrounia (Skoteni Cave)
LN 2	4800–4500	
Final Neolithic (FN)	4500–3800	Aleopotrypa Cave, Franchthi Cave, Kitsos Cave, Pevkakia, Tharrounia, Kephala

[a] Based on calibrated ages in Demoule and Perlès (1993).

integrates these conclusions to evaluate previous claims made about mortuary variability, the visibility of the dead, ritual complexity, community ideology, and social differentiation in societies located on the mainland and nearby islands of Greece.

archaeological data can highlight inconsistencies in our thinking about the Neolithic and provide a range of interpretive alternatives that are necessary to explore.

In moving towards this goal, I begin in Chapter 2 by presenting the theoretical framework for this study and the methods of analysis. I first review the anthropological literature on the directives of mortuary practices, adopt an interpretive framework based on this literature, and introduce a way old and new mortuary data from archaeological contexts can be organised and analysed to identify these directives. I have organised the discussion and interpretation of mortuary data from thirteen Neolithic sites chronologically (Table 1.1). These sites are geographically located in Greek Macedonia (Nea Nikomedia), Thessaly (Plateia Magoula Zarkou, Agia Sophia Magoula, Souphli Magoula, Dimini, and Pevkakia), the southern mainland (Kitsos Cave, Lerna, Franchthi Cave, Prosymna, and Aleopotrypa Cave), and the nearby islands of Euboea (Tharrounia) and Keos (Kephala) (Fig. 1.1). Seven of these sites have the best mortuary data for providing the empirical basis to explore similarities and differences in mortuary practices throughtime and space, and include Plateia Magoula Zarkou, Souphli Magoula, Franchthi Cave, Prosymna, Aleopotrypa Cave, Tharrounia, and Kephala. I discuss the six other mainland sites in available detail, but the lack of reported information and/or the poor quality of the mortuary data from these sites permits only general comparisons with the principal case studies. Mortuary remains from these sites date to each of the four main phases of the Neolithic in Greece, and several have remains dating to more than one phase (Table 1.1).

These data are analysed in Chapters 3 to 5: mortuary practices during the Early and Middle Neolithic phases are the subject of Chapter 3, Late Neolithic practices in Chapter 4, and the Final Neolithic in Chapter 5. Each chapter begins with a review of the culture-history of that particular phase, followed by a detailed examination of the case studies and a summary of the main trends in mortuary practices. The final chapter, Chapter 6,

CHAPTER 2
MONITORING MORTUARY RITUAL

Mortuary ritual is a set of prescribed or customary behaviours for disposing of the dead. Like other kinds of rituals, mortuary ritual practices are influenced by social, ideological, religious, and cosmological concerns. The disposal of the dead may be social if it facilitates social intercourse, ideological if it promotes a shared body of social doctrine, religious if it is intended to placate or win the favour of supernatural beings, and cosmological if it reinforces a peoples' philosophy of the universe and beliefs about the supernatural. Something of all these functions can be found in a single act of ritual (Merrifield 1987:6).

Because mortuary ritual crosses many dimensions of the cultural domain, archaeologists have used mortuary data since the late 1960s to investigate a diversity of cultural, behavioural, environmental, and historical phenomenon. Research has focused on how mortuary practices are used to express socio-economic competition (Cannon 1989; Little et al. 1992), trade and alliance formations (Carr 1992; Carr and Maslowski 1995; Trigger 1968; Winters 1968), territoriality (Chapman 1981), warfare (Owsley et al 1977; Ravesloot 1988; Seeman 1988), migrations (Brunson 1989), ideology (Hodder 1982a, 1984; McGuire 1992; Parker Pearson 1982, 1984), worldview (Emerson 1989; Gruber 1971; Hall 1979, 1983; Merbs 1989; Penney 1983; 1985; Sugiyama 1992), social interaction and ethnicity (Willey and Sabloff 1980:34-126; Seeman 1979), and osteobiological characteristics associated with these phenomenon (Ambrose and Katzenburg 2001; Blakely 1977; Buikstra 1977; Chapman and Ransborg 1981:19-23; Huss-Ashmore et al 1982; Katzenburg and Saunders 2000; Ortner and Putschar 1981; Price et al 1984; Ubelaker 1989; see also Beck [1995] for papers on the above topics). Especially during the 1970s, American mortuary archaeology came to emphasise the social dimensions of mortuary practices, and a great deal of attention centred on how mortuary variability reflects social organisation (Saxe 1970; Braun 1979; Brown 1971a; Chapman 1982). Social organisation was seen as the primary determinant of mortuary variability (Carr 1995:106) and mortuary practices and remains were largely understood as a by-product of social directives (Tainter 1978:107). However, as I show later in this chapter, empirical evidence does not support this premise.

A narrow focus on the social determinants of mortuary ritual has had several unfortunate consequences. Most importantly, it has been blamed for the slow rate of theory development during the last decade. O'Shea's

(1982, 1984) work on formation processes as they relate to mortuary remains and McGuire's (1992:126-128) ideas on quantifying energy expenditure have been heralded as the last significant contributions to American mortuary theory (Carr 1995:119). A formal theory for the study of mortuary data has remained fragmented and governed by personal preference (Tainter 1978). A bias towards the social motivations of mortuary ritual also neglected the symbolic aspects of disposing the dead, which has required the use of very different theoretical approaches geared towards the analysis of symbol systems. And, except for past societies without monumental funerary architecture, what may be learned from the very processes involved in disposing the dead—constructing and maintaining burial facilities, preparing the body, conducting feasts—and dealing with the ancestors, has been almost entirely neglected. I suspect the lack of detailed attention to the relationships that exist between ethnographic and archaeological surveys of mortuary practices are no small part of these problems, and equally because useful ethnoarchaeological sources are rare (David 1992a, 1992b; Hayden 2001). O'Shea's (1984) study remains particularly important because it establishes a bridge between ethnographic studies of mortuary customs and the archaeological study of mortuary remains, and Carr's (1995) survey of mortuary practices using ethnographic sources has questioned many of the claims made by O'Shea and qualified the proposal that philosophical-religious beliefs are an equally valid area of mortuary research.

In an area of archaeological inquiry where provisos and caveats are around every corner, how then are we to distinguish the factors that affected very ancient mortuary practices? In this chapter, I advocate an 'ethnographically-sensitive' approach, which, through a detailed description of mortuary variability, provides a means to relate certain types of variability to particular kinds of social and/or philosophical-religious behaviour. There are four steps to this approach. The first, as proposed by O'Shea (1984) involves developing (a) an orderly method of recognising and organising mortuary data from the archaeological record, and (b) a set of theoretical assumptions that provide the researcher with a way of recognising distinct structures in mortuary variability. The second step is to develop a series of interpretative correlates that can be used to explain mortuary variability. In this chapter, I proposed a number of ethnographically-derived hypotheses of the main social and philosophical-religious determinants of mortuary practices. These normative explanations act as theorems, they can be deduced as hypotheses, tested, and can therefore later be incorporated into the general analysis as theorems in a formal sense (cf. O'Shea 1984). Essentially, these are the standards that the fitness of theoretical descriptions can be put against empirical descriptions. The third step is to establish variation in mortuary practices by examining the sequence, scale, and form of mortuary rites (empirical descriptions). The final step then involves contrasting and comparing normative explanations for mortuary variation based on ethnographically-derived hypotheses against the variability observed in the archaeological cases.

2.1   MORTUARY VARIABILITY

To understand variability in mortuary practices we must first have some useful way of categorising mortuary data. The purpose of separating mortuary data into discrete categories and classes is to describe the general kinds of data best observed by archaeologists in a mortuary context. These have been proposed in different forms (Alekshin 1983; Binford 1971; Goldstein 1981; O'Shea 1984; Sprague 1968), and the list I use is derived from a synthesis of previous research. The following list, however, is expressed in somewhat more detail than earlier versions.

2.1.1   Categorising Mortuary Data

There are six categories of mortuary data where variation may be observed: (1) osteobiological, (2) the mortuary facility, (3) the preparation and treatment of the body, (4) the grave furnishings and/or burial gifts, (5) locational (spatial) variability, (6) and environmental information. Each category is composed of a number of variables, or classes. These classes can act as independent variables in later analysis. This is why it is useful to express them in detail, in order to take into account all the probable mortuary expressions.

- The osteobiological category includes such elements as the demographic factors of age and sex, dietary information, skeletal pathology, and circumstances of death.

- The mortuary facility category deals specifically with the tomb or grave itself. It includes such variables as type, shape, dimensions, orientation, and structural enhancements (such as coverings, doorways, etc.). If the facility is more elaborate, specific design and construction practices and techniques must be considered in addition to the raw materials used.

- Preparation and treatment describes how the body was prepared for disposal. It includes variables relating to the disposal type and the disposal program. The disposal type includes such factors as the form of interment, the form of the disposal area, body posture,

body orientation, pattern of bone association (scattered, articulated, etc.), and the minimum number of individuals represented in the mortuary population (MNI). I term the entire process of disposing the dead as the disposal programme, which may be separated into three parts:(1) the pre-interment treatment, (2) the burial scenario, and (3) the post-interment treatment. When discussing pre- and post-interment treatments, those practices indicative of "secondary" burial (initial mortuary treatment then final disposal) must be taken into account. These include such practices as defleshing, cremation, ritual mutilation, exposure, partial interment, and exhumation and reburial. Second, attention must be paid to the burial scenario, be they single interments, multiple burial scenarios, or proxy\cenotaph burial (there is a formal burial but no body was interred).

- The grave furnishings/burial goods category provides information on the variety (or typology), quantity, quality, and source of goods (if possible) deposited with individuals. It may also be useful to separate out, or distinguish between intentional grave inclusions (e.g., implements and furnishings) and incidental inclusions (such as clothing ornamentation) if possible.

- Locational variability, in this instance, can involve three arbitrary locations for spatial analyses. Measured at the macrolevel is the disposal area in relation to the settlement or other disposal areas. The mesolevel is a unit that can be used to describe variability within the confines of a single disposal area, such as a cemetery or house floor. The microlevel refers to relationships assessed within a single disposal unit, or a grave (for example, variation in spatial relationships between the grave goods and the body).

- Environmental information is derived from entomological, botanical, and faunal sources. Traditionally, this type of data has been rarely used, and is especially difficult to integrate into an analysis when relying on information from dated sources simply because it was not collected. Nevertheless, in the cases discussed here, there are several instances where faunal material was recovered from graves and it is imperative to discuss this significance of their presence.

Obviously, this is only one way of organising the sources of variation potentially visible in the archaeological record. Regardless of their arrangement, these variables represent a basis for the study of mortuary variation (O'Shea 1984:41). However, when faced with actual mortuary data often not all the categories or classes of information are present (i.e., were not recovered). This occurs for several reasons, such as pre- and post-depositional effects, or non-systematic or non-problem oriented approaches to excavation (see O'Shea 1981, 1984 for further discussion). Regardless of the reason, this makes it essential to break down the categories once again. O'Shea (1984:41) has presented two reasons for rationalising this reduction: first, a lack of detail in the excavation record, due to those factors noted above, and second, any particular attribute or class (such as demography) of observable mortuary practices does not provide all the potential information itself, but must also be taken in context with all of the other attributes relative to it. This final breakdown forms the irreducible basis for the study of mortuary remains.

When discussing the inter-relatedness of variables, O'Shea (1984) warned that it is important to note Taylor's (1969:112) emphasis on the importance of *affinities* in archaeological research, as archaeological data essentially 'consists of the material result of cultural behaviour, and the affinities—quantitative, qualitative, spatial, etc.—which can be found to exist among them, and between them and the natural environment'. The concept of affinities is particularly important to the study of mortuary remains, as O'Shea (1984:41) points out, because we are not really interested in the presence of only one attribute, but how the occurrence of many attributes are structured to produce a certain mortuary patterning. However, we are, at present, unable to observe the patterns produced by *all* the affinities. But, due to the work that has been done on discovering the common constraints placed on mortuary variability, we can specify a smaller set of attributes, which O'Shea termed *primary affinity categories*, that are composed of *primary referents*. The primary categories can help determine the *minimum* constraints put upon mortuary variability by a society. In whatever fashion they are designed, primary categories must *at least* include information on the age and sex of the mortuary population, the frequency with which certain traits or objects occur, how pervasive attributes are in the mortuary population, the source of the materials used in disposing the dead (architectural, grave goods and furnishings, etc.), and the spatial properties of a disposal area.

This smaller set of attributes are useful because they are fundamental and they allow the researcher to describe critical aspects in the observed mortuary patterning and they are directly relevant to the social and philosophical-religious differentiation being expressed through mortuary behaviour (O'Shea 1984:42). Perhaps most importantly, these primary categories allow any element of mortuary ritual to be monitored and described in a more standardised manner. When combined, they allow the researcher to describe the possible significance many attributes used in mortuary ritual and to make inferences on the structure and complexity of mortuary behaviour that produces the differentiation (O'Shea 1984:43).

Practically, this allows a researcher to describe the organisational principles of a mortuary program in terms of what is observable in the archaeological record. Therefore, theoretically, one can submit the observed patterns of mortuary differentiation as descriptions of particular mortuary practices that have practical, social, economic, or philosophical-religious significance. The degree to which this can be accomplished relies upon the connections that can be made between the procedures for disposing of the dead and the directives of the disposal program; that is *why* certain procedures are used in the disposal of certain individuals. This, necessarily, relies upon theoretical links that can be made between ethnographic and archaeological mortuary behaviours.

2.1.2 Sources of Variation in Mortuary Practice

The factors that effect the disposal of the dead can be placed into five main categories:social organisational, philosophical-religious, physical, circumstantial, and ecological. In his cross-cultural survey of the ethnographic literature using the Human Relations Area Files (HRAF), Carr (1995:106-107) has defined each category of factors. Social factors include age, gender, vertical and horizontal social positions, and personal identity. Philosophical-religious variables include as categories of socially institutionalised beliefs and worldview assumptions about disease, death, dying, the soul, the afterlife, and the cosmos. Circumstantial factors are those involving how and when the individual died—the location, timing, and cause of death. Physical variables include those factors relating to the physical requirements need to ensure the health of survivors, for body processing, and access to the body for interment as well as after death. Carr also included two 'ecological' variables: the practice of using of cemeteries to mark territory and variation in mortuary practices caused by land/resource variability, such as the use of caves, rock shelters, or niches when land suitable for a cemetery is unavailable.

By providing a more exhaustive companion study to previous cross-cultural surveys of mortuary practices focused on specific problems (Binford 1971; Goldstein 1976, 1981; Tainer 1975a, 1975b; Vehik 1975), Carr's analysis tested series of important premises in American mortuary archaeology with the aim of providing a more secure ethnographic base on which to build middle-range theory for interpreting mortuary practices. In this section, I will discuss the results of Carr's study and their importance for understanding the causes of mortuary variability.

Carr (1995) evaluated the number of occurrences of social organisational, philosophical-religious, physic-cal, circumstantial, and ecological determinants of mortuary practices in 31 non-state societies. He then tabulated factors are more commonly expressed in different aspects

TABLE 2.1.
THE PRINCIPLE PHYSICAL, SOCIAL, AND PHILOSOPHICAL-RELIGIOUS DETERMINANTS OF MORTUARY VARIATION BASED ON A CROSS-CULTURAL SURVEY OF ETHNOGRAPHIC CASES.

	Cause of Death	Social Position of the Deceased				Philosophical -Religious Beliefs				
		Classification at death	Vertical position	Horizontal position	Indicator of social personae	Cause of death	Health/ safety of the living	Beliefs about the afterlife	Soul's nature, journey, and its effect the living	Universal orders, mythology
Preparation & Treatment of the Body										
Preparation		•	•			•	•	•	•	••
Treatment		••	•	••		•	•	•	•	•
Position at burial			•				•			•
Orientation at burial								•		•
Form of disposal	••	••	•	•				•	•	•
Preparation of the Grave										
Grave form			•	•						•
Number of socially recognized burial types			•	••						
Grave Furniture & Goods										
Kind of grave furniture		•	•	••	••		••	••	••	•
Source of grave furniture			•							
Quantity of grave furniture										
Spatial Location and Designation										
Local grave location	•		•	•					•	•
Region, ecozone location of disposal area	•							•	•	
Regional location of disposal area relative to settlement		•	•	•					•	•
Grave formally demarked			•						•	•
Intra-cemetery grave location of burial types										
Energy Expenditure										
Overall energy expenditure			••	••						
Funeral time & duration; secondary funerals				•				•	•	•
Mourning Ritual										
Funeral dance/games				•						
Funeral meals/fasting				•						
Funeral dress ornamentation				•					•	•
Grief, bereavement, and grave visitation				•					•	•

Sources: Binford (1971), Goldstein (1976, 1982), Tainter (1975), Vehik (1975), Carr (1995). A (•) indicates strong correlation, (••) indicates strongest correlation.

9

TABLE 2.2.
MOST COMMON ASSOCIATIONS FOUND BETWEEN
MORTUARY PRACTICES AND THEIR DETERMINANTS.

Determinant	Expression in mortuary practice[a]
Social Position of the Deceased	
Social classification at death	Body treatment, form of disposal
Vertical social position	Energy expenditure, grave form, grave furniture
Horizontal social position	Corpse processors
Personal identity	Grave furniture
Gender	Grave furniture
Age	Body preparation, energy expenditure, number of burial types
Philosophical-Religious Beliefs	
Beliefs about the cause of death	Form of disposal
Beliefs about the soul	Grave furniture, body treatment
Beliefs about the afterlife	Grave furniture
Beliefs about the soul's journey	Grave furniture
Beliefs about universal orders	Body preparation, corpse processors
Beliefs about responsibilities	Bereavement

[a] Listed in decreasing order of importance for each determinant.
Source: Carr (1995:table XI).

of the disposal programme. In Table 2.1, I have divided the disposal program into six main categories and listed the main physical, social, and philosophical-religious factors influencing them. Table 2.2 summarises these findings by showing which mortuary expressions most strongly correlate to the social position of the deceased and philosophical religious beliefs. Circumstantial and ecological factors have not been included in either table because Carr found they do not as strongly determine mortuary practices in the societies he examined. The most important observation gained from these common associations is that any one mortuary practice may be influenced by more than one determinant. While this may appear to complicate matters, the fact that different social and philosophical-religious determinants are expressed through the same practices is helpful because it is possible to limit the field of determinants and focus on whether they realistically explain mortuary practices in any particular cultural context.

The aim of Carr's study was to examine eight main premises that have guided the interpretation of mortuary remains since the 1960s. He gives a full discussion of these premises and his conclusions, which I have summarised these in Table 2.3, but I wish here to discuss their implications for the study of the Neolithic in Greece.

An enduring premise in mortuary archaeology provided by Binford (1971) is that mortuary practices and remains are arbitrarily related to their determinants. In contrast, Carr's study found that specific mortuary practices may hold a wide range of meanings, but are not arbitrary.

Importantly, from this basis, it is not possible to conclude that the structure of mortuary remains and not their symbolic content should be the primary focus of mortuary analyses. It perhaps may be better to view mortuary practices as non-random, non-arbitrary, and multi-dimensional. For instance, as a grave good, the kind of chariot placed in pharaoh's tomb was *at once* determined by his vertical social position and social personae and specific Egyptian beliefs about the afterlife, the soul's journey, and the universal order of the world pertaining to living gods that has deep mythological origins. Not only are the symbolic dimensions of mortuary practices worthy of study, but it is theoretically unwarranted to assume the second premise—that social directives will more often be expressed in mortuary practices or will override philosophical-religious concerns—simply because social and philosophical-religious concerns are intricately connected to broader world-view themes.

Support for the notion that both the structure and content of mortuary practices and remains are worthy of study has important methodological implications as well. One place to start is the support for Hertz's (1907) premise that the practice of handling the corpse embodies social and symbolic principles relating the corpse of the deceased to the soul of the deceased and the society of mourners. At a methodological level, then, archaeologists may begin to unravel the determinants of mortuary practices by exploring the entire process of handling of the corpse—what I have termed here the *disposal programme*. As a first step in making inferences about the social and philosophical-religious motivations driving the disposal programme, this approach would require that we reconstruct in as much detail as possible the steps and stages of disposing the dead which are visible in the archaeological record. In the next section, I propose how the motivations of mortuary practices can be investigated using a "mortuary *chaînes opératoires*" methodology, which conceptually draws from influential ideas put forward by anthropologists of French school of *technologie*. Another important finding of Carr's study related to discerning the factors influencing the disposal of the dead is that the overall energy expenditure given an individual's mortuary treatment will reflect the social position of the deceased. While the studies by Carr (1995) and Tainter (1975a, 1978) found strong correlation between energy expenditure and vertical social position of the deceased, operationalising these observations have been roundly criticised primarily because it is just not possible to (a) determine the *overall* energy expended while disposing the dead or (b) easily quantify it in terms of labour expenditure.

I argue that it may be more useful to think of energy expenditure as a heuristic device that allows an analyst to

TABLE 2.3.

COMPARISON OF COMMON PREMISES IN AMERICAN MORTUARY ARCHAEOLOGY TESTED AGAINST ETHNOGRAPHIC DATA.

Premise	Conclusion
1. Mortuary practices and remains, as symbolic forms, are arbitrarily related to their determining causes or referents (Binford 1971).	No. There are nonrandom, semideterminant relationships between specific mortuary practices and dimension of social organization, but they are not arbitrary. There is no empirical basis to suppose the structure and not the symbolic content of mortuary remains is more productive for reconstructing the past (Carr 1995:151).
2. Mortuary practices and remains are to be understood largely as the product of social organization (Tainter 1978:107).	No. Many variables commonly used to infer social patterning, including grave form, kind of grave furniture, grave location (at local, regional and ecozonal levels), body treatment and preparation, and the form of disposal, are as commonly associated with philosophical-religious beliefs as social organization factors. Other factors may better reflect aspects of social organization: the internal organization of cemeteries, overall energy expenditure, the number of socially recognised burial types, the number of persons in the grave, and the quantity of grave furniture (Carr 1995:157-160).
3. Mortuary practices are determined in their structure and content by the relationships between the corpse of the deceased, the soul of the deceased, and the remaining society of mourners (Hertz 1907).	Yes. The handling of the corpse is determined by a wide range of philosophical-religious and social motivations, most frequently, by beliefs about the soul's nature, its effects upon the living, the nature of the afterlife, the social classification of the individual at death, and vertical social position (Carr 1995:175-178).
4. The vertical social position of the deceased is indicated by the overall energy expended while disposing the body (Tainter 1975, 1978).	Yes. The complexity of bodily treatment, construction and placement of the interment facility, the extent and duration of mortuary ritual, the material contribution to ritual (specifically the kinds of offerings placed in the grave but not likely their quantity), and human sacrifice are valuable indicators of the overall amount of energy expended on the funeral and burial which correlate directly with the vertical social position of the deceased (Carr 1995:178-180; Tainer 1978).
6. The horizontal (Goldstein 1976, 1981; Saxe 1970) and vertical (Binford 1971) social position of the deceased is often indicated by the location of the grave.	Partly. Vertical and horizontal social positions are among the variables tied into the local position of the grave and formal demarcation of cemeteries. The horizontal and vertical social position and age of the deceased are most commonly associated with local grave location, while horizontal social position and beliefs about the soul's nature more commonly affect the formal demarcation of cemeteries.
7. The regional location of the cemetery is primarily determined by the importance of cemeteries as territorial markers, cosmology, and other beliefs about the dead and the afterlife (Chapman and Randsborg 1981; Hall 1979; Renfrew 1976).	Yes. Philosophical-religious beliefs, including beliefs about universal orders, the structure of the cosmos, and beliefs about the afterlife (including location of afterlife) most strongly determine cemetery location (in 53% of cases). The premise that a cemetery's regional location is evidence of its use a territorial marker is not supported, but Carr (1995:183) believes this result to be inconclusive due to data limitations.
8. Vertical social position is symbolized by elaborate grave construction and the kinds and quantities of grave furniture (O'Shea 1981).	Yes. Vertical social position has the greatest effect on the elaboration of graves and overall energy expenditure. However, vertical and horizontal social position *does not* affect different sets of mortuary practices as shown in Table 2.1. Rather, the same practices can be affected by both horizontal and vertical social considerations, although it appears that horizontal social position is less frequently visible in mortuary patterning (Carr 1995:188).

11

place a relative value on the discrete variation in the effort expended in preparing and treating the deceased. A qualitative assessment of energy expenditure is no less valid or rigorous than a quantitative approach. I have tried both approaches using mortuary data from the Greek Neolithic (see Fowler 1997 for a quantitative approach). Operationally, the qualitative approach is in an analysis and description of the disposal programme sequence. Regardless if the analyst approaches variation qualitatively or quantitatively, there is clearly a difference between the energy expended in the burial of two adult males in separate pit graves with the same grave goods when one grave is covered with flat limestone blocks and the other is not, as we would suspect from Point 8. However, focusing attention on the disposal sequence draws our attention away from trying to explain differences in the energy expended in the burial of these two men, and on to trying to explain the significance of elaborating one man's grave by capping it with limestone blocks. This approach simply address two different of the same phenomenon: overall energy expenditure is likely determined by the vertical position of the deceased, while the specific ways the treatment of the body and the grave are elaborated leads us to consider other social and philosophical-religious determinants governing the stages in the disposal programme. In this way, the presence of vertical social position in this society is a hypothesis to be tested. Relative energy expenditure, evidenced in our example by elaborated grave construction, is one means to examine the hypothesis, while the location of the grave is another. In 18% of cases studied by Carr, vertical social position indicated by the position of an individual's grave in a cemetery, and in 27% of cases formal demarcation of the cemetery or parts of it related to the exclusive use of a disposal area by a single corporate group (Carr 1995:182, table XX). Thus, if our man in the cap-stone pit grave is also set apart from others in the cemetery, there is a greater likelihood he held a high status in this community.

We now have a series of ethnographically-tested premises about mortuary behaviour for which we can put forward testable hypotheses. In the next section, I attempt to link together (a) the sources of variation potentially visible in the archaeological record, (b) the disposal programme, and (c) the corpse, the community of the dead, and the society of mourners.

2.2   THE HERTZIAN TRIANGLE

The approach I advocate to link mortuary remains, the directives of disposal, and the relationships which define the directives, is based upon what has become known as the Hertzian triangle (Huntington and Metcalf 1979; Hertz 1907). In the triangle, three pairs of relationships are recognised (Fig. 2.1). The relationship between 'The Living and the Mourners' and 'The Corpse and its Disposal' determines the scale of mortuary rites, which distinguishes an individual's social personae—the social identity or identities of a person reflecting the rights and duties held by them during life (Goodenough 1965:1, 24). The relation ship between 'The Corpse and its Disposal' and 'The Soul and the Dead' is captured metaphorically (e.g., spring and rebirth or awakening, autumn, harvest and death) and expressed through the form and symbolism of rites. The final pair, between 'The Soul and the Dead' and 'The Living and the Mourners,' accounts for the sequence of mortuary rites, or the process whereby the social persona is transformed from the visible to the invisible society.

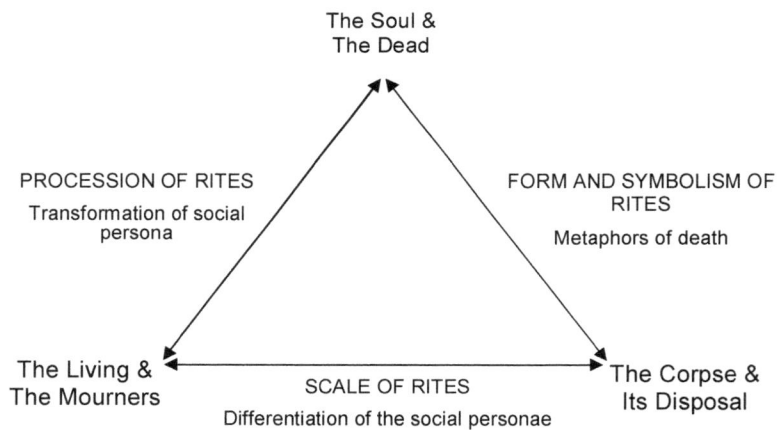

The Soul &
The Dead

PROCESSION OF RITES
Transformation of social persona

FORM AND SYMBOLISM OF RITES
Metaphors of death

The Living &
The Mourners

SCALE OF RITES
Differentiation of the social personae

The Corpse &
Its Disposal

Figure 2.1. The Hertzian triangle (based on Huntington and Metcalf 1979: fig. 2).

This model is a powerful heuristic device for the archaeological study of mortuary remains. When combined with ethnographic and archaeological observations, it allows a more elaborate model relating the domain of mortuary practices to social and ideological distinctions emphasised in mortuary practices.

The social dimension of the triangle has been given unwarranted superiority in the study of the mortuary practices. The activities involved in each stage of mortuary ritual process can and often do 'mean' something different than others. While the preparation of the body and the types of grave furniture/goods made for or used in mortuary ritual may be significant expressions of beliefs about the nature of the soul and its effect upon the living, these activities are a direct product of the physical and emotional effort involved in manipulating the corporeal and spiritual individual from the state of life to the state of death. The transformation of the dead is often captured through metaphor and symbolism that characterises the universal shift from material to immaterial, being to non-being, present to past, kinsman to ancestor, living to dead. For those most interested in the complexity of this transformation, a study of these three relationships have the potential to provide us with more than a vulgar figure of the social position of the deceased.

2.2.3 The Procession of Rites

The relationship between 'The Living and The Mourners' and 'The Soul and The Dead' addresses how the sequence of mortuary rites is used to transform the social persona from a state of living to that of death. As O'Shea (1984:34) noted, for certain cultural groups the disposal of the dead may reflect more the departure of the social individual rather than the irradication of the physical remains. This notion is related to Hertz's (1907) idea that those who are full participants in the living community must be given the appropriate rites to sever the relationship with the community once they are dead. In this way, society integrates the individual of the 'visible society' into the community of the dead, or the 'invisible society.' In these terms, mortuary ritual is understood as the final *rite of passage* that must be endured by the individual. Rites of passage have been shown by Hertz (1960), van Gennep (1960), and Leach (1982) to be a near-universal characteristic of societies. It is the main mechanism used to promote an individual from one status in society to the next (Leach 1982). Rites of passage are prohibitive rituals insofar as they act to exclude participants from the community in the process of ritual. During life, the process ultimately incorporates that individual back into society, but in death, one is forever excluded from *corporeal* participation in the living society.

The relationship between 'The Soul and the Dead' and 'The Living and the Mourners' stresses the sequence of mortuary rites. One may analytically approach this distinction as a sort of mortuary *chaînes opèratoires*, or 'operational sequence' (Cresswell 1976; Lemonnier 1986, 1992), whereby mortuary ritual is seen as a series of operation that brings an individual from a state of living to that of death—from the visible to the invisible society. Conceptually, this approach is grounded in Marcel Mauss's (1935) concept of *enchaînement organique*, or the way in which natural resources are sequentially formed through bodily gestures carried out in social milieus. The handling of the corpse is analogous to a 'raw material', in that the corpse is no longer a social individual and is sequentially formed through the bodily gestures involved in preparing the body for disposal, which are carried out in a social milieu. Matter, energy, objects, gestures in sequence, and knowledge are the five elements that mortuary rituals share with all other activities (Lemonnier 1986, 1992), and through which cultural traditions are maintained and passed on the next generation.

Operationally, a description of the process of disposing the dead—the sequential operations used to transform the dead—provides an outline of the behaviour or actions involved in that transformation. From this physical basis, we may begin to infer the kinds of acts that occurred before and after the physical transformation of the dead.

The death of an individual sets off a series of activities that contribute towards this process. Initially, a set of decisions must be made regarding the appropriate rites for an individual, and other logistical considerations, such as informing relations in other locations. There are three principle areas where attention is focused at this point: the preparation of the body, the preparation and/or construction of a disposal area (grave, ossuary, etc.), and the manufacture and/or preparation of the material objects required for the rites (such as grave furniture and goods and other ritual equipment). There may be a certain sequence in which many of these activities occur, but decisions are continuously being made throughout the process and a variety of practical, social, and philosophical-religious factors provide a *framework* within which the mortuary rites are observed. As such, pre-interment mourning observances can often occur even before death. The focus may change upon death, when for instance, concern about the state of the "soul" before death shifts to concerns about preparing the soul for its journey to the afterlife. The activities culminate in the interment of the individual, in whatever fashion is required by that society. The sequence does not end there, however, and a variety of post-interment mortuary observances may occur. These may require close family, friends, or related kin to observe certain sanctions for a time. In addition, or alternatively, they may perform certain rituals on a regular basis for some time into the future. Undoubtedly, the variety of responses to death is incredibly vast (Huntington and Metcalf 1979). Nevertheless, addressing the mortuary *chaînes opératoires* can yield insights into three dimensions of mortuary ritual:

(1) It provides a framework within which to consider the decision-making process that led to an individual's final interment, and possibly, the rites awarded that individual after their death.

(2) It allows us to highlight those aspects of mortuary practices that may have been deemed highly significant for that individual, the social group(s) to which they belonged, and to the society at large.

(3) It can inform us about the repertoire of forms and symbolism and the overall scale of rites observed in that society.

Further to this, work by Parker Pearson (1982) has shown how the physical disposal of the dead not only involves a conceptual transformation of an individual's social personae, but also of the living society as well. The physical execution of this transformation is heavily guided by philosophical and religious beliefs, and the survey by Carr (1995:190) reveals that social organisational factors may often be expressed indirectly through the belief system. Thus, mortuary practices are meaningfully constituted (Hodder 1982b) and are chosen in relation to personal intentions, social strategies, attitudes, beliefs and world-view themes.

2.2.4 Metaphors of Death

The fact that mortuary practices are meaningfully constituted contrasts Binford's (1971) position that symbols are arbitrary in any society and are less ideally suited to the study of mortuary patterning. Thus, 'the contents as well as the structure of mortuary remains hold potential for reconstructing the past' (Carr 1995:189), and, as Hodder (1982b:9) asserted, the form and meaning of mortuary ritual is therefore non-arbitrary in any particular context. The relationship between 'The Corpse and its Disposal' and 'The Soul and the Dead' stresses this dimension of mortuary ritual and directs our attention towards the metaphors of death expressed through the form and symbolism of rites. Of particular interest is how the state of the corpse and the state of the soul are related. Carr (1995) found very strong support for Hertz's (1907) hypotheses that mourners often believe that the state of the corpse is a model of the state of the soul, and that the soul can be manipulated by the way the corpse is handled. Thus, the metaphors of death should primarily reside in those features of mortuary ritual that pertain to the preparation and treatment of the body as well as the particular circumstances surrounding an individual's death. Ethnographic research suggests the former will be

most expressly visible in the handling of the body before and during interment and the latter in the location of the grave (Table 2.2).

2.2.5 The Scale of Rites

The differentiation of the social personae has received the most attention in the literature. As noted above, likely the most important observation in Carr's study was that philosophical-religious factors determine mortuary differentiation as or more often than social factors. This and other related observations have several deep theoretical implications.

First, following the assertion that social organisational factors are often expressed indirectly through the belief system, Hodder (1982a:215) has argued that beliefs are constructed through structural oppositions. Therefore, social differentiation, as it is expressed through mortuary differentiation, may be imbedded in the procession, form and symbolism of rites aimed at satisfying philosophical-religious beliefs about 'universal orders' and the soul. The definition of the social personae is therefore imbedded in a common ideological heritage (David 1992), and may operate through mortuary ritual in the ways identified by Giddens (1979:193-197): (1) by representing the dominant sections of society as universal; (2) by denial or transmutation of contradictions; and (3) through the naturalisation of the present, or structuring mortuary practices according to 'natural' statuses based upon age, gender, and so forth.

Second, the connection between the expression of social statuses and beliefs is supported by ethnographic research (Table 2.1), and provides some basis for comparing archaeologically observed patterns produced by similar types of differentiation (cf. O'Shea 1984:64). While the main dimensions of social distinctions are commonly reflected in mortuary practices, O'Shea (1981, 1984) has argued that some are more visible in the archaeological record than others. O'Shea argued that horizontal distinctions would be less visible than vertical ones. This hypothesis has not been supported through ethnographic study and may largely reflect methodological problems, as vertical and horizontal distinctions are determined quantitatively rather than qualitatively (Carr 1995:187). Furthermore, O'Shea linked body preparation and treatment to horizontal distinctions and the quantity of grave furniture to vertical social position. Neither of these assertions are supported by the present ethnography (Carr 1992), and a perusal of Table 2.1 suggests that vertical and horizontal social position may be expressed in much the same way cross-culturally.

Third, the latter observation is of considerable methodological importance. Vertical social position is most often reflected in the energy expended in disposing the dead, and there is little correlation between the frequency of grave goods and vertical position as proposed by Binford (1971), Stickel (1969) and O'Shea (1981, 1984). The premise behind this is that certain mortuary treatments using certain social symbols refer to different statuses, and these positions are of successively higher importance. Distribution pyramids (or hierarchical pyramid) have been a common technique used to relate the distribution of grave good frequencies and associations (Binford 1971; Braun 1979; Peebles and Kus 1977; Stickel 1969) to social position. It is argued that people of higher social status were given more goods, and these positions are held by a progressively decreasing number of individuals resulting in a pyramid of specific social rank categories. While the frequency of grave goods corresponds in a gross way to the total energy expenditure given a person's interment—as a material contribution to ritual—there is little basis for making a distinction between objects contributed during the precession of rites or those that were personal possessions.

However, these findings do not diminish the importance of using energy expenditures to evaluate the social position of the deceased. It has proven to be a powerful concept because one can describe qualitatively or quantitatively the effort given an individual's mortuary treatment. The notion of using energy expenditures to determine rank differentiation is grounded in systems theory and based upon premises made by Saxe (1970) and Binford (1971). Saxe (1970:6) noticed that the occasion of death calls for the participation of individuals who had entered into relationships with the deceased. Further, Binford (1971:21) noted that the *social personae* and the size and composition of the social group who endorse status responsibilities to the deceased are two very important components that aid in structuring the form of mortuary ritual. Binford (1971:21) proposed that individuals of higher rank would be entitled to greater corporate involvement in their interment, and therefore would cause a greater degree of disruption in the community for conducting the mortuary ritual. The premise for measuring energy or labour expenditure was expanded by these ideas, stating that

> we may observe that both the amount of corporate involvement, and the degree of activity disruption, will positively correspond to the amount of human labour expended in the mortuary act. Labour expenditure should in turn be reflected in such features of the burial as size and elaborateness of the interment facility, method of handling and disposal of the corpse, and the nature of the grave associations (Tainter and Cordy 1977:97).

These observable levels of energy expenditure are understood to reflect the existence of a corresponding structure of rank grading in a society (Tainter 1977a:331), as it is assumed that the archaeological evidence of energy expenditure in a mortuary treatment has a direct relationship to the hierarchical strata which the society is

divided into. However, the methodological problems raised by O'Shea (1984) regarding this procedure have limited its use.

It is now necessary to reconsider the theoretical conceptions of energy expenditure and the methods used to quantify it in light of Carr's (1995) recent addition to the cross-cultural surveys of mortuary practices made by archaeologists (cf. also Binford 1971; Goldstein 1976, 1981; Tainter 1975a; and Vehik 1975). I suggest that if energy expenditure is to have any utility in mortuary studies it must be conceived of as a cumulative measure of the archaeologically visible mortuary process—the sequence of rites involved in transforming the social personae, or what Hertz (1907) described as the relationship between 'The Living and the Mourners' and 'The Soul and the Dead.' The social dimension of this process, whereby the differentiation of the social individual is determined by the scale of rites—Hertz's relationship between 'The Living and the Mourners' and 'The Corpse and its Disposal'—has been given unwarranted superiority over the study of the mortuary process and the metaphors of death expressed through the form and symbolism of rights that define the relationship between 'The Corpse and its Disposal' and 'The Soul and the Dead.' If energy expenditures can be used to evaluate the process of mortuary ritual, then it is clear that the different stages in that process must separately and individually evaluated. As Carr's findings again stress, the activities involved in each stage of the process can and often do 'mean' something different than others. While the preparation of the body and the types of grave furniture made for or used in mortuary ritual may be significant expressions of beliefs about the nature of the soul and its effect upon the living, these activities are a direct product of the physical and emotional effort involved in manipulating the corporeal and spiritual individual from the state of life to the state of death.

2.3   SUMMARY

In this chapter, I have outlined a theoretical basis to address the three principle relationships defined by Hertz (1907) which are expressed in mortuary practices and remains and a set of analytical procedures that isolate the material differentiation in them. The main problem facing the archaeologist is to determine which aspects of a particular mortuary practice are operating in what capacity. Such analyses must consider both the structure of mortuary remains and the processes that led to mortuary practices. This has not been the norm in most analyses of mortuary ritual.

During the 1970s American mortuary archaeology was focused almost exclusively on the social dimensions of mortuary practices and remains. By the 1980s, more effort was focused upon understanding the form and symbolism of mortuary rites. Yet, surprisingly few studies have taken into account the procession of rites. For example, following Giddens (1979; see above), Shanks and Tilley (1982) proposed that the *in situ* spatial arrangement of different dismembered and disarticulated fauna in Neolithic tombs represented ideological naturalisation (linking social constructs as part of the natural order of things) and denial of contradiction (covering up or misrepresentation of social relations). An observation made by David (1992:349, n.12), noted how Shanks and Tilley ignored the precession of rites—the process of decarnalisation and ancestralisation of the deceased. Thus, they assumed the final structural arrangement of bones provided the explanation and not the process that led to that pattern.

The methodology I have described here utilises descriptions of variation in the transformation of the corporeal remains of the deceased as a means to elucidate the analogous transformation of the social personae, the metaphorical transformation of members of the living community to the community of the dead, and the social differences that existed between individuals in life. In the following chapters, I will demonstrate that this approach permits new insights into mortuary variability, the reasons for the physical visibility of the dead, the complexity of mortuary practices, community ideology, and social differentiation during the Neolithic period in Greece.

CHAPTER 3
EARLY AND MIDDLE NEOLITHIC MORTUARY PRACTICES

3.1 EARLY AND MIDDLE NEOLITHIC CULTURE-HISTORY

The Early Neolithic (EN) phase, and the following Middle Neolithic (MN) phase, are characterized by what have been termed 'classic' Neolithic traits—settled agriculture life and a diversity in the types, styles, and functions of ceramics and stone tools. However, in Greece, these phases hold some unique characteristics unlike contemporary Temperate European or Near Eastern cultures. The EN phase is similar in many ways to the subsequent MN phase, and supposes continuous development over less than two millennia.

The majority of radiocarbon dates place the Early Neolithic between 6500 and 5800 B.C., with two dates near 6800 B.C. (Demoule and Perlès 1993:368). The MN phase is comparably of shorter duration and radiocarbon dates cluster around 5800-5300 B.C. (Demoule and Perlès 1993). The MN seems to be part of a continuous development begun in the EN because there are few differences in settlement pattern and architecture, and domestic equipment. The significant differences come in the area of ceramic and stone tool production, as well as the development of a more complex system of trade and exchange during the MN phase.

3.1.1 Settlement Pattern

The settlement pattern for the EN is best known from Thessaly as a result of extensive survey conducted over twenty years (French 1972; Halstead 1984; Gallis 1989). The two striking features of the EN settlement pattern are the high number and relative stability of sites. In Thessaly alone about 120 sites are known for this period, and these are separated by a mean distance of less than 5 km (Demoule and Perlès 1993:368). Over 75% of these sites were occupied for the entire MN phase as well (cf. also van Andels and Runnels 1995 for the Larissa Basin).

The density of settlements shows two distinct patterns. In Thessaly the density was high, considering the number sites and their location. Outside of Thessaly, settlement density was low. There were less permanent settlements, with fewer long-lasting or monumental features (Cherry et al. 1988). Several explanations have been given for this pattern. For the South, it has been suggested that people sought out permanent springs that would supply a constant and reliable source of water (Runnels and van Andel 1987). Jacobsen (1984b), on the other hand, has suggested the pattern is due to the seasonal movement of

flocks in the southeastern Peloponnese, based upon traditional transhumance trails.

Generally, sites are clustered around the drainage of major rivers, in the foothills, and a few are located in the semi-mountainous areas, up to 500 m above sea level. The availability of water seems to have been the most important factor for the location of settlements, as villages were built on a variety of soil types, but the method of procuring water (through wells, cisterns, or depressions) is still a matter of debate (Demoule and Perlès 1993:368).

There are also discrepancies in the measurements of the sizes of the sites. Halstead (1984: Table 6.1, 6.6) estimated that the average site size was less than 1 hectare, based upon French's data (1972). But Demoule and Perlès (1993:370), using Gallis' (1989) data, suggest a range from 2 to 5.5 ha in size. The population of the sites is estimated to range from 100 to 300 people per settlement (Halstead 1984; Jacobsen 1981), or perhaps slightly higher in some cases (Theocharis 1973).

The majority of settlements are open-air sites. Caves were not widely used during the MN for habitation but were often used for the disposal of the dead (see below). On of the more intriguing features of MN settlements is the presence of ditches around several settlements. At Nea Nikomedia (Rodden 1965), there was an early wall which was quickly replaced by a ditch. These ditches, also found at Servia, Souphli Magoula, and Achilleion, have not been adequately explained. Jacobsen (1981) suggests that they were used for drainage. Others submit that the ditch has symbolic meaning, delimiting the inner village space (Demoule and Perlès 1993:370). Most agree, though, that the ditches were not used for defense purposes nor really had any practical significance whatsoever.

3.1.2 Settlement Architecture

The plan of most settlements is of an agglomorative type, with closely spaced free-standing houses, without common walls or bounded courtyards. The houses are typical of Neolithic Greece and the Balkans. They are small and rectangular, but each house has its own particular details (Elia 1982).

Two types of building materials were used at Greek sites. Mudbrick (which common to the Near East but mainly limited to Greece in Temperate Europe) and the wattle-and-daub technique (typical of Europe but not the Near

East) were both used at EN settlements (e.g. Sesklo). Stone was also sometimes used for foundations where it was readily accessible. However, it is the copious use of mud that may provide us with some clue as to the presence of the 'ditches.' Since earth was the most common construction material, used quite regularly in the construction or repair of the houses, why would people travel long distances to obtain it? Using the earth from around the settlement would create a ditch, and at the same time would provide defence from predators, or perhaps people. The ditch would also control and restrict access into and out of the settlement. And, therefore, perhaps as Demoule and Perlès have suggested, the ditch delimited the village centre (or the 'heart' of the village) from the outlying areas.

The actual appearance of houses is known from a few clay figures. Most seem to have two or three rooms, with double pitched, painted roofs. Several openings, serving as doors or windows, are also known. A rare find at Prodromos attests to the use of wood. At this site, squared beams were connected by wooden pegs to create the house super-structure (Hourzoumiadis 1971). On the inside, houses show a variation on two main features: floor coverings and hearths. Sometimes floors were covered in patches with pebble floors, spotted with pits of unbaked clay. Most often, though, they consist of unadorned packed clay. Hearths were pebble-lined and plastered, raised on platforms, and some look quite oven-like. The oven-like hearths have been found both inside houses and in open spaces. Actual "ovens" are quite rare, as at Nea Nikomedia (Rodden 1962), which may have been used for cooking or as ceramic kilns (Theocharis 1973).

3.1.3 Technology and Crafts

3.1.3.1 Domestic Equipment

The domestic equipment used during the Early Neolithic is typical of the period, in that it is cumbersome and quite diverse. Mats are known from sherd impressions at Servia (Carington Smith 1977), and twine-weaved mats were found at Nea Nikomedia (Rodden 1964). The presence of weaving is surmised from the rare spindle whorls. However, some artifacts of unknown function may have a connection to weaving. Small disks that have been pierced could have been used to wind and store wool, while the 'sling-bullets' made of baked or unbaked clay, are reminiscent of loom-weights. The 'sling bullets' are often found in great bundles (up to thirty) near hearths.

At all sites clay spoons and ladles, stone pestles, pounders, palettes, grinders, and querns were used. Bone tools are numerous and show quite a variety. Awls were often made from the distal end of a sheep (*Ovis aries*) or goat (*Capra hircus*) metapodials. Pins, spatulae, burnishers, and hooks were also crafted out of bone

(Moundrea-Agrafioti 1980; 1981). Polished stone tools (axes, celts, chisels) were made out of a variety of raw materials, including serpentine, jadeite, hematite, and igneous rock. The properties of these rocks suggest that the tool was cut and ground into shape, rather than flaked before polishing.

3.1.3.2 Ceramic Production

New ideas of EN ceramic production come from recent work done in the Peloponnese and from archaeometric analyses. EN ceramics are typically small and consist primarily of convex bowls with rounded bases. Recent studies suggest that the base was modeled and then the walls were built with coils or slabs, particularly at Franchthi Cave and Sesklo (Vitelli 1984; 1993). The bowls were slipped, rarely painted with iron oxide pigments, and were well burnished (Vitelli 1984, 1993). Temperatures less than 650°C were used for firing, and the pots show direct contact with the fuel (Vitelli 1991; Maniatis and Tite 1981). The pots seem to have been fired individually, and made only when needed. Casual, seasonal production would account for the irregularities in shape and the small sizes of the pots.

Ceramic decoration is quite scarce and is limited to geometric motifs. These motifs are painted in red or brown on a light background. This type of decoration, known as 'proto-Sesklo,' is common in Thessaly (Sesklo, Prodromos, Otzaki), and to a few sites in the south (Elatia, Boeotia, and Franchthi Cave, Argolid) (Demoule and Perlès 1993:381). Impressed wares are also known during the EN in northern Greece. Although rare in the northeast, it dominates types in the northwest. Despite these differences, there are no sharp stylistic boundaries during the EN.

In the MN phase, ceramic technology appears to have been more aggressively explored, producing impressive developments and innovations. Unlike the EN, however, the ceramics are not as homogeneous throughout Greece (Demoule and Perlès 1993:377). Different fabrics were used for different types of wares for the first time in Greek prehistory (Vitelli 1989). This allowed a greater variety of more difficult shapes to be produced, such as carinated vessels, pyriform vases, basins with pedestals, and collared jars. As well, the size of the vessels greatly increased. The firing temperatures were increased by several hundred degrees over the EN (above 800°C) (Maniatis and Tite 1981; Vitelli 1991), and numerous pots were now being fired together (Vitelli 1993).

The MN phase is also characterised by a greater diversity in decoration, which became more common and covered most of the pots. Different regional styles also began to develop. In the Peloponnese, monochrome, pattern-painted, and pattern-burnished Urfirnis wares were made, using iron-oxide pigments exclusively (Cullen 1985a,

1985b; Vitelli 1974, 1993). In Boeotia, painted and unpainted backgrounds were used for ceramics (Weinberg 1962). In Thessaly, the Sesklo pottery tradition continues, with geometric decoration in brown-red painted on a white to cream background (Kotsakis 1983; Mottier 1981). At Nea Nikomedia, in western Macedonia, a new range of decorations in brown-red on a light slip predominates (Washburn 1984). Besides the painted wares, the first coarse wares make their appearance into ceramic assemblages. These were repeatedly used on fires, based on repetitive burn marks (Vitelli 1989, 1991), but are still very uncommon, totalling only 5-10% of all types (Demoule and Perlès 1993:381).

The more extensive labour investment required to make these ceramics suggests that production was no longer a casual undertaking. Instead, it appears that potters were at least part-time craft specialists (e.g., Vitelli 1989, 1991). During the MN, potters may have been less constrained by subsistence and other duties, allowing them the time and resources to explore different manufacturing techniques (Arnold 1985). Regardless of the opportunities that potters had to explore different avenues of manufacture, there must also have been a economic and social demand for the greater diversity of ceramics. The dichotomy between 'fine' and 'coarse' wares has led researchers to consider socio-economic reasons for greater variability in ceramic types during the MN. The distinctiveness of local fabrics has been interpreted as having the intensive objective of creating visible, characterising social symbols (Vitelli 1991), or as displaying links within growing local and regional social systems (Cullen 1985a, 1985b; Perlès 1992), rather than local experimentation and trade in technology. It has further been argued that the small and selective exchange of local ceramics was a mechanism used to avoid inter-settlement conflicts (Cullen 1985a, 1985b). However, there should be caution taken in such interpretive approaches, as symbolic or reciprocal exchange is far more difficult to monitor than simply tracing the goods that are exchanged (Greenfield 1991). Nevertheless, it is apparent at this point that some degree of craft specialisation is shown by the range and high level of craftsmanship needed to produce the ceramic wares developed in the MN.

3.1.3.3 *Stone Tool Production*

The flaked stone tools of the EN have often been described as simple. However, the simplicity of the tools is based upon complex strategies of procuring raw material and sophisticated production techniques. A wide variety of raw material was used for tools and these were crafted using an equally wide range of techniques. Local raw materials (low quality chert and jasper) were rarely used and tools were made from odd-shaped flakes

produced by direct percussion using a hammer (Demoule and Perlès 1993:382). The non-local materials, which make up the majority of assemblages, were obtained from great distances and worked by a variety of techniques (Moundrea-Agrafioti 1981, 1983; Perlès 1990; Perlès and Vaughan 1983). Obsidian was gained from the Cycladic island of Melos and was pressure flaked into fine blades and microblades. Finer-grained cherts, although not common, were worked much the same way as the obsidian to produce the same goods. The larger blades were made of honey flints, introduced as blanks, and used for plant processing. The jasper blades were produced by indirect percussion and were used for processing plants. Stone tool assemblages in the EN, then, consist mainly of unretouched obsidian blades and retouched flint and jasper blades with little retouch and a sickle gloss (Moundrea-Agrafioti 1981, 1983; Perlès 1990; Perlès and Vaughan 1983). The number of drills, borers, and points varies greatly between sites, and the rare trapeze blades are the only tool that could be considered arrowheads (Demoule and Perlès 1993:382).

The tool-kit from the MN differs significantly from the EN kit in that retouching was employed with greater frequency (Elster 1989; Moundrea Agrafioti 1981, 1993; Perlès and Vaughan 1983). Obsidian blades and sickle blades were now commonly retouched, undergoing numerous periods of use and reuse. Due to the nature of obsidian, it was retouched only marginally. During this phase, bifacial, transverse arrowheads were commonly used, and eventually were worked into asymmetrical points with a lateral notch by the end of the phase. As with the ceramic assemblage, craft specialization is apparent in the making of the flaked tools. As flint-knappers know, the technique of pressure-flaking is a difficult one. It is noteworthy that even with a low production rate, the frequency of errors in the blades is almost undetectable (Demoule and Perlès 1993:383).

3.1.4 Trade and Exchange

The peculiar aspect of the EN lithic industry is that there is no regional variability in non-local raw material use. The relatively small amount of non-local material suggests that direct procurement of exotic materials by the inhabitants is unlikely, as land and sea trips of several hundred kilometres would have been necessary to obtain the raw materials (Perlès 1990). The long-distance exchange of EN lithics contrasts with the near absence of trade in ceramics. This implies the abundant use of local raw materials for making ceramics, and is supported by ethnographic evidence that potters rarely venture over two or three kilometres to obtain clay (Arnold 1985). The exchange of ornaments and "prestige items," such as stone seals or vases, are again different. These were traded in much the same way as lithics, but in less quantity. Still, at the beginning of the Neolithic we see a

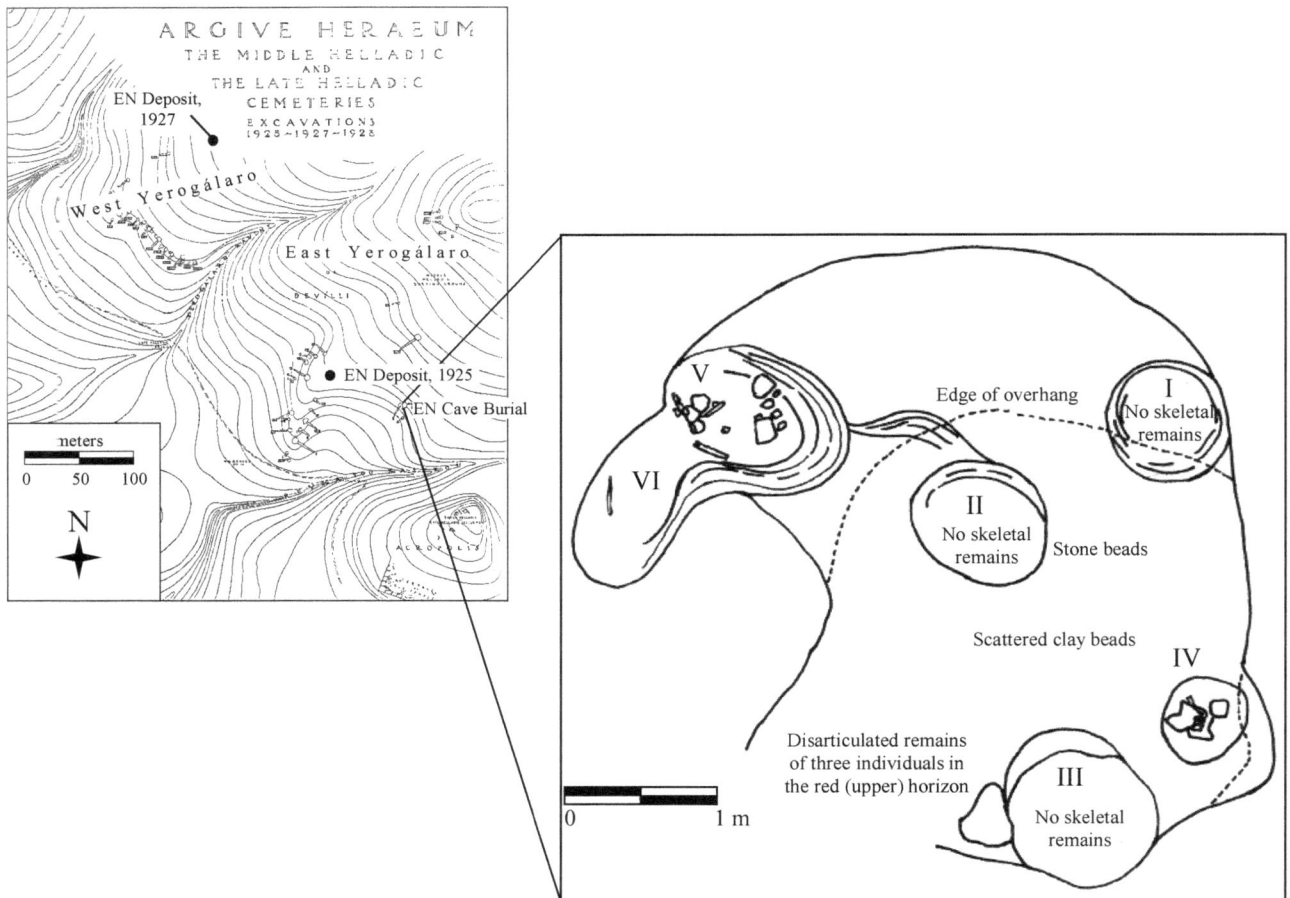

Figure 3.1. Plan of the cave with Early Neolithic burials and human skeletal remains at Prosymna (redrawn from Blegen 1937: fig. 28). Inset shows the location of deposits with Early Neolithic remains at Prosymna (modified after Blegen 1937: plan 1).

pattern of complex trade and exchange relationships between neighbouring sites.

The exchange of ceramics during the MN suggests that relationships between neighbouring Neolithic societies were becoming more manifest in terms of cultural material. How this relates to the more specific workings of social systems has yet to be significantly addressed. Still, in the MN, the range of trade in lithics was comparable to other artefact types. Although the origins and patterns of circulation for all the flaked stone have yet to be studied, Demoule and Perlès (1993:383-384) have suggested three systems of exchange that took place during the MN:

- Stone tools: including flaked, polished, or ground stone tools. These are considered utilitarian goods with a common "style" throughout Greece. The material was circulated over a large area, and was probably procured and produced by a small group of part-time specialists.

- Ceramics: including the decorated and coarse wares. These are characterised by clear and deliberate styles which fall into distinct regional boundaries, and small amounts of were circulated. All types were manufactured locally with local materials.

- Speciality Items: including stone seals and vases, and stone and shell ornaments. These are thought to be symbolic or prestige items (Demoule and Perlès 1993:384), with no real stylistic distinctions. The unusual characteristic of these items is the rarity of the materials, which, once manufactured, were not exchanged over wide distances. Perhaps also significant is the rarity with which these items appear in the grave assemblages.

3.2   PROSYMNA

The area around Prosymna was a location favoured for habitation from the Neolithic to Classical times. During three field seasons (1925, 1927, and 1928), Carl Blegen laid out numerous exploratory trenches in the hopes of uncovering unknown areas of the Bronze Age settlements and the associated tombs (Blegen 1937). Blegen's excavations revealed five Neolithic deposits (Fig. 3.1, inset) that suggest Early Neolithic habitation of the area (Demoule and Perlès 1993:385). On the West Yerogálaro ridge, a rectangular depression (2.6 x 2.8 x 0.55 m) running from east to west was filled with small stones, pieces of charcoal, several wares of broken EN pottery, 80 flakes and fragments of obsidian, faunal remains, and the floor and walls were burned (Blegen 1937:28-29). The pit was interpreted as a hearth and the area surrounding it marked a tool-processing and domestic area (Blegen 1937:28).

In the central area of the East Yerogálaro ridge, three further Neolithic deposits were found. One of these was a small deposit containing sherds of Early Neolithic date (Blegen 1937:23-24). Traces of Neolithic occupations were more visible on the east side of Chamber Tomb X. Here, a large irregularly shaped circular depression (4 m in diameter and 0.8 m deep) held animal bones, numerous pottery sherds, and charcoal. The monochrome (black, red, and brown) and polychrome wares ('rainbow' ware) found in the depression are characteristic of EN pottery wares in southern Greece. A thick deposit of carbonized material and ashes indicates that this area also acted as a large open hearth. The size of the depression also suggested that the hearth was located inside a moderately-sized hut (Blegen 1937:25). However, the ash deposit was thick and filled the entire depression, so it is unlikely that it was used a residence. Four smaller depressions (from 0.8 m to 1.25 m) were found in the immediate vicinity of this feature—to the north, south and two to the east—and are thought to be smaller fire pits (Blegen 1937:25).

The Neolithic burials were found very near the group of fire pits. While tracing the southeastern extent of Neolithic habitation debris associated with the fire pits, excavation revealed the entrance to a small cave and three disturbed skeletons. Two strata of relatively thick layers of ash (0.3 m and 0.2 m) were found further into the cave. Pottery dating to the EN phase was found within and below the ash layer. Further into the small cave were six graves. Three graves were empty and the other three contained human skeletal remains.

The habitation and mortuary remains suggest a small population. Although it is problematic to relate the different deposits precisely, they are all of EN date and it is possible that the same people used the habitation site and disposed of their dead in the cave. Judging from the faunal remains deposited in the fire pits this group had a different subsistence focus than is characteristic of Neolithic agropastoralists. There was an emphasis on wild game and there is no clear indication of cultigens or domesticated stock. The lack of more permanent stone-built structures (walls or foundations) or evidence of substantial wooden structures found at other EN sites, while not entirely characteristic of highly mobile groups, at least indicate less permanent occupation. There is every indication that the EN inhabitants of Prosymna did not practice a mixed-farming economy. These observations do not agree with the characteristics of other EN settlements in the southeastern Peloponnese. While some (e.g., Cauvin 1992; Sherratt 1981, 1983; van Andel and Runnels 1987) have observed that Neolithic groups in this region practiced a pastoral economy and were more mobile, this only occurred later during the Late Neolithic phase.

3.2.1 Mortuary Remains

The cave containing mortuary remains is about four meters in diameter and a meter high rock outcrop remains of the original the cave ceiling (Fig. 3.1). Five discrete strata were identified at the entrance and within the cave (Blegen 1937:25- 27):

(1) Immediately below the surface of the entrance was a mass of broken conglomerate over a half metre thick (ca. 60 cm). This was interpreted as the original overhang of the cave that had collapsed in antiquity sealing the cave.

(2) Below this was a reddish sandy soil of similar thickness. The very disturbed and scattered remains of three skulls and other human bone fragments were found at this level in the southwest corner at the cave entrance (Fig. 3.1).

(3) The remains were badly weathered and could not be handled.

(4) Below the reddish horizon was a layer of very black soil containing carbonised organic matter. The layer was of variable thickness, but averaged 30 cm.

(5) A third soil horizon at the lowest level was a ca. 20 cm thick greyish mixture of earth and ash.

(6) Below the ash layer was the basal layer of the cave floor and it is at this level where six deliberately constructed depressions were found.

The six depressions are circular, or slightly oval, pits that vary in size (Table 3.1). They have an average radius of 0.635 m and a volume of 0.686 m^3. The smallest and largest graves differ slightly from 0.36 m in radius to 0.58 m3 in volume. There is some disparity, then, between the sizes of the graves.

Of the six identified depressions, only three held skeletal remains. Grave IV is located in the southeast corner of the cave and contained the disturbed remains of a juvenile. The burned and broken bones were arranged

TABLE 3.1
THE EARLY NEOLITHIC MORTUARY REMAINS AT PROSYMNA

Grave No.	Location	Grave Type	Grave Shape	Grave Dimensions				Interment Form	Pattern of Bone Association	Burial Scenario	Age	Grave Goods	Associated Features or Objects
				L	W	Depth	Volume						
I	cave interior	pit	circular	0.85	0.85	0.45	0.26	no remains		cenotaph?			
II	cave interior	pit	circular	0.97	0.82	0.25	0.18	no remains		cenotaph?			clay beads
III	cave interior	pit	circular	1.15	1.0	0.4	0.42	no remains		cenotaph?			
IV	cave interior	pit	circular	0.65	0.55	0.4	0.13	cremation	bone fragments around skull	secondary	juvenile	.	covering stones
V	cave interior	pit	oval	1.5	0.85	0.45	1.95	cremation	bone fragments around skull	secondary	adult	broken stone bead, obsidian blade, 2 red monochrome sherds	covering stones
VI	cave interior	pit	oval	1.0	0.65	0.55	1.18	inhumation?	single humerus	secondary? (extramural)	adult		
--	cave entrance									secondary? (extramural)			
--	cave entrance									secondary? (extramural)			
--	cave entrance									secondary? (extramural)			

Source: Blegen (1937).

around the skull in the centre of the depression and no objects were associated with the burial. Graves V and VI are located in a depression and niche, respectfully, under a rock overhang in the northwest corner of the cave. Grave V contained the fragmentary and partially burned skeleton of an adult. As with Grave IV, broken arm and leg bones were arranged around skull fragments. Small stones had been incorporated in the grave fill and were placed over the remains. This is the only burial with grave goods, which included a blade of obsidian, a broken stone bead and two sherds of red monochrome ware. Grave VI held only the broken long bone of another adult (perhaps a femur). The bone was not burned and no objects were associated with it. Graves I, II, and III did not contain any skeletal remains but have the same shape as the others. Graves I and III were filled with grey earth and small stones but did not contain any objects. Grave II is a shallow depression also containing grey earth and stones and four stone beads were found beside it at a depth level with the cave floor at the time the depression was made. In the central area of the cave, where no pits were located, several clay beads were scattered about the area.

3.2.2   Mortuary Practices

The burials at Prosymna present an interesting set of preparation and treatment techniques. Most notable is the evidence for partial cremation. Not all the remains found were burned, and the single bone in Grave VI and the skeletal remains at the cave entrance do not appear to have subjected to firing. In Graves IV and V, both cranial and post-cranial bone elements were burnt and were highly carbonised and blackish in appearance. This suggests that they had been subjected to direct intense heat for a long duration of time. Blegen reported no pathologies or cut marks on the burnt bone, but their characteristics suggest that the bodies were burned "dry" or after all the flesh decayed or was removed. Considering Buikstra and Swegle's (1989) experimental data, it would have taken more than an hour of intense heat to achieve this degree of thermal alteration. Also, contrary to Bennett's (1999) experimental work, it is not likely that the bones were burned *after* being interred— the character of the bone does not correspond to the intensity of the fire necessary to achieve that state of alteration.

Besides being partially cremated, only certain portions of the bodies—fragmented pieces of long bones and skulls—were placed in Graves IV and V and arranged around the skull in the middle of the grave. While each grave is somewhat disturbed, having two burials arranged in such a fashion is more likely to be intentional than due to chance. Clearly, the bodies were cremated before being placed in the depressions. The thick layers of carbonised organic debris indicate that fires were constructed in the small cave after bodies were placed in the grave and sealed with earth and stones. Whether the cremations and the ashy debris in the cave are connected is debatable.

Blegen suggested that the fire pits excavated near the cave and on the West Yerogálaro ridge would have acted as cremation pyres (Blegen 1937:25, 29). However, the deep ash layers inside the cave suggest other possibilities. In all other cases of cremation during the Neolithic in Greece, burned human bone is found in two contexts other than grave pits. They either occur in so-called 'cremation pits', as at Souphli Magoula and Plateia Magoula Zarkou (Gallis 1982), or they become incorporated in habitation debris, such as at Franchthi Cave (Cullen 1995), Aleopotrypa Cave (Papathanasopoulos 1971; Lambert 1972) and Kitsos Cave (Lambert 1981). The great distance between the deposit on the West Yerogálaro ridge and the cave site, located over 300 m apart, does not make it the most practicable place to carry out a cremation. To transport the cremated remains would have required a container of some sort. It would follow, as is represented in other cases of cremation during this phase (e.g., Souphli Magoula), that the cremated remains would have been given final interment still in the container, most likely a ceramic vessel. Further, while the fire pits on the East Yerogálaro are closer (some 70 m) no human skeletal remains were discovered in the deposits or the vicinity that could be attributed to the EN occupation of the area. It is improbable, then, that the hearth located on the West Yerogálaro ridge would have acted as a funerary pyre. If the bodies were cremated outside of the cave, it is unlikely that this was done in fires used for domestic purposes. It is more likely that cremations would have taken place at the entrance to the cave. If the cremations occurred here, all the bones could be easily recovered and transported to the pit for burial. Not all of the bone elements of the dead were placed in the burial pits, however, and it appears they were selectively culled before final interment. The remaining body parts were not found during excavation.

Although the exact details followed in disposing of the dead are elusive, the amount of fuel needed to accomplish even partial cremation would shortly create very thick deposits of ash and charred organic debris in the cave. This may go some way to explaining the gross thickness of the ashy strata in the cave. Blegen did originally interpret the ashy layers as the remnants of a shrine where sacrifices were offered to the dead. Blegen's report does not make it clear that charred faunal remains were incorporated into the ashy deposit and this makes it difficult to suggest that animal sacrifice was part of the mortuary ritual. Alternatively, we could expect such debris if ash and other burned organic debris from domestic fires were dumped in the cave. What can be gleaned from these data is that the thickness of the ashy layer accumulated from repeated activity post-dating the burials. The presence of numerous sherds of EN pottery strewn about the entrance of the cave may indicate an in-cave ritual, but this may also be unrelated to the techniques used to dispose the dead. However, the stratigraphy, similarities in the disposal of the dead, and the pattern of artefact scatter do suggest some type of post-interment mortuary ritual occurred within the cave.

The highly weathered and fragile human remains found in the reddish, sandy soil at the entrance of the cave are not easily associated with the lower ash deposit and other burial features. There is no evidence that the entrance had been deliberately covered in any fashion, by a wall, stones, etc. Given these circumstances, it is likely that, as Blegen (1937:26) proposed, the cave was accessible when the burials occurred. It may be suggested that the three empty graves may have once held the remains of the three individuals at the cave entrance and their dislocation was a result of carnivore activity. This is unlikely for both stratigraphic and taphonomic reasons.

Stratigraphically, some 50 cm of soil and ash separate the pit burials from the disturbed skeletal material in the upper level. It is only possible to suggest that the pit burials occurred before the skeletal remains were deposited in the more recent red sediment. The empty graves may be viewed as either cenotaph burials or cases where the contents have simply disintegrated. The latter is not plausible in light of the environment within the cave. The hardpan and ashy layer are an alkaline environment and the bones found in the graves, while fragmented and broken, were not in such a fragile condition as those found in the red sediment at the mouth of the cave. Reddish soils in Mediterranean and semi-tropical environments are more acidic due to the mineral content of the soils. This is probably a major contributing factor to the preservation and recovery of Neolithic burials in Greece and other area with similar soil types (e.g., sub-Saharan Africa). Both these lines of evidence suggest that only three burials occurred in the cave, but preparations were conducted for three others. The three bodies found at the cave entrance may then represent extramural burials, or the first stage in preparing the body for cremation (defleshing) and then subsequent interment in the pit graves. However, there are two problems with this hypothesis. First, it is difficult to suggest why the process was not completed and bodies at the entrance of the cave were never cremated and placed in the pit graves. Second, while the skeletal remains do come from a level with EN debris, there remain no reasonable grounds to connect these remains with the stratigraphically earlier burials. The only other option is to suggest that three people were unceremoniously caught in the debris as the overhang of the small cave collapsed. Without a detailed understanding of the skeletal remains, the fate of these individuals remains enigmatic.

The grave goods and other artefacts found in the cave circumstantially support a scenario where the empty graves acted as cenotaphs. The beads in the central part of the cave and near the southwest edge of Grave II indicate a type of personal ornamentation used in the community and may have originally been placed over the empty graves as part of the ritual requirements for cenotaph burials. In contrast, the only grave goods were given to the adult in Grave V. This implies that this individual received greater corporate involvement in the material contribution to ritual, and may have held some measure of prestige in the small community. Alternatively, such treatment may be characteristic of adult burials. It is clear, though, that the energy expended in disposing of the dead was not uniform. Comparatively, lower energy expenditures were involved in interring the juvenile in Grave IV and the individual in Grave VI, while the adult in Grave V had the greatest amount of energy expenditure. Also of considerable interest is the inclusion of broken red sherds amongst the goods in Grave V. The practice of placing deliberately broken objects does occur in other Neolithic mortuary contexts, but the purposeful inclusion of red-coloured pottery is limited to the EN-MN phases (e.g., Souphli Magoula, Franchthi Cave). The significance of this pattern will be discussed later in this chapter.

3.2.3 Conclusions

In general, mortuary differentiation at Prosymna is characterised by: (1) the same set of techniques used to prepare the body and the grave; (2) a disproportionate distribution of grave goods and the exclusive allocation of specific types of goods; (3) the differential location of skeletal remains; and (4) at least two discernible levels of energy expended in the overall mortuary treatment of the dead. The impetus behind these different treatments is speculative considering the size of the sample and any suggestions can only be offered with caution, but two patterns do stand out.

First, the evidence suggests that two completely different scenarios were used to dispose of the dead at Prosymna: cenotaph burials and extramural secondary burials. The secondary burials are characterised by the deliberate destruction of the integrity of the corpse (Bloch 1971). Such treatment of the dead is surely linked to the society's perception of the dead, the circumstances surrounding the person's death and the perceived relationship between the living and the dead. The underlying theme of such a disposal program is that the mortal remains of the dead must be sufficiently transformed so that the dead individual does not remotely resemble the living individual. In this sense, the transformation of the individual's social personae is complete and irreversible. Practically, more effort (both in terms of time and resources) would be required to dispose of the remains of an adult than that of a child, and this may account for the differences in energy expenditure. The treatment of the dead and the form of burial are uniform and involve the same process. In contrast, the grave goods given the adult are 'individualistic'; that is, they do not form part of a repeated theme. The social or philosophical-religious motivation driving such behaviour is exceedingly difficult if not impossible to isolate, and likely a complex mix of forces became manifest in what appears to be a rather simple mortuary assemblage.

Second, what is perhaps most striking about the burials at Prosymna is that they are disassociated from the space used by the living. Often the formal and exclusive burial of the dead away from living areas is taken to be indicative of a corporate group membership (Saxe 1970; Goldstein 1979, 1980, 1981; Charles and Buikstra 1983). Formal burial space is often thought to be emblematic (in the sense of Wiessner 1984) and is used by sedentary lineage groups to indicate and legitimise their rights or control over resources by burying their dead at key points on the landscape. As competition for the resources intensifies, the spatial differences within the cemetery will become more elaborate. The corporate group has two important characteristics (Murphy 1989:118). First, they may be a kinship or descent group that collectively holds assets or rights to certain valued economic and non-economic holdings. Second, the term designates a continuing group of people that have developed rules of membership and exclusion and do not define themselves on an *ad hoc* basis according to their residence preferences. Although so much remains unknown about the EN habitation at Prosymna, the mortuary evidence conforms to this pattern in its broad outlines. However, to identify a corporate group at Prosymna really does not tell us much about EN social organisation. This is because, like most ethnographic concepts, it refers to types of interactions and beliefs, and not entities or concrete, material 'things.' The concept of a corporate group is thus a difficult one to put into operation in archaeological situations. How can we say the people of Prosymna do not conform to such criteria? Given the signposts of corporate membership that are present at Prosymna, it is surprising that they have not been detected in the Early Bronze Age (Pullen 1985).

3.3   EARLY AND MIDDLE NEOLITHIC FRANCHTHI CAVE

Franchthi Cave is located on a rocky headland on the southern coast of the Argive peninsula in the Peloponnese. The cave is rather large—being some 150 m long—and would have offered excellent protection from predators and the elements. Franchthi Cave is unique amongst early Holocene sites in Greece for

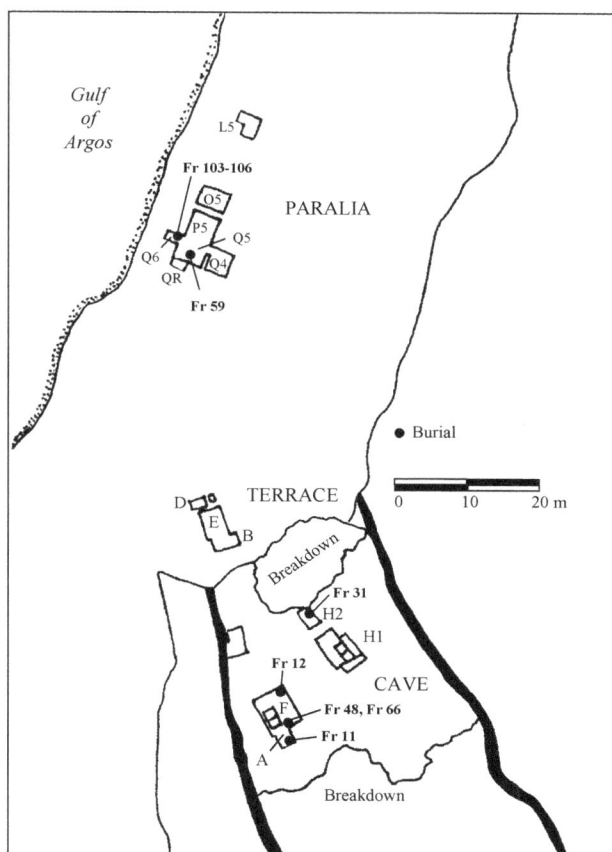

Figure 3.2. Plan of the Franchthi Cave showing the locations of the Early and Middle Neolithic burials (redrawn after Jacobsen and Cullen 1981:figure 1 and Hansen 1991:figure 5).

several reasons: a long and rich record of human habitation; the high standards of fieldwork conducted by the University of Indiana team between 1967 and 1979; the presence of early-dated built structures within and outside the cave; and the earliest dated mortuary remains in Greece. The complex stratigraphy of the site shows that it was used for some 25,000 years (ca. 28,000 to 3,200 B.C.), a time range spanning the Upper Palaeolithic, Mesolithic and Neolithic periods (and perhaps even an earlier occupation). Palaeolithic and Mesolithic habitation occurred only within the cave, but Neolithic and later material was also recovered outside the cave entrance on the beach front, or *paralia* (Fig. 3.3).

Excavations within the cave were limited due to rock falls from the roof and brow of the cave but work along the paralia was less constrained. However, geoarchaeological research indicates a substantial rise of sea level and consequent decrease in the available coastal lowland at the beginning of the Holocene (Bottema 1986, 1994; van Andel, Runnels and Pope 1986; van Andel and Sutton 1987; Gifford 1990; van Andel, Zangger and Demitrack 1990; van Andel and Runnels 1995). There is

TABLE 3.2
THE EARLY AND MIDDLE NEOLITHIC MORTUARY REMAINS AT FRANCHTHI CAVE

Date	Fr[1]	Location	Provenance	Grave Type	Structural Enhancements	Burial Scenario	Interment Form	Body Position	Body Posture	Body Orientation	Age and Sex	Pathology	Grave Goods
EN	11	cave	A:62	pit?		single	inhumation	Left	semi-flexed	N-S	juvenile female? (5-6 yrs.)	slight porotic hyperostosis?	stone "pillow"
EN	12	cave	F/F-1:41D	??		single	inhumation	back	semi-flexed	N-S	juvenile male? (8 yrs.)	porotic hyperostosis?	
EN/early MN	103	paralia	Q6	pit?	cover stones	single	inhumation	left	semi-flexed	NW-SE	foetus		
EN/early MN	104	paralia	Q6	pit		single	inhumation	right	disarticulated	S-N	infant male??		
EN/early MN	105	paralia	Q6	pit?	cover stones	single	inhumation	left	semi-flexed	SW-NE	infant male??		
EN/early MN	106	paralia	Q6	pit	cover stones	single	inhumation	left	semi-flexed	NE-SW	infant male??		
Early MN	48	cave	F/A	lined/pit?	cover stones	single	inhumation	left	semi-flexed	S-N	infant female??		monochrome burnished hole-mouthed, footed marble bowl
Early MN	66	cave	F/A	pit	cover stones	single	inhumation	right	semi-flexed	SW-NE	infant male??		rubbing stone
Early MN	31	cave	H-2 A:95	??		single	inhumation	front	disarticulated	SE-NW	adolescent female (17 yrs.)		
MN	59	paralia	Q5	pit		single	inhumation	right	flexed	NE	adult female (39 yrs.)		monochrome Urfirnis carinated bowl, six bone points, three obsidian blades, and obsidian burin spall?

[1] Fr = Angel (1969) field record number
Source: Jacbosen and Cullen (1981); Angel (1969); T. Cullen, personal communication 1996.

little doubt that any residues of human coastal occupation post-dating the last glacial maximum have long since been covered by the waters of the Bay of Koilada.

3.3.1 The Neolithic at Franchthi Cave

The deposits at Franchthi represent each phase of the Neolithic, a span of time covering some 3,500 years. During the EN, there was a dramatic change from previous Mesolithic subsistence practices. The exploitation of maritime (especially tuna) and wild resources (e.g., red deer) dropped dramatically in comparison with the Mesolithic. Instead, sheep (mainly) and goat came to dominate the faunal record (less so pig and cattle), and certain cereals (emmer and einkorn wheat and two-row barley) were rapidly adopted into the diet.

The new material culture associated with a Neolithic mixed-farming economy—pottery, flaked tools of flint/chert and obsidian—was also introduced, and has many similarities with other EN assemblages throughout the Peloponnese. Materials such as obsidian were somehow (likely indirectly) obtained from the Aegean island of Melos, but other resources, such as marble and andesite, were likely gained from local sources (Jacobsen 1981; Perles 1992). Substantive differences between Mesolithic and Neolithic subsistence strategies have been shown, but the mixed-agriculture of the early Neolithic at Franchthi did change throughout the period. In particular, Jacobsen (1979, 1981, 1984b) has suggested that the broad-spectrum strategies of the EN and MN changed by the Late Neolithic (LN), when seasonal pastoralism became a more significant component of the local economy.

3.3.2 Neolithic Mortuary Remains

The excavations at Franchthi are a story of evolving field methodology. Both excavation and recording methods improved during each of the eight field seasons, and this research remains a model for prehistoric excavation in the country (Cullen 1995:270). Nevertheless, several problems have affected the nature of the remains recovered from Franchthi, and in particular, those relating to the mortuary sample.

Human mortuary remains at Franchthi have been dated to the Mesolithic period and the Early, Middle, and Final Neolithic phases. No remains have yet been dated to the Late Neolithic period, although there is substantial evidence for the habitation of the cave and paralia during this time. Whether this is an artefact of excavation or a case of changing mortuary practices due to increased mobility (i.e., people where buried in locations other than Franchthi) is uncertain, but the former explanation has been considered more plausible (Jacobsen and Cullen 1981; Cullen 1995).

The skeletal remains have been recovered from two contexts: (1) intact or disturbed individual or multiple burials lain out in shallow pits in the cave or paralia; and (2) fragments of human bone that became incorporated into habitation debris. Both the Mesolithic and Neolithic remains both adhere to this general pattern, although Mesolithic burials are found only in the cave (Cullen 1995). Reconciling Angel's (1969, 1973) practice of assigning 'Fr' numbers to single burials or bone fragments has been a large task (see Cullen 1995:274-275 for discussion), and they cannot be equated with the number of individual skeletons at the site. In this assessment, an effort was made to include only partially complete or complete skeletons or bone fragments found directly in an inhumation context which represent single individuals. This practice, combined with the reassessed chronology by Vitelli (1993), has produced a sample of eighteen individuals most securely dated to the EN/Early MN (n=6), early MN (n=3), MN (n=1), and the FN (n=8). The EN-MN remains are the best preserved, and the nature and problems specific to the FN remains will be discussed later (Chapter 5).

The study of human bone scatter has identified several other possible burials. Della Cook's work on the bones stored in Nauplion has identified several other burials, defined by five or more associated bones from at least three different body parts (Cullen, personal communication, 1996). These bone 'groups' were from the same unit and possibly from the same individual, but the excavators designated no formal burial. Five groups of bone scatter have been identified on the Paralia and seven in the cave. The remains belong to five neonates, three juveniles and four adults (possible all female) that date to the EN-MN (n=9), maybe the FN (n=1), and two others could not be assigned to a phase. Only the fragmented remains of an adolescent male (designated here as Fr 18.1) found in association with Fr 18 was included in the FN sample considered here. The remainder of the bone scatter is discussed below separately from the more securely contextualized bone material. Despite early pondering by Jacobsen and Cullen (1981), the presence of secondary burial at Franchthi is unlikely (Cullen, personal communication, 1997).

Also problematic is the nature of the burial facilities at Franchthi. The sediments in the cave are rocky and often no change in soil color was detected around the skeletal remains, so the existence of burial pits was sometimes assumed rather than being physically observed (Cullen, personal communication, 1996). Therefore, no data on grave shape or dimensions were recorded and these attributes are notably absent in the table (Table 3.2). Nevertheless, all of the graves are thought to be pits, as there is no certain evidence of stone-lined graves (but see below), or any other type of elaborate (e.g., stone-built) burial facility. Several burials were elaborated by covering the body with rocks or stone slabs (recorded as 'covering stones' in Table 3.2), but this appears to be restricted to the very young. It should be noted that with one burial (Fr 48) the body may have been interred in a stone-lined pit, but it could not be determined if the stones were placed around the body intentionally.

3.3.5 Early and Middle Neolithic Mortuary Practices

Although the EN and MN samples are collapsed out of necessity, there is surprising consistency in the treatment of the dead over this rather long time span. At least two types of graves can be identified: grave pits with or without covering stones. A possible stone-lined pit (containing Fr 48) would be a variant of the covered grave pit. However, I do not include it here as a third type for the reasons discussed above. Both uncovered and stone-covered grave types occur in the cave and on the paralia. There is no apparent structural elaboration of the pits, but in once case a juvenile's (Fr 11) head was rested on a 'pillow' of pebbles placed there before the funerary ceremony began. It is also most likely that the covering stones were gathered before the body was interred and that the burial itself and completion of the grave was confined to a single event.

The bodies of the dead were carefully laid on either their left or right side in a semi- or fully-flexed position oriented in a northerly-southerly direction. No individual was found oriented along an east-west axis. Although the sample is small, the position of the deceased does follow certain constraints. The bodies of children (juvenile, infant, or neonate) were always interred in a semi-flexed and not a flexed position like adults. While the bones of children are more readily affected by taphonomic factors than adult skeletons, all children's burials were not from the same location at Franchthi, and as such, they experienced different post-depositional conditions. Given these factors, the uniformity of children's body position makes it clear that this aspect of mortuary ritual was important and the restrictions surrounding it were consistently observed.

Only two burials do not fit the general pattern: one young female was found in the cave lying on her front (Fr 31), and a young male (Fr 12) is unusual for no other reason than he was found on his back in an EN/early MN grave on the paralia. The adolescent female (Fr 31) is the greatest anomaly to this pattern. She was found inside the cave, lying on her front, with a rubbing stone nearby. Her upper body was disarticulated and covered with rocks, her arms extended over her head, and the lower half of the skeleton was missing and never recovered (at least together) during later excavation (Jacobsen 1981). Jacobsen and Cullen (1981:87) have suggested that this aberrant example of burial at Franchthi may be a result of sacrifice, punishment by death, or deliberate disturbance

by later occupants of the site. The condition of the skeletal remains does suggest later disturbance and, overall, the peculiar nature of the find indicates that this may not represent a burial at all. Equally plausible is that the woman may have suffered some sort of accident, and only later did carnivore activity remove her lower extremities (not covered by rock) from its original context. Cut marks or other modification of the bone would go some way to resolving the fate of this young woman, but are presently not available. It is clear, though, that this woman did not receive the same treatment as others at Franchthi during any period.

Grave goods are not common at Franchthi, but associating them with specific individuals is problematic. Intact Mesolithic burials at Franchthi (Cullen 1995) indicate that a variety of (perhaps) personal ornaments made of shell and bone was associated with the dead. Although bone and shell items are also abundant in Neolithic levels, they could not be associated directly with the events surrounding the disposal of the corpse and cannot be attributed to mortuary proceedings (Jacobsen and Cullen 1981). Discounting the questionable 'burial' of the adolescent female discussed above, only two individuals appear to have been given grave goods or furnishings (Jacobson 1979:269, 271). In the cave, a neonate burial (Fr 48) of early MN date included two gifts: a monochrome burnished hole-mouthed jar and a small, footed marble bowl. The jar appears to have been deliberately broken and less half the pot was recovered. The marble bowl was also damaged, although not to the same degree. Outside the cave, on the paralia, a MN burial of an adult female (Fr 59) received an exceptionally (in this context) large number of grave goods: a monochrome Urfirnis carinated bowl, six worked bone points, three obsidian blades, and possibly a burin spall of obsidian. The bone and stone artefacts are not extraordinary in comparison to similar finds in habitation areas, but the bowl appears to have had a substantial life-use before becoming a burial gift, which is evidenced by mend holes near the rim. There is no obvious connection between these individuals: they are of different ages, were not buried in the same location, are probably not contemporary, and differ in the particular type of grave, body position, and orientation.

The special funerary treatment of the two individuals with grave goods raises several important issues concerning the significance of these objects, not only at Franchthi, but also during the Neolithic in general. It is very difficult to come to some understanding of the value of these goods, both for the individuals they were interred with and to the community as a whole. Jacobsen and Cullen's (1981:93-95) attempted to assess the significance these goods in terms of socio-economic value. They noted that 'the function of the object..., the raw material used in manufacture, the material's availability, the amount of labour and craftsmanship expended in creating the object and, more difficult to discern, the personal association of an object' (Jacobsen and Cullen 1981:94) are all important factors weighed in permanently moving material goods to a mortuary context. Vitelli (1993), I believe, has convincingly shown that pottery was not frequently made during the EN or MN phases at Franchthi. Only 12 or 13 pots were manufactured in a year (Vitelli 1993:210). At least from the perspective of the inhabitants of Franchthi, we cannot assume that objects fashioned of rarer materials would be of any less value than those that are more readily available. The fact the Urfirnis bowl was repaired may testify to this value system, as does the willingness of the community and a family to leave a rare marble bowl with the neonate.

There is ample ethnographic evidence to suggest that very young individuals are largely disconnected from the formal social organisation in which they are born. Very young children have these unique statuses because they have not yet been imbued with socio-economic roles. Thus, their status is not associated with the rules and responsibilities by which the community at large is defined. Therefore, it is reasonable to suggest that the gifts given the neonate refer more to the state of the family and the community at the time of this young person's death, than any social status that would have been held by the neonate itself. This leads us into the psychological realm of mortuary ritual, an aspect with which archaeology remains ill-suited to deal with. However, because the treatment of this individual is so different from the other children at Franchthi, we cannot assume that this was a normative mortuary practice. The themes expressed here are simply not repeated elsewhere. These practices appear to be particular to this individual, and may represent the psychological state of the parents of the child and the small community at Franchthi in relation to the events surrounding this baby's death.

In contrast, there is more direct evidence that the gifts given the adult woman (Fr 59) reflect her socio-economic standing. A study of this woman's skeletal pathology provides some clue of the activities she was involved in while alive (see Jacobsen and Cullen 1981:94, n. 14). The tooth wear associated with the woman is consistent with those resulting from thread-biting, spindle-holding, spinning, and weaving. As well as these typical domestic activities, the pathological evidence associated with the hands and shoulders of the woman suggests she may have been a potter. Do the grave goods found with her represent a pot-making tool-kit, or a portion of one? Vitelli (1999) has recently suggested that potters during the EN, and maybe the MN, may have been more than just potters. She argues the transformation of clay to pottery could have been seen as an example of all natural transformation processes, such as the changing of the

seasons, day to night, and life to death. Knowledge of these transformations and the different realities in which they occur is akin to the esoteric knowledge often associated with shamans. Thus, Vitelli proposes that potters during these phases may also have acted as shamans. The unique attributes of this woman's mortuary treatment circumstantially support such a hypothesis. However, since this is the only burial of its kind in the entire Neolithic period, great caution must be taken in this instance.

Beyond the completion of the grave, however, there are no other indications of post-interment activities. This lack of visibility does not necessarily mean that none occurred, and it is quite possible that some sort of post-interment rituals were observed, but they were not of an enduring material nature.

3.3.4   Conclusions

Individuals at Franchthi all received the same form of burial and there is little variation in the techniques used to execute the burial program. The principle difference is that there were two graves types. Consequently, it may be suggested that there were two socially recognized grave types: pit graves with or without covering stones. Overall, mortuary ritual was not implemented to create highly visible graves (Jacobsen and Cullen 1981), but was intended to emphasise biological differences (in this case, age) and the activities of daily life. Because very young children are seldom imbued with social responsibilities, their mortuary treatment can be a significant marker in how they differ from other members of the community. This is reflected in both the disposal of the corpse and the distribution and types of grave goods. The types of graves and grave goods are also indicative of the energy expended in mortuary treatment. At Franchthi, there are four levels of energy expenditure. In sequential order, the different levels of energy expenditure are characterized by (1) graves with covering stones and burial gifts; (2) graves with covering stones; (3) uncovered graves with burial gifts; and (4) graves without covering stones or burial gifts. In this calculation, the neonate (Fr 48) received the highest amount of energy expenditure, while the woman (Fr 59) is second. The other burials are segmented according to age. There is clear evidence that the adult woman's mortuary treatment may have more to do with socio-economic considerations than the psychological factors involved in children's funerary proceedings and associated beliefs about the dead. By this statement, I do not mean that psychological factors were less important in the burial of adults, just that at Franchthi these may not have been expressed in mortuary ritual, or were simply not expressed in a way that would have been preserved in the archaeological record. From an analytical perspective, these possibilities are not always mutually exclusive.

Also of particular interest is that mortuary remains are incorporated into living areas. In some ethnographic cases, such behaviour can be associated with the cause of death or the social position of the deceased (see Table 2.1). At Franchthi, however, most burials occur adjacent to domestic areas. This does not imply that this was a prohibitive treatment used to differentiate members of the community. Instead, it may be better understood as a prescriptive method used to incorporate the dead into the physical realm of the living. While such a practice may have been used to symbolise social cohesiveness and continuity, it was probably also guided by beliefs about the relationship between the dead and the living and the effect they have on each other. The use of burial coverings for children may also reflect this belief system. Beyond the more practical functions of burial coverings (to deter carnivore activity, to alleviate the stench of a decaying corpse, etc.), burial coverings can also be symbolic of the desire to segregate the living from the dead. Thus, the covering stones used at Franchthi may have more to do with perceptions about the differences between the deaths of children and adults. Perhaps it was believed that children would become malevolent spirits. Child mortality rates characteristically drop during the European Neolithic (e.g., Jakes 1988; Larsen 1995; Lewthwaite 1986; Meiklejohn and Zvelebil 1991), and with the death of children becoming less frequent at this time, such an attitude may have been pervasive amongst Neolithic groups. In this case, the stone coverings could have been used to protect the living community, but the practice did not break from the tradition of burying the dead in close proximity to daily activity areas. These suggestions are admittedly speculative, but the relationships between the living and the dead that can be drawn from the mortuary treatments at Franchthi are conspicuously different from those expressed in other EN and MN mortuary programs to which we now turn.

3.4   SOUPHLI MAGOULA

The prehistoric site of Souphli Magoula is located on the eastern bank of the Peneios River, about 5km northeast of Larisa. Demetrios Theocharis (1958:78, 1960:71) first examined the site in 1958, and later that same year Hegan Beisantz discovered urns containing cremated remains near the western slope of the *magoula* (hill) (for a history of excavations see Theocharis 1958, 1960). Unfortunately, the urns and their contents were badly damaged by erosion and the recent excavation of an irrigation ditch in the area. During the early 1970s, the construction of another irrigation ditch below the eastern slope of the *magoula* revealed several more burial urns (Fig. 3.3). K. Gallis (1979, 1989) began salvage excavations in 1974 in response to these events. The soundings made in 1974 revealed nine EN burials, four of which were partially or completely destroyed by a

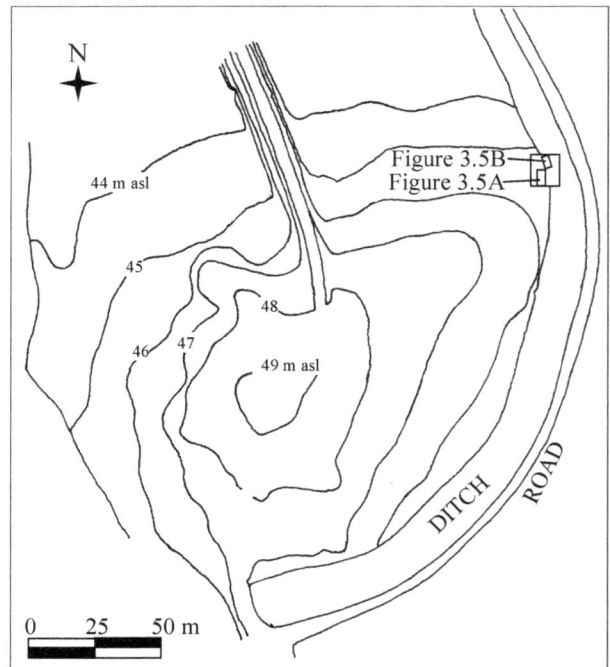

Figure 3.3. Simplified topographic plan of Souphli Magoula showing the location of the Early Neolithic cremation burials and mortuary features in relation to the magoula, modern irrigation ditches, and road (redrawn from Gallis 1982: fig. 2).

bulldozer in the process of excavating the ditch. Further excavation in 1975 revealed four other cremation burials as operations proceeded along the wall of the ditch. A longer field season in 1976 was dedicated to clarifying the stratigraphy of the burial area and exposing deposits that had not been damaged by recent construction activity in the area. Investigations during this year found two inhumation burials, two more cremation burials and several features that may have some association with EN cremation practices.

3.4.1   Mortuary Remains

The excavations 60 m east of the summit of the *magoula* revealed several types of archaeological features associated with EN mortuary activity (Tables 3.3 and 3.4). These features, which include burial pits, urns and other more specialised facilities, can be dated to at least two different phases of the EN occupation on stratigraphic grounds (Fig. 3.4). The earliest levels are from *c.* 2 m to 2.5 m below the surface. The later levels are represented by a deposit roughly a meter thick, and extend to bedrock at 3 to 3.5 m below the surface. Two discrete occupation floors dating to the later phase separate the two sets of strata. For the sake of brevity, these two horizons will be termed Horizon 1 (early levels,

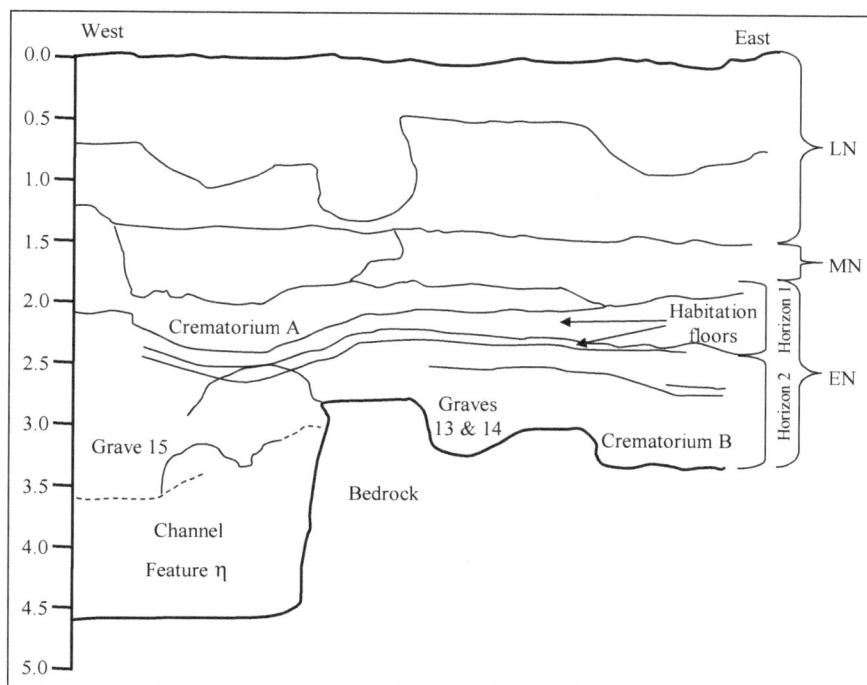

Figure 3.4. Stratigraphy of the Neolithic deposits containing the Early Neolithic cremation burials, mortuary features, and habitation floors at Souphli Magoula (redrawn from Gallis 1982: fig. 9).

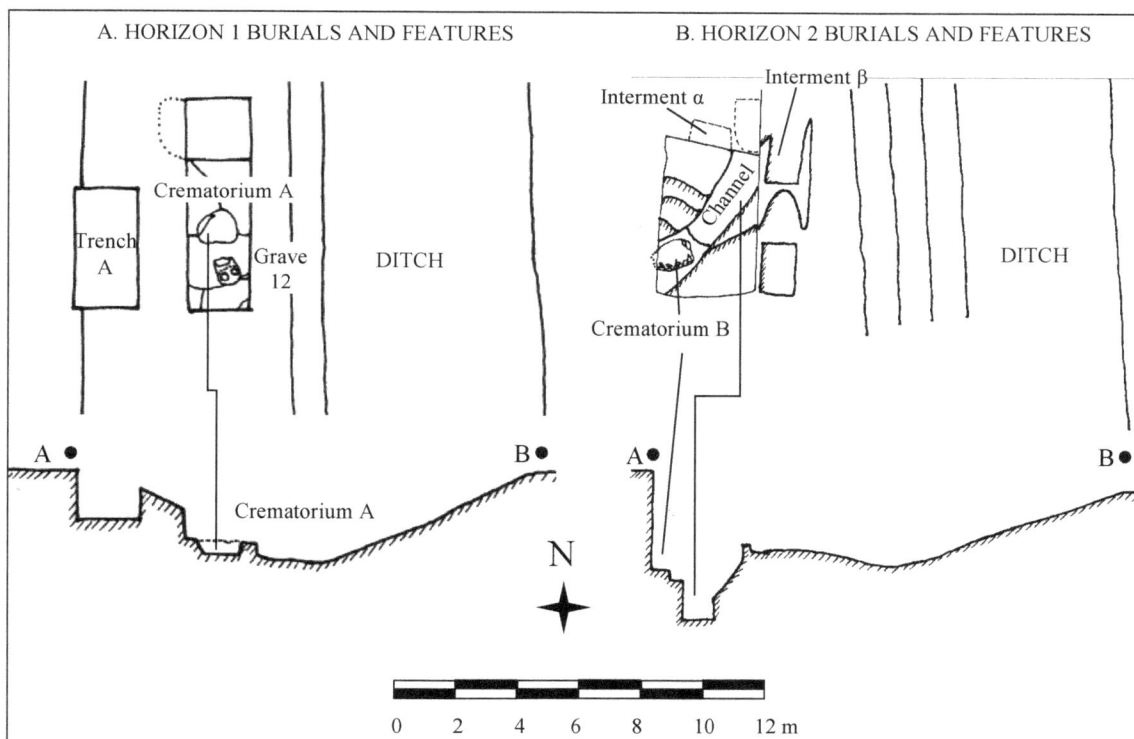

Figure 3.5. Plans of the Horizon 1 (A, redrawn from Gallis 1982:fig. 6) and Horizon 2 (B, redrawn from Gallis 1982: fig. 8) Neolithic burials and mortuary features in and around Trench A at Souphli Magoula.

TABLE 3.3
THE EARLY NEOLITHIC MORTUARY REMAINS AT SOUPHLI MAGOULA

Grave/Feature Number	Skeleton Number[1]	Location	Grave Type	Interment Form	Posture	Burial Scenario	Bones in Grave Area[2]		Age and Sex	Grave Goods	Associated Features/Objects
							Human	Animal			
HORIZON 2											
Grave 1	--	Test Pit, 1974	Pit	cremation		secondary; single			--	skyphos?	charcoal, pot-sherds
Grave 2	1	Test Pit, 1974	Pit	cremation		secondary; single	C, P	●	--	skyphos?	charcoal, pot-sherds
Grave 3	--	Test Pit, 1974	Pit	cremation		secondary; single	C, P		--	skyphos?	
Grave 4	2	Test Pit, 1974	Pit	cremation		secondary; single	C, P		--	skyphos?	
Grave 5	3	Test Pit, 1974	Pit	cremation		primary; single	C, P		juvenile	skyphoi (2), mini-vase	charcoal, traces of burning in pit
Grave 6	4	Test Pit, 1974	Pit	cremation		secondary; single	C, P		adolescent? female?	skyphos?	
Grave 7 (upper)	5a	Test Pit, 1974	Pit	cremation		secondary; double	C, P		--		Mycenaean chamber tomb intrusive into this burial
Grave 7 (lower)	5b	Test Pit, 1974	Pit	cremation		secondary; double	C, P		juvenile/adolescent? female?	3 mini-vases	charcoal
Grave 8	6	Test Pit, 1974	Pit	cremation		secondary; single	C, P	●?	adult? male?	rim sherd with matt impression	disturbed by Interment α
Grave 9	--	Test Pit, 1975		cremation							
Grave 10a (upper)	7a	Test Pit, 1975	Pit	cremation		secondary; double	C, P		adult? male?	4 broken skyphoi, mini-vase	charcoal
Grave 10b (lower)	8₁	Test Pit, 1975	Pit	cremation		secondary; double	C, P		adult? female?	skyphos, sherds, rubbing stone	charcoal
Grave 11	9	Test Pit, 1975	Pit	cremation		secondary; single	C, P	●	adult? female?	2 broken skyphoi, mini-vase	charcoal
Grave 12	10	Test Pit, 1975	Pit	cremation		secondary; single	C, P		infant?	skyphos?	figurine; grave below occupation level
Interment α	--	Trench A, η	Pit	inhumation	flexed	primary, single			Adult		grave below occupation level
Interment β	--	Trench A, η	Pit	inhumation	semi-flexed	primary, single			Juvenile? (6–8 yrs)		
HORIZON 1											
Grave 13	12	Trench A, 1976	Pit	cremation		secondary; single	C, P		juvenile?	skyphos, unknown pot type	charcoal, gravel
Grave 14	13	Trench A, 1976	Pit	cremation		secondary; single	C, P	●	--	skyphos?, sherds, mini-vase, "fruit stand"	charcoal
13/14-1	14	Level 1 fill	Pit?	bone scatter		?	C, P	●	remains of 1 person		
13/14-2	15	Level 2 fill	Pit?	bone scatter		?	C, P	●	remains of 1 person		

[1] The skeleton number refers to those assigned by Dr. N. Xirotiris (1982).
[2] C = cranial bone fragments, P = post-cranial bone fragments, ● indicates presence of animal bone.
Source: Gallis (1982) and Xirotiris (1982).

from 1.5 to 2.5 m below surface) and Horizon 2 (late levels, 2.5 to 3.5 m below surface. Deposits dating to the Middle Neolithic (1.5 to *c*. 2 m) and Late Neolithic (surface to 1.5 m) phases compose the remaining Neolithic strata. The discussion below begins with the earliest remains found in Horizon 2.

3.4.1.1   Horizon 2 Mortuary Remains

The earliest Neolithic mortuary remains at Souphli were detected during the 1976 excavation of Trench A (Fig. 3.5A). At the lowest levels, a large trench or channel was cut some 1.5 m into the bedrock (from 3.0 to 4.5 m below the surface) (Fig. 3.4). The precise extent of the channel was not determined, but it would have extended beyond the excavation trench in a southwest to northeast direction, undercutting later deposits. Two different fill deposits in the channel contained an EN skyphos, an ovoid bowl, numerous pottery sherds, bone and stone tools, animal bones, much charcoal and ash, and several fragments of burned human bone. The uppermost level also held the burned human remains of at least two individuals (Skeleton Nos. 14 and 15) as well as faunal remains. The human remains likely represent cremation burials that had been disturbed by the construction of the later (Horizon 2) floors above this (Gallis 1989:35).

Immediately above the channel were two preserved cremation burials partially cut into bedrock (Grave 13 and 14). Grave 14 contained a skyphos burial urn with fragments of burned human and faunal remains. In the burial pit, pottery sherds, charcoal and two burial gifts, a small crudely made U-shaped bowl (mini-vase), and a shallow bowl with a pedestal ('fruit- stand') was found. Grave 13 was also a pit burial that included a skyphos containing the remains of a juvenile. A badly damaged pottery vessel was found next to the burial urn and the pit was filled with charcoal fragments and gravel. Near the burials, at the southwest corner of Trench A, a large circular pit 1.2 to 1.3 m in diameter was uncovered. It was partially cut into bedrock and had walls constructed of rough brick that had been repeatedly burnt. Five different concentrations of incinerated cranial and post-cranial human bone fragments and faunal remains were found within the pit (Figs. 3.4, 3.5A, Table 3.4). Only slightly burnt bones were found around the rim of the pit, and a complete figurine and a stone 'earstud' were found on the floor (Gallis 1989:226). The feature was considered to be a place were cremations occurred and was designated Crematorium B by the excavators.

3.4.1.2   Horizon 1 Mortuary Remains

Above the two successive occupation floors that distinguish the Horizon 1 and 2 levels, there is more abundant evidence of mortuary activity (Fig. 3.5B). Hollowed into the ground at this level was a shallow pit similar to Crematorium B (Fig. 3.4, 3.5B Table 3.4). The

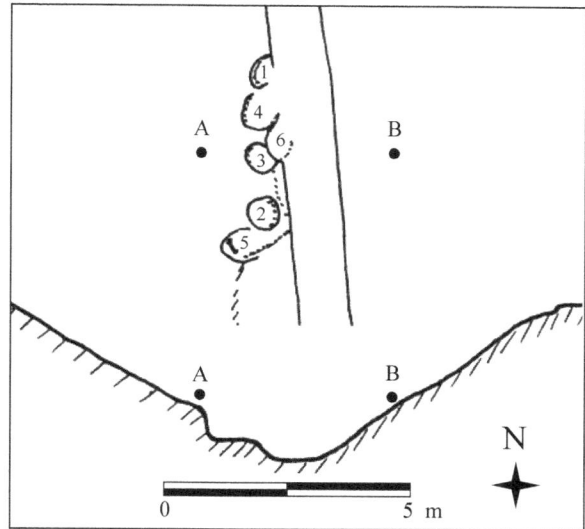

Figure 3.6. Early Neolithic cremation burials 1 to 6 located along the ditch north of Trench A at Souphli Magoula (redrawn from Gallis 1982: fig. 3).

circular pit is 1.1 m in diameter and 0.3 m in depth. Its earthen walls had been repeatedly burnt and it contained a large amount of charcoal, carbon fragments, and small fragmented human bones (skull fragments and several hand and foot bones). On the edges of the pit, three post-holes were noticed, that many have been used to support a funeral pyre (Gallis 1989:224, Plate 9). This feature was termed Crematorium A.

Surrounding the pit were eight cremation burials (Graves 7 to 12). One burial was badly damaged due to the construction of the irrigation ditch (Grave 9), but the other burials were shallow pits with burial urns containing fragmentary, burnt human remains. All the graves had fragments of charcoal, but only four graves had any burial goods. Two of these graves had upper and lower components (Graves 7a, 10a, 10b) and only one was a single burial (Grave 11). Burial goods consisted of broken pottery, mini-vases, and one individual (Grave 10b, Skeleton No. $8a_I$) received a stone tool. An interesting feature of Horizon 2 is the presence of inhumation burials (Fig. 3.5, A and B). Two inhumations (Interment α and Interment β) were dug almost a meter through the Horizon 2 deposits and into the earlier EN occupation floors. There has been some question if these burials date to the EN occupation of Souphli (Demoule and Perlés 1993; Andreou et. al 1996). Because one of the most recent cremation burials (Grave 8) was disturbed during the construction of Interment α, it is likely that both of the inhumations are intrusive and do not date to the EN phase. Besides the obvious differences in burial form, most telling is that the inhumations disturbed the latest burials. This did not occur with any of the cremation burials, even though they are often very close together and some were deposited on top of one another

TABLE 3.4

THE EARLY NEOLITHIC MORTUARY FEATURES AND OTHER ASSOCIATED REMAINS AT SOUPHLI MAGOULA

Date	Mortuary Feature	Skeleton Number[1]	Location	Interment Form	Bones in Grave Area[2]		Number of Individual Represented	Associated Features/Objects
					Human	Animal		
Late EN	Crematorium A	11	Test Pit, 1975			present	?	broken skyphos
Late EN	Crematorium B	16	Trench A, Level 1 fill	bone scatter	C, P	present	?	
Late EN	Crematorium B	17	Trench A, Level 2 fill	bone scatter	C, P	present	remains of 2 people	
Late EN	Crematorium B	18	Trench A, Level 3 fill	bone scatter	C		?	
Late EN	Crematorium B	19	Trench A, Level 4 fill	bone scatter	P	present	?	
Late EN	Crematorium B	20	Trench A, Level 5 fill	bone scatter	P		?	head of figurine below this level
Late EN	Locus 15	21	Test Pit, 1975, Locus 15	bone scatter	C? and P?	present	?	skyphos, ovoid bowl, sherds, bone and stone tools; charcoal, ash

Source: Gallis (1982) and Xirotiris (1982).

TABLE 3.5

THE TYPES OF BONE INCINERATION AND TIME ESTIMATED TO ACHIEVE THE DEGREE OF INCINERATION OBSERVED FOR THE CREMATIONS AT SOUPHLI MAGOULA

Bone Incineration	Time Estimate for Bone Incineration (in min.)				Total	
	12-60	60-70	7-70	Indeterminate	Frequency of Incineration Types	Total % of Incineration Type
Completely carbonised		2			2	12.50%
Completely calcined		1			1	6.25%
Partly carbonised and calcined	4				4	25.00%
Partly carbonised and smoked	3				3	18.75%
Partly carbonised, calcined, and smoked			2		2	12.50%
Indeterminable (highly fragmented)				4	4	25.00%
Total Frequency of Time Estimate Category	7	3	2	4	16	100.00%
Total % of Time Estimate Category	43.75%	18.75%	12.5%	25.0%		

Source: time estimates based upon Buikstra and Swegle (1989). The frequencies refer to the number of individuals.

without disturbing the lower burial. It is, therefore, more probable that the inhumation burials date to the Middle Neolithic phase.

The six cremation burials recovered during the salvage operation along the irrigation ditch were found at levels consistent with Horizon 2 (Fig. 3.6). These graves were more poorly preserved than those in Trench A. Only Graves 5 and 6 contained identifiable skeletal remains, and only Grave 5 had burial goods. Grave 5 is also unusual because the burial goods, burial urn and the pit were burned, and Gallis (1989:30, 224) suggested that the artefacts and the body were burned right inside the pit. The plausibility of this scenario will be taken up further below.

3.4.1.3 Cremated Remains

From the wide range of cranial and post-cranial human bone elements found in the Souphli disposal area, 16 cremated individuals were identified. Thirteen partial skeletons were studied in more detail (Xirotiris 1989), and three other burials held very fragmented remains that precluded any precise identification.

All the recovered human bone remains were burnt to various degrees. The bones were either carbonised (black), calcined (white), smoked (grey), or combinations of the three (Table 3.5). Most individuals had partly carbonised and calcined bones and there are lower frequencies of partly carbonised or calcined bone, and combinations of all three degrees of bone incineration (carbonised, calcined and smoked).

Several cremation burials also had incompletely incinerated bones with a brown colouring. While this can indicate that the bone was burnt 'dry,' or with the flesh removed before burning (Buikstra and Swegle 1989), these bones may also have been affected by the surrounding soil. All the bones at Souphli came into contact with soil when the pits were filled and earth entered the jars sitting on their bases. The minerals in the soil may have stained the portions of the bone surface not already burned. These conditions cast doubt on whether flesh was removed from the body before incineration.

Due to the practice of cremation, a large number of the human bone elements that are key referents for identifying age and sex characteristics (cranium, pelvis, etc.) were too burnt, fragmented, or simply not present in the sample. Therefore, determining the age or sex of individuals was often impossible, and many classifications remain tentative. What is instructive, however, is that only faunal remains (which were burned to the same degree as human bones) were found with the adult remains in Grave 8 and 11, and with individuals of indeterminate age or sex.

3.4.1.4 Burial Goods and Associated Objects

Over half of the burial urns were damaged due to the post-depositional factors noted above (Table 3.6). Those urns located in the ditch were mostly destroyed or severely fragmented, but the graves and artefacts located farther away from the irrigation ditch were better preserved. Therefore, the precise type and shape of many vessels could often not be determined. All indications suggest, however, that there was only one type of burial urn at Souphli—the skyphos—although it came in a variety of sizes. Because the preservation of the both the osteological remains and skyphoi is poor, it is not possible to consider the factors (such as age or sex) that may have constrained the distribution of burial urns, or if in fact there were any such constraints.

Several types of burial goods appear in the Souphli cemetery, the most frequent of which is pottery. There is one instance where a rubbing stone was left for an adult male (Grave 10b). Otherwise, most burial gifts are of two types: a skyphos (Gallis 1989:Plate 10, nos. 7-10) or the crudely made mini-vases (Gallis 1989:Plate 10, nos. 2 and 12). One unique find is the so-called 'fruit-stand' found in Grave 14 (Gallis 1989:Plate 10, no. 13). One other pottery vessel, likely a grave good, was destroyed to such a point that the type was not identifiable (Grave 13). Determining the constraints on artefact distribution is limited because of the problems associated with ageing and sexing individuals, and no patterns are immediately apparent. It is notable, however, that the same grave goods appear in graves assigned to both Horizon I and II.

There is a range of other artefact types that may have been associated in some way with mortuary activity at Souphli:

- In the area of Crematorium A, one pot (a skyphos?) was discovered.

- On the floor of Crematorium B, the head of a figurine and a stone ear-stud were found.

- In the channel, a skyphos, several sherds, bone and stone tools, and an ovoid vase were recovered.

- A complete figurine was also found in the northern edge of Trench A near Inhumation α.

Artefacts were made and used for specific purposes in the mortuary ritual. This specialisation in artefact function (perhaps production?) is not considered characteristic of the EN phase. Most tools were used for multiple tasks, and only in the subsequent MN phase is there believed to be any strong evidence for either craft specialisation or purposeful production of specific artefact types (see Chapter 4.1).

TABLE 3.6
POTENTIAL FUNCTIONS OF THE ARTEFACTS ASSOCIATED WITH
MORTUARY FEATURES AT SOUPHLI MAGOULA

Artefact Class and Type		Function in Mortuary Ritual	
Class	Type	Burial Good	Ritual Equipment?
Pottery	Skyphos	●	●
	Mini-vase	●	
	Figurine	●	
	Fruit stand	●	
	Ovoid vase		●
	Indeterminate	●	●
Bone	Various tools		●
Stone	Rubbing stone	●	
	Various tools		●

TABLE 3.7
THE DEGREE OF BONE INCINERATION AND REPRESENTATIVENESS OF HUMAN BONE ELEMENTS AND
FAUNAL REMAINS ASSOCIATED WITH GRAVE FEATURES AT SOUPHLI MAGOULA

Degree of Bone Incineration	Bone Elements[1]						Individuals with faunal remains
	Cranial fragments	Vertebrae	Rib fragments	Scapulae	Phalanges	Post-cranial fragments	
calcined	2	1			2	2	
partly calcined	1				1	1	
carbonised	1		1		2	2	
partly carbonised	1	1			1	1	1
partly carbonised and calcined	3	1	2		2	3	1
partly carbonised and smoked	2	1	1		2	2	1
partly carbonised, calcined and smoked	2	1			2	2	2
smoked	1	1			1	1	1
indeterminate	3			1	6	4	1
Total MNI	16	6	4	1	19	18	7

[1]The numbers refer to MNI.
Source: Xirotiris (1982).

TABLE 3.8
THE DISTRIBUTION OF BURIAL GOODS IN THE AGE AND SEX CATEGORIES REPRESENTED
AT SOUPHLI MAGOULA

	Sex		
Age	Male	Female	Indeterminate
Adult	mini-vase (1) □ skyphoi (4) ●	rubbing stone ■ mini-vase (1) □ skyphoi (3) ●	
Adolescent		skyphos □	
Juvenile		mini-vase (3) □	vessel (type unknown) ■? skyphos (2) ● mini-vase (1) □
Infant			
Indeterminate			skyphos □ fruit-stand ■? mini-vase (1) □

● Age constrained.   ○ Sex constrained.   ■ Constrained to this age/sex category.   □ Not likely constrained by age or sex

3.4.2   Mortuary Practices

The degree of bone incineration represented at Souphli, the bone elements found in the burial urns, and the absence of other types of bone modification (e.g., cut-marks) provide two insights into the procedure followed in disposing of the corpse (Table 3.7). First, in general, there are more carbonised than calcined bones. This indicates that few bone elements came into direct contact with fire for a long duration. Thus, the fires were likely of intense heat for a relatively short duration of time; that is, fuel was not continually added to the fire until the body was completely incinerated. The bones had to be subjected to fire and not just heat in order to carbonise them, so it is unlikely that the corpses were cremated while suspended over the fire. While the three post-holes around Crematorium A could imply such a practice, I am uncertain how an irregular tripod-like structure would have been used to support a platform for cremating the dead. Second, the osteological data indicate how the cremated remains were processed for final interment. As mentioned above, only certain parts of the body were found in the containers: cranial fragments, vertebrae, ribs, scapula and assorted fragments of the post-crania. Delicate facial bones are nearly absent in the containers, and only fragments the denser bones of the cranium were placed in the burial urns. It is probable that certain bones, such as scapula and other large bone elements, occur in very low frequencies in the graves because they were too large to fit in the burial urns. For example, only the fragment of one scapula was put in a burial urn (Grave 7b). Thus, it seems likely that the most intensely burned bone elements, or fragments of them, were culled for interment in the burial urn.

The question of fragmentation is an important one, as it must be determined if the fragmented bones found in the urns were in such a state before being burned. As noted above, the lack of cut marks suggest that the bodies of the dead were not prepared for cremation by defleshing the body. Thus, the cremated body, although not completely incinerated by the fire, must have been further broken up before placed in the burial urn. Bones burned to such a state as these will become more brittle and can be broken with a stone or bone tool relatively easily. However, the presence of much ash and charcoal in the burial urns and pits suggest that the bones were simply culled while still in the crematorium, gathered up along with charcoal and ash, and placed in the urn for final burial.

This reconstruction of the cremation procedures at Souphli suggests that the disposal of the dead was minimally a three- stage process:

(1) The body was first cremated in a crematorium. At this point, the mini-vases may have been included and fired while the body was being incinerated. Live or dead animals, or perhaps just their bones, were also included in the cremation at this stage.

(2) Certain burnt human bones and some animal bones were then culled and placed with charcoal and ash in a specific burial urn (a skyphos).

(3) Finally, the burial urn was placed in a small pit on the outskirts of the settlement with or without grave goods and burned animal bone. Charcoal and ash was then scattered about the burial pit. Because numerous graves were found close together, and none were damaged by later burials, it is likely that some type of grave marker was placed over the graves.

Only one burial does not follow this pattern. The juvenile interred in Grave 5 appears to have received somewhat different treatment. The burial urn and pit were both burned, and Gallis (1982:30, 224) suggested that the urn, mini-vase and possibly the body itself were cremated right in the pit. This suggestion is somewhat problematic. The bone elements and burials gifts do not markedly differ from other burials. If the juvenile were cremated inside the pit, we would expect a complete skeleton to be represented. However, only certain portion of the cranium and post-cranium were present. Where did the other parts of the skeleton go? The urn, on the other hand, may simply have had a use-life, perhaps as a cooking vessel, before it was used in burial. This would account for the traces of burning on its surface. While the process that led to the cremation of this young person may have been somewhat different, the result was nevertheless the same, and there is no basis to suggest that this treatment can be linked to the age of the individual.

The material contribution to mortuary ritual is an important key for identifying differences in mortuary treatment, because the incineration process is so similar at Souphli Magoula. The burial process outlined above suggests that at least four different levels of energy were expended in the disposal of the dead:

(1) faunal remains, mini-vases and broken pottery were included in the cremation fire and placed with the dead in the burial pit (Graves 9, 13);

(2) mini-vases were included in the cremation fire and placed with other pottery or stone artefacts in the burial pit with the dead (Graves 3, 7b, 10a, 10b, 14);

(3) only pottery was included as a grave good with the burial (Grave 13);

(4) the person was cremated, their remains were put in an urn, which was then placed in the burial pit with no grave goods or animal bones (Graves 1-4, 6, 7a, 8, 12).

The energy expended in mortuary treatment indicates the importance of the types of objects and the faunal remains found in the graves and the burial area. It must be asked what factors may have played a role in constraining the use of the grave goods.

While we cannot presume that mini-vases occur with people of certain ages or sex, their distribution is certainly restricted and they are not found in every grave. Perhaps more important than their distribution, is the nature of the vessels and their inclusion in the burial pits in general. The mini-vases are poorly made and there is no reason to doubt they were fired when the body was being cremated then moved with the body for final interment (Gallis 1982:32). The fact they are not elaborately made or decorated may be irrelevant. From a symbolic viewpoint, the transformation of clay may be seen to parallel the cremation of the body—as the plastic and malleable clay changes into a durable vessel through the use of fire, so does the body transform from a creature that was alive, creative, innovative, etc., to something inert and unchangeable. In this sense, the pot is seen to mirror the human body (David et al. 1988). Once fire is used, the process cannot be reversed—pottery cannot again become clay, and the dead cannot again live. Clearly, there is an emphasis on the transformation process.

Pottery vessels included as grave goods were not found in a complete state. Most sherds do not show traces of fire (except Grave 5) and were not included in the cremation. Although it could be suggested that vessels were intentionally broken at some point in the mortuary ritual, this is unlikely. Few EN ceramic vessels are found completely intact, and it is more probable that the vessels were placed beside the burial urns. The pots broke as a result of later activity in the area and as the weight of the overlying deposits eventually crushed them.

Faunal remains also do not occur in each burial, but instead are plentiful in Crematorium A, Crematorium B, and in the channel below Crematorium B. An abundance of faunal remains in areas of mortuary activity immediately conjures images of ritual feasting and perhaps animal sacrifice. If this were the case at Souphli, such mortuary rituals are apparently rare in Neolithic contexts (cf. Jacobsen and Cullen 1981:90). But why would these animal remains also be in the burials urns and pits, and why would such feasting occur in the same place the bodies of the dead were cremated? The answer could lie in how the pits were used.

Crematorium B has two features not found in Crematorium A. First, on floor of the pit the head of a figurine and a stone ear- stud was found. Second, the facility does not have post-holes. While the ear-stud may have once been worn by an individual cremated in the pit, the figurine and the lack of post-holes requires some explanation.

In a number of ways, Crematorium B parallels ethnographic cases documenting how special purpose facilities are constructed. For example, the construction of Crematorium B is somewhat similar to the way smelting furnaces are constructed in West and East Africa. Before construction, medicinal bark or other medicines, animal bones and pottery (in a variety of combinations) are placed in the bottom of the furnace (Schmitd 1997). These objects and medicines are part of a redundant set of symbolic and curative practices used outside iron smelting. They are part of a symbolic repertoire linked to healing in general, more specifically with fertility cures, and protection against malevolent spirits. While the same meanings of course, cannot be attached to Crematorium B or the objects associated with it, we should expect that potent symbolism and specific observances would have surrounded the construction and use of such an important facility.

With these thoughts in mind, designating Crematorium A as a place where cremations occurred may be problematic. It differs in a number of ways from Crematorium B:

- It is not associated with the same artefacts (no pottery or figurine fragments).

- It was not constructed the same way as Crematorium B.

- The pit itself is rather 'clean' of skeletal material in comparison to Crematorium B even though more cremation burials are dated to Horizon 1. The pit contained faunal remains but only a few small human bones, including a fragment of a cranial vault and several phalanges and tarsals (Xirotiris 1982:Table 1).

It is difficult to determine if the human bones in Crematorium A occur due to activities other than cremation. The present data do not suggest that erosion of the hill slope washed the bones into the pit after the site was abandoned; and it is also difficult to argue that the bones may have been displaced from the surface and fell into the pit as a consequence of activity in the area, although this is quite plausible. In general, Crematorium A better resembles a large cooking pit, rather than place for cremating the dead. However, because it occurs later than Crematorium B and is associated with the latest Early Neolithic strata in the area, it is the best candidate for a cremation facility. Thus, there is no substantial basis to suggest that Crematorium A was used exclusively as a place to cremate the dead. In sum, while the osteological data indicate that there was no change in incineration methods during the EN occupations of Souphli, there was certainly a shift in the maintenance and type of cremation facilities.

But what is the significance of the faunal remains? Of the sixteen burials at Souphli only three, or 19%, had animal bones included in the burial urn. Most faunal remains are not found in graves, but around the burial area and in the crematoriums. For all intensive purposes, there is no way to determine if the animal and human bones in the burial pit resulted from the same firing event. In the process of collecting the bones for burial, the animal bones could have been inadvertently collected in the mass of bone and ash that accumulated in the pit and subsequently placed in the burial urn. Alternatively, given the low frequency and incidence of faunal remains, the occurrence of animal bone in the burial urns may also be accidental.

Even if faunal remains were not intentionally placed within the burial urns, their presence is nevertheless significant. Animals may have been roasted before cremation as part of a purifying ritual to prepare the crematorium, or after cremation as part of a feasting ritual. Perhaps they were used in both capacities. In either scenario, these data indicate one of the few cases during the Neolithic in Greece of any mourning rituals surrounding the event of death. But what is the broad significance of these practices? Might they have some connection to the symbolic distinction Hodder (1990) has made between *domus* and *agros*? If this distinction is take too literally (e.g., Whittle 1996:69-70) then we are left to squabble over details. However, the theme expressed in the model—a distinction between 'the house,' arguably the centre of Neolithic social life, and 'nature,' that which exists beyond the 'the house'—may be more indicative of a general motif expressed in all human culture: that which distinguishes, for lack of a better term, the 'cultural' (the 'domesticated') from that which is not (the 'wild'). Certainly, a number of ways in which cultures focus upon the interrelationship and points of contact between these two broad concepts have been studied. What better context is there to express such connections and differences than in mortuary ritual?

3.4.3 Conclusions

For some time Souphli Magoula was generally regarded as the earliest case of urn burial (urnfield) and cremation in Greece (Renfrew 1972:79; Gallis 1989). While the site continues to have the earliest dated urnfield in Greece, the excavations at Franchthi Cave (Cullen 1995) have revealed Mesolithic burials with evidence of cremation. Despite these new finds, it has often been remarked that the greatest contribution Souphli Magoula can make to the understanding of the Early Neolithic is in the area of funerary ritual and ideology (e.g., Demoule and Perlés 1993:385-386; Andreou et al. 1996:559).

All individuals at Souphli received the same form of burial. A study of the cremation practices suggests there is very little variation in the way the body was prepared for burial. The process itself appears to have been long

and complex, but a specific formula was followed closely every time. Graves were placed closely together, and several were quite close to the crematoriums. But new burials did not disturb older ones, even when new burials were placed directly above older ones. If one considers the small size of the population, and how infrequent death would have been in this community, the graves must have been marked in some fashion to avoid destroying older burials. These observations imply that there was only one socially recognised burial type at Souphli Magoula. This casts further doubt on the dating of the inhumation burials found in the area. Although they parallel other EN mortuary practices in Thessaly (Nea Nikomedia and Dimini; see below), the stratigraphic evidence and mortuary customs do not provide a clear association with the Early Neolithic occupation.

Individuals were differentiated at Souphli on the basis of the type and quantity of burial goods rather than burial form (Table 3.8). Only certain types of goods have a restricted distribution. Skyphoi, for example, were only found in graves belonging to adults and a juvenile. However, the adults had several vessels each and the juvenile received only one. Skyphoi were probably not restricted to individuals of a particular age group, but multiple vessels were only given to adults, thus indicating their age status. The types of goods and the four levels of energy expenditure also reflect social differences drawn on biological lines. However, this tendency suggested by the data is hampered by poor identifiability of the skeletal remains. Other objects have fewer obvious constraints on their distribution. For instance, the peculiar mini-vases appear to have a ubiquitous distribution. While they may not have been used to socially differentiate individuals at Souphli, I have argued that they would have acted in other symbolic fashions. The transformation of clay to ceramic may have acted both as a metaphor for death and as a physical manifestation of the transformation of the social personae. This dual role indicates how an object may have multiple meanings and how deeply intertwined social and ideological mortuary directives may be. However, because the mini-vases are not found in every burial this symbolism was not attached to every person. What these individuals had in common is not indicated by the either the osteological or archaeological data. One may speculate that the mini-vases were used to aid the dead or protect the living, but they may just as likely have been items that were a necessary part of rites pertaining to the specific circumstances surrounding these deaths. What these circumstances were would require a far better understanding of EN life at Souphli Magoula than is currently known.

Perhaps what is so unique about the EN mortuary practices at Souphli Magoula is the direct evidence for how the dead were prepared for final interment. The crematoriums yield a special glimpse into the process of mortuary ritual at Souphli. The evidence for burned animal bone and a broken figurine in Crematorium B allow us to envision some of the specific rites that may have taken place during the funerary process. What is particularly interesting is that all of these activities appear to have taken place outside of the settlement. Thus, the location of the disposal area and the place where rituals took place was physically removed from the area of the village. This is quite unlike the practices followed at other EN sites, and likely indicates a very different attitude towards the dead than that displayed by other EN groups.

3.5   NEA NIKOMEDIA

Despite being one of the richest but most poorly published EN settlements in Greece, the burials at Nea Nikomedia provide an additional source of information about mortuary practices during the EN on the Greek Mainland (see Fig. 1.1). During two long field seasons in 1961 and 1963, Grahame Clark and Robert Rodden recovered unprecedented remains of a very early farming village on the Greek Macedonian plain dating from *ca.* 5800 to 5300 BC. These excavations are most noted for the recovery of well-preserved EN architecture and mortuary remains.

Excavations at Nea Nikomedia revealed four building levels that could be divided into two building phases during the EN (Rodden 1962, 1964, 1965). Buildings were rectangular, freestanding structures built by covering the exterior and interior of a wooden framework linked by reeds and rushes with mud. They were oriented in an east to west direction to provide protection by the prevailing northerly winds. The buildings are rather all large, but smaller structures were arranged around the largest building (8 x 11 m). This large building was segmented into three separate rooms by two buttresses creating a spacious central room that contained figurines, polished stone axes, 400 unworked flint blades, stamp seals, unusual gourd-shaped pottery vessels, and several hundred clay "roundels" or "earplugs."

The final assessment of the EN mortuary remains has not yet been published in detail, but reports have included some general information about the types of graves used and their location. Angel (1973) published a report on the skeletal remains, which is unfortunately flawed in a number of respects. First, Angel reported that 105 individuals were recovered during excavations, but only data for 87 skeletons was reported. Whether this is a product of the recording methods used by Angel (see Franchthi Cave discussion above, Sec. 3.6.2) has not yet been determined. The available data does indicate that people were interred in irregular pits near houses or within abandoned buildings. Thus, burials appear to have been purposefully placed outside houses while they were

being used. Bodies were placed in the graves in either a flexed or semi-flexed position. Presently, there is no data to indicate the basis upon which individuals were accorded this positioning. The graves contain either single or multiple primary interments. Single burials were probably reserved for adults and adolescents and multiple burials were used for infants and juveniles. There is one case, however, were an adult female was interred with two juveniles. Another peculiar burial was of a young man (8 NN) who had a large polished stone between his teeth. Angel (1973:105) suggested that this man suffered some type of head trauma and may have died a violent death. Perhaps most peculiar about the mortuary practices at Nea Nikomedia is that no burial goods were found in the graves. Although burial gifts are not common during the Early Neolithic, in each of the cases discussed above some individuals did received a material contribution to their mortuary ritual.

3.6   TRENDS IN EARLY AND MIDDLE NEOLITHIC MORTUARY PRACTICES

Table 3-9 summarises the variation in mortuary practices observed in the EN and MN case studies. The details and differences between these four cases show several important trends regarding the procession, scale, form, and symbolism of mortuary rites during the EN to MN.

3.6.1   Scale of Rites

During the EN, the differences in the way the dead were disposed of can be linked to statuses based on age, gender, and social identity. There are three aspects of EN mortuary practices that most visibly express these distinctions: (1) the grave forms and number of socially recognised burial types; (2) the kinds of grave goods; and (3) the energy expended in mortuary ritual. For example, at Franchthi Cave primary inhumation in graves with or without covering stones was made on the basis of age—adults were buried in graves without covering stones and children were interred in graves with covering stones. Also, the position of the body at Franchthi appears to be based on age. This is interesting because such a practice is not strongly predicted by ethnographic data (Table 2.1). Grave goods are usually utilitarian in nature and are most often found with adult women. These goods designate females of a particular age category and are probably indicative of the types of activities undertaken by women. When these aspects of mortuary treatment are combined and considered in terms of the overall energy expended in mortuary treatment, there is no indication for structurally unequal social positions cross-cutting age, gender and social identity. In sum, the scale of mortuary rites served to distinguish individuals on the basis of horizontal or 'natural' statuses: age, sex, the duties linked to the division of labour based upon these biological criteria and social identity.

TABLE 3.9
EARLY AND MIDDLE NEOLITHIC MORTUARY PRACTICES

Categories of Observable Mortuary Variation		EN-MN Mortuary Sites			
		Prosymna	Franchthi Cave	Souphli Magoula	Nea Nikomedia
Preparation & Treatment of the Body					
Preparation	extramural burial and exhumation	●		●	
	not preparation indicated		●		●
Treatment	inhumation		●		●
	cremation	●		●	
Position at burial	flexed		●		●
	semi-flexed		●		●
	disarticulated and arranged	●		●	
Orientation at burial	northerly		●		?
	southerly		●		?
	not applicable	●		●	
Form of disposal	primary		●		●
	secondary	●		●	
Preparation of the Grave					
Grave form	pit grave	●	●	●	●
Number of socially recognised burial types		1	2	1	2
Grave Furniture & Goods					
Kinds of grave furniture	ceramics	●	●	●	
	terracotta	●		●	
	lithics	●	●	●	
	bone		●		
	shell				
	wood				
Source of grave furniture	local area	●	●	●	
	extra-local trade item	●	●		
Quantity of grave furniture		low	low	low	no goods
Spatial Location and Designation					
Local grave location	disposal area in cave	●	●		
	open-air disposal area		●	●	
Regional location of disposal area relative to settlement	spatial separated	●		●	
	incorporated		●		
Grave formally demarked		No	no	No	
Intra-cemetery grave location of burial types	differentiated				
	not differentiated		●		●
	not applicable (i.e., one grave type)	●		●	
Energy Expenditure					
Levels of energy expenditure		2	2	4	1?
Funeral time & duration; secondary funerals		●		●	
Mourning Ritual					
Funeral dance/games					
Funeral meals/fasting		●?		●?	
Funeral dress and ornamentation				●	
Grief, bereavement and grave visitation		●			

Mortuary differentiation is achieved by making minor modifications to the construction of the grave (Franchthi), positioning the body (Franchthi), or by adding grave goods (Franchthi, Souphli, Prosymna). Because the scale of mortuary rites in small, and differences are often quite subtle, the procession of mortuary rites during the EN stress the process of disposing the corpse rather than acting as a means to elaborately differentiating individuals or groups in material ways. It can be suggested that the disposal of the dead concentrated on the conceptual and physical transformation of the social personae. Both aspects of this transformation are often heavily guided by philosophical and religious beliefs about universal orders, the soul, the afterlife, the health and safety of the living community, and the cause of death (Parker Pearson 1982; Carr 1995). The handling of the corpse and the location of the graves at all the sites, and the duration of the mortuary rites at Prosymna and Souphli indicate that mortuary practices were more heavily guided by these beliefs. Only at Franchthi Cave is there evidence that the positioning of the body was directed by social differences based upon age.

3.6.2 Procession of Rites

Because these mortuary practices are meaningfully constituted, the form of these mortuary rites is non-arbitrary and directly related to personal objectives, general social strategies, attitudes, beliefs and world view themes. Thus, also embedded in the transformation of the corpse and the social individual are other beliefs that specifically concern the relationship between the disposal of the corpse, the soul and the community of the dead.

The way the corpse is handled is commonly seen to model of the state of the soul (Hertz 1907). Because the soul is required to be in a particular state to enter the community of the dead, the body must be prepared and treated certain ways. This aspect of EN mortuary practices shows the greatest amount of variation. For example, the handling of the body at Prosymna and Souphli Magoula are similar in some ways, but are very different in certain aspects of actual execution. Bodies are partially cremated in both places then disarticulated and arranged. But at Souphli, the bodies are placed in ceramic vessels and then pits, while at Prosymna the remains are interred in shallow graves. These practices differ from those at Franchthi Cave where primary inhumations in pits on the paralia and in the cave are the norm. The pattern at Franchthi is similar to what is generally known about Nea Nikomedia, but burials did not take place within caves.

3.6.3 Form and Symbolism of Rites

Are there any common symbolic themes expressed in EN-MN mortuary ritual? I first address this question by examining if common metaphors are used in the form and symbolism of mortuary rites, and then ask where the ancestors would reside.

In the first instance, an understanding of the contents as well as the structure of the mortuary remains is important (e.g., Hodder 1982b, 1986). Beginning with Souphli, we find that pottery vessels are not only used as burial gifts but also as containers for the cremated remains of the dead. Since this is only one of two known urnfields during the Greek Neolithic (the other at Plateia Magoula Zarkou), it must be asked if the burial urns have any symbolic significance. To this end, a study of the metaphors attached to ceramics in particularly relevant (e.g., David et al. 1988; Thass-Thienemann 1973; Welbourne 1984). Pottery is often viewed as a metaphor for the human body, and in fact, the parts of vessels are commonly given human attributes, such as bottom, shoulder, and mouth (a practice followed also by ceramic specialists). In places where women are potters, the pots themselves are often seen to mirror the female body and their interiors can be equated with the womb and extended to beliefs about fertility. This metaphor is part of a larger "symbolic repertoire," or sets of symbols repeated in other types of material culture and conceptions about the landscape (McIntosh 1989; cf. Sterner 1992). For example, caves are sometimes seen as places of birth or rebirth, analogous to the womb.

Apart from the possible connections between pottery and the human body, the placement of the dead in relation to habitation areas may provide one clue as to where Neolithic peoples thought their ancestors resided. The 'community of the dead' may be indicated by the location of the burials in relation to settlement and surrounding area. During the EN-MN, burials are located either within the confines of the settlement or outside the periphery of the settlement. The location of the burials can be seen to symbolise the location of the community of the dead, which reflects beliefs about how ancestors should be integrated into the community of the living. This proposition rests on the assumption that settlements did not expand around the burial areas during the occupation of the settlements masking an earlier separation of burial ground and settlement. Since this did not occur at these EN and MN sites, these spatial data suggest a simple binary opposition principle was in place during the EN-MN phases:

(1) If the dead are included in living areas, so too are the ancestors regularly included within the operations of community life. Such a connection may indicate rather harmonious relationships between the living and the dead. The opposition would thus be: dead/inside : ancestors/solidarity.

(2) Alternatively, if the dead are segregated from living areas, ancestors are believe to occupy a separate realm from the living, and one might suppose that

access to either realm for either group may be limited. This circumstance may reflect the notion that the dead are more harmful to the living, and that there is tension, conflict or dissonance between the living and dead communities. This opposition would thus be: dead/outside : ancestors/dissonance.

If we apply these concepts to the EN-MN mortuary data, the following relationships are suggested:

EN Souphli:
A) outside settlement → place of ancestors (all) → separate realm

EN Nea Nikomedia:
A) abandoned buildings → adjacent to living areas → place of ancestors (?)→ same realm

B) extramural in settlement → adjacent to living areas place of ancestors (?)→ same realm

EN Prosymna:
A) cave → outside settlement → place of ancestors (all) → separate realm

EN-MN Franchthi:
A) cave → adjacent to living areas → place of ancestors (only infant, juveniles, adolescents) → same realm

B) paralia → adjacent to living areas → place of ancestors (only foetus, infants, adult) → same realm

3.6.4   Conclusions

What is most interesting about this exercise is that there are no apparent geographical or temporal relationships between either the EN-MN mortuary practices or the symbolism expressed through the form of mortuary rites. The mortuary practices in northern Greece (Souphli and Nea Nikomedia) and in southern Greece (Franchthi and Prosymna) have little in common. Prosymna and Souphli are similar in terms of the symbolic themes expressed and in the way the dead are segregated from the living community, although they are separated in time by several centuries and in space by over 230 km. The form of mortuary practices at Franchthi and Nea Nikomedia are grossly similar, but differ in their details. The dead were included within the confines of the living areas at both these sites. Even though the mortuary sample at Franchthi is small and limits the ability to study changes in mortuary practices over time, it does appear that this practice was used during the entire EN-MN habitation of the site. Only at Souphli is this transformation expressed in another way. Gallis (1982) has suggested that the firing of the small ceramic mini-vases probably occurred when the body was cremated. I have suggested that transformation of clay to ceramic may have acted both as

a metaphor for death and as a physical manifestation of the transformation of the social personae. Such a practice is strongly supported by the ethnographic data.

CHAPTER 4
LATE NEOLITHIC MORTUARY PRACTICES

4.1   LATE NEOLITHIC CULTURE-HISTORY

This Late Neolithic phase covers approximately a millennium, from 5300 to 4500 BC. Originally, this phase was thought to be much longer, but in recent schemes it has been divided into two separate phases, the Late Neolithic and Final Neolithic (Sampson 1989; Zachos 1987). The Final Neolithic, also known as the Late Neolithic II, as originally conceived by Diamant (1974), Phelps (1975), and Renfrew (1972), corresponds to the Chalcolithic in the Balkans. The Late Neolithic has also been sub-divided into two sub-phases by Demoule and Perlès (1993:386-388), Phase 3 and Phase 4, each covering about a half a millennium. For our purposes, it is useful to retain the traditional phasing of the Late and Final Neolithic, while distinguishing the *c.* 500 year subphases of the Late Neolithic. In the following discussion, I use the terms Late Neolithic 1 and Late Neolithic 2 to respectively refer to Phase 3 and 4 defined by Demoule and Perlès.

The Late Neolithic 1 (LN 1) dates from about 5300 to 4800 BC. Few radiocarbon dates or published sequences support this division, but various stylistic changes in pottery provide useful chronological indicators. In particular, the black burnished ware and the 'matt-painted' ware (Weinberg 1970) best help define the LN 1. Also during this time the Cycladic islands, from Keos to Amorgos, were first inhabited by farming populations. Known as the 'Saliagos' group, these islands were inhabited on and off throughout the following Late Neolithic 2 (LN 2), and perhaps into the Final Neolithic (Demoule and Perlès 1993:388).

In contrast to the LN 1, the LN 2 is largely known through reference to stratigraphic and typological evidence, and reciprocal imports, which do not date to the LN 1 or Final Neolithic. This places the LN 2 to a very brief time span between 4800-4500 B.C. The LN 2 is most clearly identified in Greece north and east of the Pindus mountain range. Close similarities develop between the central area of Greek Macedonia and the Vinča province in the former Yugoslavia, Bulgaria and northeastern Greece (Thrace), Albania, and the 'Classical' Dhimini culture in Thessaly. The picture is not so clear in southern Greece, but there are certainly distinct differences at this time in the assemblages between LN 1 and the Final Neolithic. In particular, there are certain groups of ceramics not identified with either the earlier or later phases.

4.1.1   Settlement Pattern

The LN was a time of settlement expansion in northern Greece and the Aegean islands, pockmarked by occasional hiatuses at each site. Parts of Macedonia, Thrace, and the islands were inhabited more permanently. Although most sites are large (50-100 ha in area), they are far less conspicuous than the immense tell-sites in Thessaly. In Thessaly, about half of the sites in the LN 1 are new, and represent a shift from the hills to the alluvial plains beside older settlements (Demoule et al. 1988; Gallis 1989; Halstead 1984). The new settlements are more regularly spaced across the landscape, and numerous small settlements and 'farmsteads' became common in the dry Larisa plain (Halstead 1989a). The changes in southern Greece are equally marked, but quite different from the north. Increasingly, caves became occupied, and some older villages were abandoned. It is thought, however, that the actual number of sites did not decrease significantly (Diamant 1974; Phelps 1975, 1981-1982).

During the LN 2, settlement patterns continue to change, but are differ locally. In Thessaly, the new, smaller sites settled in the LN 1 were abandoned and the population aggregated into larger settlements (Halstead 1984). At the same time, almost no new sites have been discovered for this sub-phase (Gallis 1989; Halstead 1984, 1989a). In the south, the major settlements in Boeotia were abandoned, and no new sites have yet been discovered through surface survey (Cherry 1990).

It has been suggested that these localized changes in settlement pattern reflect the first significant disparities in regional subsistence and economy. Some, such as Cauvin (1992), suggest that mobile pastoralism developed in southern Greece at this time, similar to the Near East. Van Andel and Runnels (1987) further propose that there is a connection with the development of wool production and an increasing demand for sheep. However, the available faunal data do not imply such a scenario (Boessneck 1955; Halstead 1981, 1984, 1989a; Von den Driesch and Enderle 1976). The 'secondary products revolution,' as proposed by Sherratt (1981, 1983) has not occurred yet. On the contrary, the evidence from Thrace, including Sitagroi (Bökönyi 1986) and Paradeisos (Larje 1987), and Macedonia (Greenfield and Fowler 2003), where we would particularly expect to see this development, indicates that domesticated species were still being utilized for primary products. The secondary products revolution, and more mobile pastoral adaptations, characterizes the subsequent Bronze Age phase.

4.1.2 Settlement Architecture and Planning

Most of what is known of settlements during the Late Neolithic come from LN 2 occupations of Dhimini and Sesklo. These sites have various features in common with others during the LN. The ditches, circuit walls, and central buildings are the most significant. Only at Sesklo (Tsountas 1908; Theocharis 1968, 1973) and Dhimini (Hourmouziadis 1979) are circuit walls known. These were built and rebuilt around a courtyard at the centre of the settlement. Other settlements, such as Agia Sofia, Arapi, Souphli, Otzaki, Argissa, Servia, and Nea Nikomedia all have ditches during the LN phase. These sites are located on alluvial plains with little available stone, and the walls may have served the same function (defence?) as the circuit walls (Demoule and Perlès 1993: 390). The ditches are paralleled in Balkan settlements to the north during this period (Vinça A to C).

The other significant architectural feature of the large LN settlements is a central building, perhaps incorrectly termed the "megaron" (Darque 1990). The structures all have their basic shape, large size, and location in common. They were placed in the centre of the village and had access constricted by either a ditch or circuit walls. The size and central location of these structures provides some of the best supporting evidence for emergence status differences within LN communities (Demoule and Perlès 1993:391), but possible ceremonial or communal functions of these structures cannot presently be ruled out.

4.1.3 Technology and Crafts

4.1.3.1 Domestic Equipment

During the Late Neolithic, three new features characterize the common domestic equipment. Storage jars, such as pithoi and domed ovens, are now regular domestic features. The use of stools and armchairs has been implied from seated figures (Demoule and Perlès 1993:391). Large, flat hearths know from earlier periods are still the focus of domestic activities. From the evidence at Dhimini, the ovens and hearths seem to be primarily used for cooking, but kilns have also been identified (Hourmouziadis 1977). Querns, grinding stones, and flaked tools compose the domestic stone tool-kit, and red deer antlers become more common in the LN bone tool-kit (Moudrea-Agrafioti 1987). Wide ranges of pots (see below) continue to be the major class of domestic equipment.

Throughout the LN, a wider range of weaving equipment and weaving techniques appear to have been used. Spindle whorls, clay and stone spools, and loom weights are far more common compared to previous phases (Demoule and Perlès 1993:391). From impressions on pots and house floors, both plain weaves and simple swill techniques were used to make mats and baskets (Renfrew 1973), and there area few instances of mats made using a coiling technique rather than by weaving (Evans and Renfrew 1968). It may also be that fur rugs were being used on the floors of some houses at this time. Particularly at Dhimini and Pevkakia, bear carpal bones have been discovered, leading Halstead (1984) and Hinz (1979) to conclude that the skins were used with the paws still attached. It could be a question of debate, though, whether these represent rugs or blankets, as their context within the household reveals little about their actual function.

4.1.3.2 Ceramic Production

The LN shows distinct changes in ceramic styles brought about largely by new innovations. Complex decoration is characteristic of this long phase, and painting often covers the entire vessel both inside and out. Never before has the density of decoration, as well as the intricacy and precision of the craft, been so well expressed (Otto 1985; Washburn 1983).

Particular to this phase are the larger vessels, such as pithoi. These are similar to the MN Franchthi vessels in size, and would have been made using much the same methods (Vitelli 1993). Bowls continue to be the most common type of ceramics, but now show greater variety (shallow, flat-based, open straight-sided, carinated). Jugs, jars with open handles, and stands are now regularly part of production (Hauptmann 1981; Hauptmann and Milojĉić 1969; Theochares 1973; Wace and Thompson 1912).

The innovations in decoration show that more time was spent on the development of unique and fine styles of pottery, perhaps demonstrating that potting had become a specialized craft (Demoule and Perlès 1993:392). Certain styles, such as the black Larisa ware (LN 1), are unprecedented in the polishing and ripple effect given to vessels. The Polychrome (LN 1, LN 2) wares of central Greece and Thessaly were made possible by the use of new maganese and graphite pigments (Demoule and Perlès 1993: 392). These new wares were made available by the more sophisticated use of kilns and saggars (Renfrew 1973; Vitelli 1993), which allowed for the three stage firing process needed for making polychrome wares. This firing process was, however, unnecessary for making the black-on-light wares using iron oxides (Frierman 1969; Jones 1986). Therefore, it seems to have been an innovation geared solely towards the production of an original local style.

In the LN 1, two interaction spheres for the distribution of ceramics have been noted (Demoule and Perlès 1993:392). First, the most common pottery found during this time includes the black-burnished and matt-painted wares, which are found throughout the mainland. Other styles had quite a limited distribution, such as the red burnished, black-and-white, and Arapi polychrome wares. Some styles were confined to Thessaly alone, while others were regional or local (Halstead 1984; Rondiri 1985).

During the LN 2, the situation is quite different. During this phase, specific forms of pottery were only used at certain sites. A good example is the "Classical Dhimini" ware (Wace and Thompson 1912). Using chemical analyses, it has been determined that particular types of local clays were used in manufacturing specific pottery styles. These styles were produced specific functions in mind. For example, the grey-on-grey ware was largely confined to graves at Plateia Magoula Zarkou (Demoule et. al. 1988), and the Larisa black ware was deposited in pits with only wild, and not domesticated animals (Watson, cited in Halstead 1984). Therefore, this sub-phase represents a new diversification in production techniques. The purpose of these techniques appears to be focused on producing a diverse group of pottery for an equally wide range of functions.

4.1.3.3 Flaked Stone Production

Two different patterns of flaked stone production appear for northern and southern Greece during the LN. The primary differences lie in the procurement of raw materials and the production of specialized tools. In the south there is a large increase in the use of obsidian, and a considerable decrease in the use of local raw materials, such as jasper and black flint. The increase in "exotic" materials is perhaps due to the simultaneous colonisation of the Cyclades at this time, which could have put more obsidian in circulation (Cherry 1981, 1990). Flint and jasper were no longer used for simple utilitarian tools in the south. Fine arrowheads were being made of these materials by indirect percussion using plain butts in the LN 1, and platform preparation using faceted butts by the LN 2. It is also noteworthy that very few sickle blades have been found during the LN in the south. This has led some to suggest that pastoral agriculture came to dominate subsistence activities (Demoule and Perlès 1993:394).

In the north, different strategies are being adopted and some old strategies continue. The dominant use of local raw materials continues, including the wide use of flint and jasper tools formed by pressure flaking, and obsidian is still imported as preformed or flaked cores. The striking feature in the north is the paucity of any new, specialized, refined stone tools when compared to earlier phases. As well, it is only by the LN 2 that sickle blades become less common, and this phenomenon is confined to Thessaly alone.

4.1.3.4 The First Metal Objects

There has been much ado about the initial appearance of metal artefacts in Greece. Authors such as Renfrew (1972) have seen it as a pivotal technology in the formation of civilization in Greece, while others view these scarce finds in a less grandiose fashion. A review of Renfrew's (1973) and Gimbutas' (1989) data reveals an incredible scarcity of metal finds in LN Greece. The only object dating to the LN 1 phase, is a small copper head from Dikili Tash (Séfériadès 1992). Although copper extraction is very common in the LN 2 at Aï Bunar in Bulgaria and throughout the Balkans, c. 4800-4500 B.C. (Demoule and Perlès 1993:395), only 12 metal artefacts can be positively dated the LN 2 (Dikili Tash, 9 copper pins; Paradeisos, 2 copper pins, Kitsos 1 copper pin). Metal artefacts of questionable date have also been reported from Dhimini and Sesklo (McGeehan-Lurtzis and Gale 1988; Tsountas 1908), and Corinth (Kosmopoulos 1948). There has been some debate over the metal finds from Zas Cave (Zachos 1990). While the variety of copper objects and an exaple of gold sheet were thought to date to the Final Neolithic (Demoule and Perlès 1993: 395), Zachos (1996a, 1996b) argues for a secure LN date. The rarity and condition of these objects implies that they were traded as finished products and not as raw materials (Demoule and Perlès 1993:395). The social implications of acquiring these rare objects have yet to be fully explored.

4.1.4 Trade and Exchange

Including the metal objects, three classes of artefacts were exchanged during the Late Neolithic phase, although the rate of exchange and their distribution differed. The utilitarian tools of the LN (ceramics, obsidian, flint and jasper, celts, grinding tools) mainly circulated between neighbouring communities (especially ceramics, Schneider et al. 1991). Melian obsidian, however, now reached Macedonia (Servia: Ridley and Wardle 1979; the Ptolemais basin: Fotiadis 1987, 1988; Demoule and Perlès 1993: 395; Nea Nikomedia: Rodden 1962, 1964), and Thessaly in small quantities. Demoule and Perlès (1993:396) have noted that trade in Melian obsidian in north Greece conforms to Renfrew's (1984b) hypothesis that trade by middlemen is culturally bounded. The frequencies of obsidian from the source (Melos) show that over 80% of the total obsidian comes from sites closest to Melos, while a sharp boundary is notable as one enters eastern Macedonia. However, it is with the "rare goods" that the most significant changes in trade appear. Shell bracelets of spondylus (Spondylus gaedoporus) are now more common (Renfrew 1973) and were made at coastal sites and traded inland (Hourmouziadis 1979, Renfrew 1973; Runnels 1983; Shackleton 1988; Tsuneki 1989). Stone vases, rare marble figurines, celts, and grinding tools also became more abundant, but exchange seems to have been made in progressively smaller areas (as with ceramics; Demoule and Perlès 1993: 395- 396).

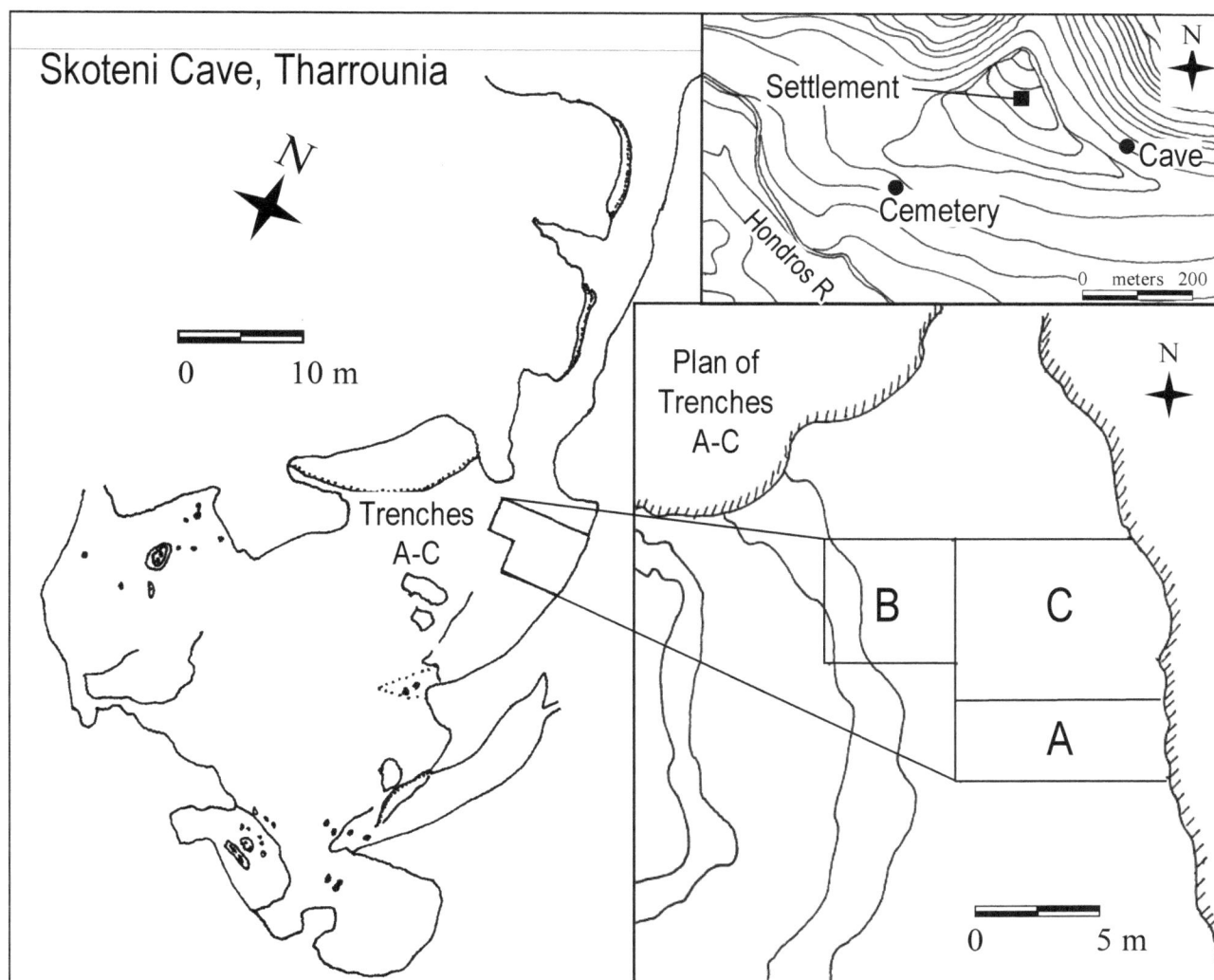

Figure 4.1. Plan of the Late Neolithic burials at Skoteni Cave, Tharrounia (redrawn and modified after Sampson 1992: figs 2 [right insert], 4 [left], and 5 [right detail]).

4.1.5 Conclusions

Overall, during the LN period the differences between northern and southern Greece become more pronounced. Increased population density and peculiar distributions of artefacts throughout settlements characterise the north, while no population increase and a specific localism in pottery styles define the south. We may therefore expect to find discrete differences in mortuary practices during this phase north and south of the Pindus mountain range. In the following section, we first look at mortuary practices in the southern mainland.

4.2 THARROUNIA

The site of Tharrounia is situated in central Euboea. Three different areas at Tharrounia were used during the Late and Final Neolithic: a cemetery, a settlement, and the Skoteni Cave (Fig. 4.1). All lie in an area about three

kilometres away from Tharrounia village, and one kilometre from the Panagia settlement. The cemetery and settlement were occupied only during the FN phase. The cave has material dating to both the LN and FN phases, but most finds belong to the LN phase (5300-4500 B.C.). Although occupied successively during the LN, habitation appears to have been irregular and sporadic (Sampson 1993:299).

The cave itself is found within a low rocky plateau (450 m asl), opening north onto a deep gorge where the Hondros river flows out to the Aegean Sea. The cave is the largest in Euboea (Sampson 1993:288), with a narrow entrance leading into an expansive inner chamber, and is quite old geologically as shown by the massive columns formed by connected stalactites and stalagmites. The cave seems to have been used for both storage and burial of the dead during the Neolithic. Judging from the abundance of large storage vessels (more than 700 pithoi) placed in the

TABLE 4.1
THE SPATIAL DISTRIBUTION AND CHRONOLOGICAL PLACEMENT OF MORTUARY REMAINS AT THARROUNIA

Location	Data	Phase		Total
		Late Neolithic	Final Neolithic	
Cave	No. of Individuals	8	5	13
	% of Location	61.54%	38.46%	100.00%
	% of Phase	100.00%	15.63%	32.50%
	Total % of All Remains	20.00%	12.50%	32.50%
Cemetery	No. of Individuals		27	27
	% of Location		100.00%	100.00%
	% of Phase		84.38%	67.50%
	Total % of All Remains		67.50%	67.50%
Total No. of Individuals		8	32	40
Total % of Phase		20.00%	80.00%	100.00%

Source: Sampson (1992).

TABLE 4.2
ATTRIBUTES OF THE LATE NEOLITHIC MORTUARY REMAINS IN SKOTENI CAVE

Phase	Location	Trench	MNI	Grave Type	Burial Form	Pattern of Bone Association	Bone Elements Present[1]	Age and Sex	Pathology	Special Features
LN2	cave	Trench A	1?	pit?	inhumation	Scatter	C, CA, L, M, isolated V	infant	--	
LN2	cave	Trench A	1?	pit?	inhumation	Scatter	C, P, F	juvenile	--	
LN2	cave	Trench A	1?	pit?	inhumation	Scatter	C, P, F	juvenile	--	
LN2	cave	Trench A	1?	pit?	inhumation	Scatter	C, P, F	adult	--	
LN2	cave	Trench C	1?	pit?	inhumation	Scatter	C, P, F	juvenile female	porotic hyperstosis or hemolytic anemia	skull placed in wall niche
LN2	cave	Trench C	1?	pit?	inhumation	Scatter	C, V, R, T, CA	juvenile female	--	
LN2	cave	Trench C	1?	pit?	inhumation	Scatter	C, P, F	adolescent	--	
LN2	cave	Trench C	1?	pit?	inhumation	Scatter	C, P, F	adult male	--	

[1] Abrreviations for bone elements areas follows: C = cranial bone fragments, CA = carpals, F = indeterminate fragments, L = long bones, M = metatarsals, P = post-cranial bone fragments, T = tarsals, V = vertebrae.
Source: Sampson (1992) and Stravopodi (1992).

cave during the LN and FN phases, it seems to have had a role in a well-organised storage system (Sampson 1993:300). Skeletal remains belonging to the LN and FN phases were found in the northeast corner of the main inner chamber (Sampson 1993: 289). Thus, it also played a significant part in mortuary ritual during both the LN and FN settlement of the area.

4.2.1 Neolithic Mortuary Remains at Skoteni Cave

There is some confusion about the precise nature of the Neolithic mortuary remains in the cave. The site reports do not describe the location of the remains precisely, and

there is seldom any correspondence between the archaeological assessment (Sampson 1992, 1993) and the osteological analysis (Stravapodi 1993). There is also some confusion as to whether the skeletal remains can be associated with LN occupation floors in the cave (Sampson 1993:289). For example, while Sampson (1993:299) insists that burials would have been placed in the cave when it was not used for other purposes, stratigraphic correlations clearly indicate that human skeletal material and LN occupation debris where found together. Despite these difficulties, the variety of available evidence does indicate some of the general directives of the disposal program.

During the Neolithic occupation of Tharrounia approximately 40 individuals were buried in the cave and the cemetery (Stravopodi 1993): 13 individuals were identified within the cave and 27 people were interred in the cemetery (Table 4.1). Eight of the cave burials date to the LN phase and five to the FN phase. All of the LN burials therefore took place within the cave in an area that is situated immediately to the left (east) as one enters the main chamber of the cave (Fig. 4.1). Their disturbed state is considered to be a result of later occupations of the cave (Sampson 1993:289). These later activities also affected the preservation of other features of the burial area. The outlines of graves were not detectable, and there is no indication that any individual received burial goods.

The osteological study was unable to differentiate many individuals according to age or sex. The remains of an infant, two juveniles and an adult were identified from Trench A, while two juvenile females, an adolescent, and an adult male were identified in Trench C. These remains differ from those found in FN deposits in the cave and the later cemetery in two respects. First, in the cave there is a somewhat more limited range of bone elements: one skull, some cranial bones, long bones, ribs, isolated vertebrae, metatarsals, and carpals (Table 4.2). There was apparently several bone fragments found in Trench B (Stravopodi 1993:381), but it is unknown if these represent a single person or the displaced bones of individuals from the other trenches. Second, the LN

remains have very little identifiable pathology when compared to other Neolithic skeletal remains. There are few cases suggesting endemic or congenital sources, and no specimens show signs of trauma or post-mortem modification, such as cut marks (Stravopodi 1993). Only one young female showed signs of porotic hyperstosis. Caution should be taken with these conclusions because few adult remains dating to the Neolithic are found without arthritis, osteoarthritis, or other signs of occupation stresses typical in other mortuary assemblages.

4.2.2 Mortuary Practices

Post-Neolithic disturbance of the disposal area and the limited osteological evidence constrain any assessment of the mortuary program operating during the LN. We are thus limited to three general observations.

From the available data, it seems that little modification was made to the body before interment and there is no indication that different amounts of energy expended in their mortuary treatment. LN burials are represented by a small range of cranial and post-cranial bone elements, suggesting that the bones of the dead may have been moved from elsewhere to receive final interment in the cave. There is no evidence, either pathological or spatial, to suggest mass burial of these individuals, so interments must have been successive.

Also of particular interest is the skull belonging to a juvenile female found in a niche in the eastern wall of the cave. The skull was found in association with a LN occupation floor. It does not seem likely that the skull was unintentionally unearthed and subsequently placed in a natural wall niche to take it out of the way. Rather, it seems to have been purposefully placed within the niche. It is noteworthy that the skull was not discarded, but that its later disposal is reminiscent of other practices in Greece during the LN where skulls of the dead receive special treatment (cf. Hourmouziadis 1973; Jacobsen and Cullen 1981). Also, this individual had a rather severe pathology termed porotic hyperstosis. Angel (1950, 1964, 1966, 1967, 1969, 1972, 1975, 1978, 1984) has repeatedly suggested that these abnormal alterations in the bony structure of the skeleton were a result of thalassemia or sickle-cell anaemia that developed in resistance to endemic malaria.

Sickle-cell anaemia is a fatal recessive genetic disorder common in populations of West Africa (or people of West African heritage) and the Mediterranean basin. Both thalassemia and sickle-cell anaemia are autosomal recessive genetic traits characterised by abnormal hemoglobin, a protein found in red blood cells that transport oxygen from the lungs to the rest of the body. Thalassemias are actually a group of heritable hemoglobin diseases associated with either a decrease or

TABLE 4.3
INHERITANCE OF SICKLE-CELL ANAEMIA IN NORMAL AND
MALARIAL ENVIRONMENTS

	Normal Environment	Malarial Environment
AA	Normal	Normal, high malarial morbidity
As	Mildly anaemic	Mildly anaemic, low to no malarial morbidity
Ss	Highly anaemic, usually fatal	Highly anaemic, usually fatal

an absence of hemoglobins (Cummings 1991:241). The effects produced by sickle-cell anaemia cause a weakening of the red blood cells. The cells are fragile and easily broken, and cannot be replaced as quickly as they die (Cummings 1991:73). Therefore, this makes sickle-cell anaemia quite lethal. Most individuals that have sickle-cell anaemia die in childhood, or at the latest, in adolescence (Cummings 1991:74).

However, these diseases are not simple dominant/recessive traits, as Table 4.3 shows. For example, an individual who is a carrier (As) of sickle-cell anaemia will prove to be mildly anaemic, and there is low to no malarial morbidity of these individuals in populations living in a malarial environment. However, if the individual is a recessive homozygote (ss), sickle-cell anaemia is fatal, regardless if the environment is normal or malarial. Occasionally, recessive homozygote (ss) individuals can appear in these populations and they would most likely die in infancy or early childhood. Stravopodi (1993:385) has suggested that these same lesions may represent an iron deficiency anaemia based on a growing body of evidence indicating that iron-deficiency may in fact strengthen the body's ability to fight off infection, rather than acting detrimentally (for recent discussions and bibliography see Holland and O'Brien 1997; Hershkovitz et al. 1997; Buckley 2000; Schultz 2001). However, this does not explain the death of this young individual at Tharrounia. It is more likely that this individual was homozygous recessive (ss) for sickle-cell or thallassemia and died as a result of it. Also telling is that this child's skull was placed in a niche in the wall of the cave and no other skeletal remains were found belonging to this individual. Therefore, the remains of this child was not treated the same as other members of the community and it was likely segregated as a result of this malady.

The location of the burials within Skoteni Cave suggests that mortuary remains, and perhaps the associated rituals, were spatially segregated from the living areas. At an even finer spatial level, the mortuary remains themselves may have been spatially separated. While the discrete location of the burials in the cave may appear to be a product of excavation, over 2 m separates the remains found in Trenches A and C. Inclusion is this burial area does seem to have been made on the basis of age or sex,

and the burials in the cave may have been differentiated on the basis of family groups. The pattern reflects exigency, and this area of the cave may have only been used as a disposal area used during short, perhaps seasonal occupations of the cave (Sampson 1992, 1993).

4.2.3 Conclusions

In considering the condition and range of skeletal remains found in Skoteni Cave, Sampson (1993:299) suggested that the cave acted as the first place of burial for secondary burial practices located elsewhere. However, there is some evidence that the LN burials in Skoteni Cave are primary. Most practitioners of secondary burials will tend to favour burial or special treatment of the skull over most other post-cranial remains. This practice is best represented by the treatment of the young child's skull placed in a wall niche. However, at Skoteni there are three crania and a number of cranial fragments associated with other post-cranial remains. There is insubstantial spatial, bio-osteological and taphonomic evidence to confidently propose that secondary burial was normally practised during the LN. The remains may just as easily represent disturbed primary inhumation burials, as has been argued for EN Franchthi Cave, and the secondary disposal of the child's skull may indicate a non-normative treatment of the body remains due to the circumstances surrounding her death. Perhaps most surprising, however, it the lack of evidence for any burial goods associated with these individuals. A great number of artefacts, especially pottery, were found in trenches in the cave, but none were linked with the funerary remains. As we will see from the cases examined next, it is quite uncommon for individuals to receive no burial goods of any kind during the LN.

4.3   PLATEIA MAGOULA ZARKOU

In the spring of 1974, a salvage excavation team headed by Christos Gallis made trial excavations at Souphli Magoula and in the vicinity of Plateia Magoula Zarkou (Gallis 1975, 1979, 1982). Plateia Magoula Zarkou is located about 30 km west of Larisa on the north side of the Peneios river. The prehistoric settlement at Zarkou has been known for quite some time (Wace and Thompson 1912; Gallis 1979:226). However, only with the opening of an irrigation ditch in the area in 1974, were burials recognized at the site. The Neolithic settlement formed a *magoula*, or hill, about 200 m in diameter and 4 to 5 m high. The Neolithic finds at Plateia Magoula Zarkou are confined to the Late Neolithic, and the black-burnished Larisa ware is the taken as the best chronological indicator of this phase (Gallis 1982; Andreou et al. 1996).

The cemetery is located near a modern field some 300 m north-west of the *magoula* (Fig. 4.2.). A number of circumstances have affected the quality of some finds.

TABLE 4.4

CHARACTERISTICS OF THE LATE NEOLITHIC CREMATION BURIALS AT PLATEIA MAGOULA ZARKOU

Grave Location	Excavation Year	Cluster[1]	Skeleton No.	Grave Type	Interment Form	Burial Scenario	Bones in Grave Area[2] — Human	Fauna	Age-Sex	No.	Burial Urn Characteristics	Burial Goods Characteristics
NE ditch	1974	1	--	pit	cremation	secondary; single?	P		--		black handled jar, disturbed	
NE ditch	1974	2	--	pit	cremation	secondary; single?	P		--		black handled jar, disturbed	
NE ditch	1974	3	--	pit	cremation	secondary; single?	P		--		black handled jar, disturbed	
NE ditch	1974	4	--	pit	cremation	secondary; single?	P		--	No. 4	black handled-jar, disturbed	
NE ditch	1974	5	--	pit	cremation	secondary; single?	P		--	No. 5	black large bowl, disturbed	
NE ditch	1974	A 6	1	pit	cremation	secondary; single	P		juvenile	No. 6	black single-handled amphora, upright	
NE ditch	1974	B 7	--	pit	cremation	secondary; single	C, P		--	No. 7	orange single-handled amphora, upright	Beside No. 7: No. 10, red bowl, upright
NE ditch	1974	B 8	--	pit	cremation	secondary; single	F		--	No. 8	single-handled amphora, upright	
NE ditch	1974	B 9	2	pit	cremation	secondary; single	C		juvenile	No. 9	cup, upright	
NE ditch	1974	B 11	--	pit	cremation	secondary; single	F		--	No. 11	gray bi-conical-handled vessel, disturbed	
NE ditch	1974	B 12	--	pit	cremation	secondary; single	F		--	No. 12	gray handled bell-shaped cup, disturbed	
NE ditch	1974	B 13	--	pit	cremation	secondary; single	F		--	No. 13	bi-conical handled vessel, disturbed	
NE ditch	1974	Γ 14	--	pit	cremation	secondary; single	F		--	No. 14	red single-handled amphora, disturbed	
NE ditch	1974	Δ 15	--	pit	cremation	secondary; single	F		--	No. 15	amphora, disturbed	
NE ditch	1974	Δ 16	--	pit	cremation	secondary; single	F		--	No. 16	gray conical cup, lower body only	
NE ditch	1974	Δ 17	3	pit	cremation	secondary; single	C, P		--	No. 17	gray amphora, disturbed	
NE ditch	1974	E 18	4	pit	cremation	secondary; single	C, P		--	No. 18	gray amphora, lower body only, upright	No. 19, red cup inverted over No. 18
NE ditch	1974	E 20	5	pit	cremation	secondary; single	C, P		--	No. 20	red handled cup, upright	red sherd
NE ditch	1974	E 21	--	pit	cremation	secondary; single	P??		--	No. 21	red amphora, upright	No. 22, handled cup inverted over No. 21; gray anthropomorphic figurine (3 cm)
NE ditch	1974	E 23	6	pit	cremation	secondary; single	C, P		adolescent	No. 23	red skyphos, upright	
NE ditch	1974	E 24	7	pit	cremation	secondary; single	C, P		--	No. 24	black single-handled amphora, upright	No. 25, red cup once inverted over No. 24
NE ditch	1976	ΣT 26	8	pit	cremation	secondary; single	C, P		adolescent	No. 26	black amphora, upright	
NE ditch	1976	ΣT 27	10	pit	cremation	secondary; single	C, P		Adult	No. 27	gray amphora?, upright	Beside No. 27: No. 28, black amphora; red amphora?; gray amphora?; gray anthropomorphic figurine, head missing (0.3 cm preserved height); flake of white flint

[1] All 1974 and Group ΣT burials recovered in 1976 were all located on north-east side of the irrigation ditch. These letters A, B, Γ, Δ, and ΣT were used to designate discrete clusters of burials.

[2] C = cranial bone fragments, P = post-cranial bone fragments, F = indeterminate fragments, ● indicates presence of animal bone. *Source:* Gallis (1982) and Xirotiris (1982).

51

TABLE 4.4 Continued.
CHARACTERISTICS OF THE LATE NEOLITHIC CREMATION BURIALS AT PLATEIA MAGOULA ZARKOU

Grave Location	Excavation Year	Grave No.[1]	Skeleton No.	Grave Type	Interment Form	Burial Scenario	Bones in Grave Area Human	Fauna	Age-Sex	Burial Urn	Burial Urn Characteristics	Burial Goods Characteristics
Trench A	1976	7	16	pit	cremation	secondary; single	C, P		--	No. 29	gray pithos, upright	one red sherd on top, one inside
Trench A	1976	8	17	pit	cremation	secondary; single	C, P		--	No. 30	gray bi-conical bowl, upright	
Trench B	1976	10	18	pit	cremation	secondary; single	F		adult	No. 31	bell-shaped cup, disturbed	
Trench B	1976	11	19	pit	cremation	secondary; single	C, P		adult	No. 32	bell-shaped cup, disturbed	
Trench Γ	1976	4	14	pit	cremation	secondary; single	C, P		juvenile	No. 34	gray bell-shaped jar, upright	No. 33, gray bell-shaped jar, inverted over No. 34
Trench Γ	1976	5	--	pit	cremation	secondary; single	F		--	No. 36	gray amphora	No. 35, gray amphora, inverted over No. 36
Trench Γ	1976	6	15	pit	cremation	secondary; single	C, F	●	adult	No. 37	gray amphora, disturbed	gray bell-shaped cup
Trench Γ	1976	16	23	pit	cremation	secondary; single	C, P		adult	No. 38	red amphora, upright	
Trench Δ	1976	12	--	pit	cremation	secondary; single	F			--		
Trench Δ	1976	13	20	pit	cremation	secondary; single	C, P			No. 46	red bowl, upright	
Trench Δ	1976	14	21	pit	cremation	secondary; single	C, P			No. 40	gray bell-shaped cup, inverted	No. 41, red conical dish, inverted beside No. 40; No. 42, red amphora, inverted over No. 40
Trench Δ	1976	15	22	pit	cremation	secondary; single	C, P	●		No. 45	gray bell-shaped cup, inverted	one red sherd inside No. 45
Trench Δ	1976	17	24	pit	cremation	secondary; single	C, P			--		
Trench Δ	1976	25	29	pit	cremation	secondary; single	C, P			--		
Trench Δ	1976	26	--	pit	cremation	secondary; single	F		juvenile	No. 43	gray bell-shaped cup, inverted	No. 44, gray bell-shaped cup, inverted over No. 43
Trench Δ	1976	27	30	pit	cremation	secondary; single	C, P		adult	No. 39	gray amphora, inverted	red sherd inside and red clay mass at mouth of No. 39
E of wall	1976	30	--	pit	cremation	secondary; single	F		adult	--		
E of wall	1976	31	destroyed	pit	cremation	secondary; single	F		adult	--		
E of wall	1976	32	33	pit	cremation	secondary; single	C, P			--		
E of wall	1976	33	--	pit	cremation	secondary; single	C?, P			No. 52	gray bell-shaped cup, previously broken handle	No. 53, small cup; No. 54, gray bell-shaped amphora, inverted inside No. 52
E of wall	1976	34	34	pit	cremation	secondary; single	C, P			No. 55	red amphora, inverted	No. 56, red bowl
E of wall	1976	35a	35	pit	cremation	secondary; double	C, P			No. 50	gray amphora, inverted	
E of wall	1976	35b	35	pit	cremation	secondary; double	C, P			No. 50	gray amphora	
NE ditch	1976	1	12	pit	cremation	secondary; single	C, P		adult male	No. 48	gray handled bell-shaped cup, upright	
NE ditch	1976	2	13	pit	cremation	secondary; single	C, P	●	adult	No. 49	orange handled cup, upright	
NE ditch	1976	28a	31	pit	cremation	secondary; single	C, P		adult	No. 57	gray amphora, disturbed	No. 58, black bowl
NE ditch	1976	28b	32	pit	cremation	secondary; single	C, P		adult	No. 59	Larissa ware, single-handled, upright on No. 57	red sherd inside
NE ditch	1976	29	--	pit	cremation	secondary; single	F		adult male	--		
SW ditch	1976	18	25	pit	cremation	secondary; single	C, P		adult	No. 63	gray single-handled amphora, inverted; repair holes	

TABLE 4.4 Continued.
CHARACTERISTICS OF THE LATE NEOLITHIC CREMATION BURIALS AT PLATEIA MAGOULA ZARKOU

Grave Location	Excavation Year	Grave No.[1]	Skeleton No.	Grave Type	Interment Form	Burial Scenario	Bones in Grave Area		Age-Sex		Burial Urn Characteristics	Burial Goods Characteristics
							Human	Fauna				
SW ditch	1976	19	--	pit	cremation	secondary; single	F		adult		--	
SW ditch	1976	20	--	pit	cremation	secondary; single	F				--	
SW ditch	1976	21	26	pit	cremation	secondary; single		C, P		No.69	gray single-handled amphora, inverted	
SW ditch	1976	22	27	pit	cremation	secondary; single		C, P	juvenile	No.75	black vessel (Larrisa ware?), disturbed	red sherd inside No. 75; No. 76, orange vase inverted over No. 75
SW ditch	1976	23	--	pit	cremation	secondary; single	F				--	
SW ditch	1976	24a	28	pit	cremation	secondary; single		C, P	juvenile	No.74	black zoomorphic vessel; ovricaprid features	No. 72, gray conical vessel, inverted beside No. 74; No. 73, gray single-handled amphora, upright beside No. 74
SW ditch	1976	24b	--	pit	cremation	secondary; single?	F		adult?	No.70	gray amphora, inverted	No. 71, red skyphos beside No.70
SW of ditch	1976	36	36	pit	cremation	secondary; single		C, P	juvenile	No.61	gray single-handled amphora, inverted	No. 60, gray, bell-shaped cup, inverted over No. 61
SW of ditch	1976	37	destroyed	pit	cremation	secondary; single	F		infant		--	
SW of ditch	1976	38	--	pit	cremation	secondary; single		C, P	adult	?	--	
SW of ditch	1976	39	--	pit	cremation	secondary; single	F		juvenile	No.64	gray single-handled amphora, inverted	No. 65, gray bowl
SW of ditch	1976	40	--	pit	cremation	secondary; single	F		--		gray, bell-shaped cup, inverted, repair holes	
SW of ditch	1976	41	38	pit	cremation	secondary; single		C, P	--	No.66	gray bell-shaped cup, inverted	
SW of ditch	1976	42	destroyed	pit	cremation	secondary; single	F		--		--	

Source: Gallis (1982); Xirotiris (1982).

53

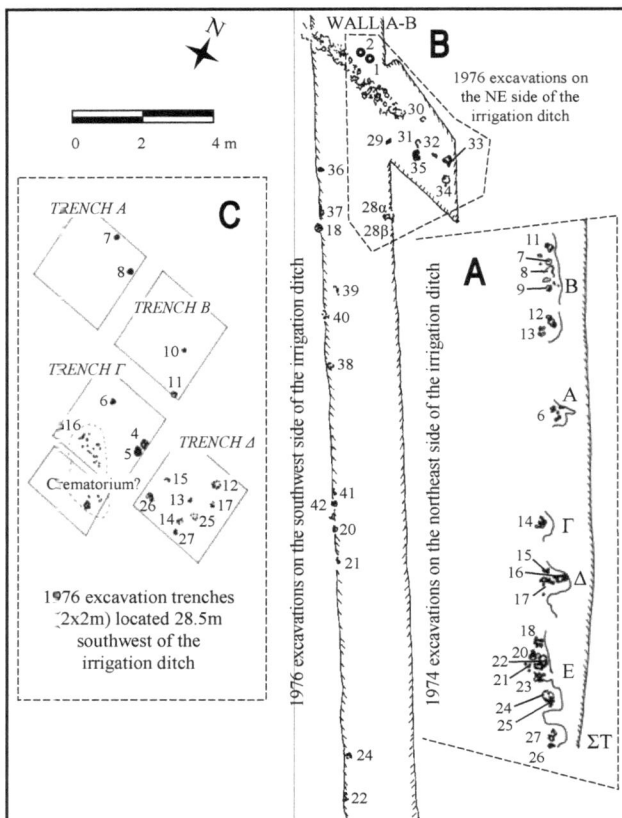

Figure 4.2. Composite plan of the cremation burials excavated during 1974 and 1976 at Plateia Magoula Zarkou. Redrawn and modified after Gallis (1982:figs. 11[B-C] and 15 [A]).

Being located next to a field both modern and prehistoric ploughing has damaged the Neolithic deposits. Further, excavation of the irrigation ditch with a bulldozer (Gallis 1982:227 n.5) resulted in the loss of some urn burials. This situation mainly affected the 1974 investigation. Later excavation proceeded northeast and east of the irrigation ditch. However, the abundance of high quality data from this cemetery far outweighs the few destroyed examples. This cemetery remains the only "urnfield", or cremation cemetery, known during the Late Neolithic, but it is remarkably similar to the earlier-dated cremation burials at Souphli Magoula excavated by Hagan Beisantz in the late 1950s and Gallis (1975, 1979, 1982; see Gallis for history of excavations). Excavations in the cemetery area revealed 67 burial urns containing the cremated bones of as many individuals situated within and to the northeast of the irrigation ditch (Gallis. 1979:69). The salvage excavations in 1974 were confined to recovering and preserving the burials found along the bottom and the sides of the irrigation ditch. As at Souphli Magoula, further work during 1976 was dedicated to clarifying the stratigraphy and exposing deposits not affected by the excavation of the irrigation ditch.

4.3.1 Mortuary Remains

The information regarding each of the cremation burials given in Table 4.4 is organized by location because vessels that contained skeletal remains and those that were burial goods were number sequentially. Thus, the excavators did not initially distinguish between urns containing skeletal remains and other pottery vessels. The 1974 salvage operation located some 23 burials on the bottom and along the northeast side of the irrigation ditch (Fig. 4.2A). The remains of five burials (Graves 1 to 5) were found along the bottom of the ditch, but were badly damaged (Table 4.4). Most of the graves on the north-east side of the ditch were poorly preserved, but in better condition that those directly in the path of the irrigation ditch. These graves were assigned to six clusters. The first five clusters, designated A, B, Γ, Δ, and E, were recovered during 1974, while two further graves were recovered from cluster ΣT in 1976 (Table 4.4).

The other graves located in 1976 were found in two places, within or near the ditch and some distance to the southwest of the ditch. Two burials were located on the northeast side of the ditch, seven graves were uncovered just east of a wall on the northern side of the ditch, and another 12 burials were found on the southwest side of the ditch. Also in 1976, four trenches (A, B, Γ, and Δ) were opened in a field some 28 m southeast of the irrigation ditch and contained a further 16 cremation burials (Fig. 4.2C). Along the south side of Trench Γ, the remains of a structure were found nearby that probably have some association with mortuary practices. Within the structure, burnt soil, a dense scatter of burnt human bone, pot sherds, and roughly-made bricks and brick fragments were found. The deposit continued further to the south. Gallis (1982) has suggested that this area was used as a crematorium, originally located on the surface, but subsequently destroyed by ploughing.

Excavations in both areas showed five discrete strata (A to E) extending from the present surface to 2.10 m below the surface. The stratigraphic sequence is as follows (cf. Gallis 1982:fig. 14):

- Stratum A was from the modern surface to 0.5 m,
- Stratum B ranged from 0.5 m to 1.0 m,
- Stratum Γ fell between 1.0 and 1.5 m, and
- the final two strata, Stratum Δ (1.5 to 1.7/1.8) and Stratum E (1.7/1.8 to 2.1 m) were alluvial sediments containing no cultural material.

All burials were found between 1.3 and 1.5 m along the ditch and in the trenches. The cremated remains were placed in pottery vessels and then in pits dug just over half a meter into Stratum Γ. The original surface of the LN phase was Stratum B, so all the burials are contemporary. The pits were circular and range from 0.6

TABLE 4.5

CONDITION AND MODIFICATION OF HUMAN SKELETAL REMAINS PRIOR TO CREMATION INFERRED FROM THE SURFACE COLOURING PATTERNS[1]

Bone colour	Pre-interment condition	Cultural modification	Burial Cluster								Total MNI	
			Cluster 1		Cluster 2		Cluster 3		Cluster 4			
			N	%	N	%	N	%	N	%	N	%
Grey-white	Fleshed or green	Not modified?	0	0.0%	1	5.0%	0	0.0%	0	0.0%	1	1.5%
White	Fleshed, green or dry	Indeterminate	1	4.8%	2	10.0%	3	27.3%	0	0.0%	6	9.0%
White-brown	Dry	Defleshed	5	23.8%	8	40.0%	2	18.2%	11	73.3%	26	38.8%
White-grey-brown	Dry	Defleshed	0	0.0%	0	0.0%	2	18.2%	0	0.0%	2	3.0%
Indeterminate	Indeterminate	Unknown	3	14.3%	5	25.0%	4	36.4%	2	13.3%	14	20.9%
Not applicable	--	--	12	57.1%	4	20.0%	0	0.0%	2	13.3%	18	26.9%
Total MNI			21	100.0%	20	100.0%	11	100.0%	15	100.0%	67	100.0%

[1] Inferences based upon the experimental data of Buikstra and Swegle (1989).

55

to 0.8 m in circumference with an average volume of 0.27 m³. The small size of the graves may reflect the expeditious directives of this part of the disposal program, as it would have certainly taken less than an hour to dig each pit. There is no indication that the grave pits were constructed with anything in mind beyond providing an essential cavity to house the burial urn and the accompanying burial gifts. Thus, there is no indication for any elaborate burial facilities. This situation contrasts dramatically with the amount of time and effort with which the bodies of the dead were prepared for burial.

4.3.'.1 Cremated Remains

The range of human bone elements represented in the burial urns is limited (Table 4.4). Discounting the unidentifiable remains in Grave 74-E21 (i.e., using a total sample of 66 individuals), over 50% (n=34) of the remains are represented by a small number of bones from the cranium and post-cranium (Xirotiris 1982:Appendix A). Almost half the burials only had elements of the post-crania represented (n=31; 47%), and one grave (74-B9) had only cranial bones in the burial urn. The low frequency of many cranial and smaller post-cranial bones in the sample shows that only a select number and type of bones were placed in the burial urn. As well, animal bones were found in three graves (76-2, 76-Γ6, and 76-Δ15), but no faunal remains were found within the burial urns.

Many larger elements of the post-cranial skeleton are represented in the burials urns, but seldom were isolated vertebra, ribs and scapula identified (Xirotiris 1982). Since the entire skeleton of a single person was not found in an urn, we know that the cremated remains were culled for final interment. Also important is to determine how the body was potentially processed before being cremated. The only available data to investigate this aspect of the mortuary treatment comes from the fortunate recording of the bone colouring by Xirotiris (1982). While bone colour can certainly be modified prior to and after burial, the urns containing the burned bones at Plateia Magoula Zarkou were often covered by other jars or bowls and then buried in pits. Loosely sealing the urn contents greatly decreased the influence that many post-depositional agents, such as soil conditions, groundwater percolation, burrowing animals, etc., could have had on modifying the colour of the bones. Despite these positive attributes, caution must be taken in applying the experimental data of Buikstra and Swegle (1989) to investigate how the corpse was processed prior to cremation.

With the Zarkou sample, the bone colouring for almost half of the individuals (n=32; 47.8% of total) could not be determined with any accuracy (Table 4.5). The remains of six other individuals (9.0% of total) were white in

colour and their pre-interment modification could not be determined. For the remaining 29 individuals, there are two patterns in bone colouring. First, bones with a white-brown (n=26; 38.8%) or white-grey-brown (n=2; 3.0%) colouring suggest that bones were in a dry condition before being cremated. "Dry" bones have had the flesh removed some time before cremation and typically exhibit a brown or tan colour after being burned. Also, these bones are highly calcined in areas, suggested it would have taken between 60 or 70 minutes to bring them to this state (Buikstra and Swegle (1989). One individual, the adult from the SW side of the ditch (76-18) exhibited bones with a grey-white colouring (Table 4.5). The absence of a brown/tan colour eliminates the possibility of the bones being burned in a dry condition, and instead implies they were fleshed, partially fleshed, or had the flesh recently removed (i.e., "green") before being cremated. These data suggest there were two ways in which the body was prepared for cremation. The first, and most common, method was to cremate only the bones of the corpse. This implies that the dead were allowed to decompose completely before their skeletal remains were cremated. The second method was to cremate bones that were partly fleshed or recently defleshed. However, it is also possible that the body was not completely decomposed before being cremated in this instance and some soft tissue still covered the skeleton before it was burned. Since there were no cut-marks on the bones that would suggest a practice of defleshing the body before cremation, it is more likely that this individual's remains were subjected to cremation before the soft tissue was completely decomposed. If the anomalous case of grave 76-18 can be explained in this way, then all the burials exhibit a similar pattern of pre-cremation treatment in which the body was allowed to decompose before all or most of the bones were subjected to intense burning. The skeletal evidence therefore implies a very long process involved in treating the dead before final disposal in the cemetery. This observation contrasts Gallis' (1982:243) opinion that cremation is a rather quick means of disposing the dead.

With cremated skeletal remains it is often exceedingly difficult to assign both age and sex to isolated individuals. The fragmentation of the remains and the distortion of key surface features both played a role in making identification difficult. Only 28 individuals (38.8% of total) could be identified to an age category, and only two adults may be male (3% of total). Using this limited sample, adults dominate (61.5%) over adolescents (7.7%), juveniles (26.9%) and the single infant identified (3.9%). From the classified material, the ratio of adult/adolescents to juveniles/infants stands at roughly 2:1. This distribution is clearly the result of the cultural choice of cremation and attrition resulting from burning human bone. As a result, these numbers hardly stand as a normative age-sex distribution. Nevertheless, because

TABLE 4.6
THE PRINCIPLE TYPES AND STYLES OF BURIAL FURNITURE, BURIAL URNS AND BURIAL
GOODS REPRESENTED AT ZARKOU

Primary Type	Undecorated	Handled	Handleless	Bell-shaped	Conical	Biconical	Zoomorphic
Types of Burial Furniture (Urns and Goods)							
Amphora	●	●	●	●		●	
Bowl	●		●	●		●	
Cup		●	●	●			
Jar		●		●			●
Pithos			●				
Skyphos			●				
Dish	●						
Sherd(s)	●						
Figurine	●						
Undetermined type	●	●			●		
White flint flake	●						
Types of Burial Urns							
Amphora	●	●	●	●		●	
Bowl	●					●	
Cup		●	●	●			
Jar		●		●			●
Pithos			●				
Skyphos			●				
Undetermined type	●	●					
Types of Burial Goods							
Amphora	●			●			
Bowl	●		●				
Cup		●	●	●			
Jar				●			
Skyphos	●						
Dish	●						
Figurine	●						
Sherd(s)	●						
Undetermined type					●		
White flint flake	●						

about 40% of the remains could be identified, it is still possible to try and identify general patterns of age-based constraint. Since there is little variation in the preparation and treatment of the corpse, the variation in burial gifts must be explored as one avenue for expressing age-based constraint in mortuary treatment.

4.3.1.2 Burial Urns and Goods.

There is a relatively high frequency of objects present in the Zarkou cemetery in comparison to other Neolithic cemeteries. Only pottery was associated with skeletal remains in the cemetery, but it appears to have had two main functions. Some vessels served as containers, or *urns*, for the cremated remains, and others were used as covering for the urns to prevent the remains from falling out. Other pottery vessels and fragments (such as single red-burnished sherds) acted as burial *gifts*, and were placed on top of, beside, or within the urns.

A very wide range of pottery types were used as burial urns (Table 4.6).There is no indication that certain types were made specifically for mortuary ritual. Some vessels even have repair holes (No. 63 and 64; Table 4.4), indicating a life-use before being used in mortuary rites. Almost half the urns are larger vessels, like amphorae, and it appears that smaller vessels were less frequently used to hold cremated remains. The distribution of urn types is rather ubiquitous. There is no concentration of particular types of burial urns in particular parts of the cemetery, or any discrete association of urn types with individuals of particular ages. It is clear, though, that burial urns were oriented differently. Some vessels were left upright, while others in an upright position had another vessel inverted to cover the mouth. In other cases, a pot was placed over the mouth of the urn and both were then inverted and placed in the grave. The gravel found in many of these graves was probably used to keep the urn stable. The data on the distribution of upright or inverted vessels is uneven as there is no data for over 50% of the burial urns throughout the entire cemetery (Table 4.4). Despite this, there appears to be a clear preference for orienting vessels in an upright position (N=23, 69.7% of vessels with determinable orientation).

Burial gifts are almost exclusively pottery vessels. A terracotta figure is associated with adult remains in grave 76-ΣT27 and with grave 74-E21, and the only other type of object that could be considered a burial gift is the flake of white flint associated with burial 76-ΣT27 (Table 4.6). Nearly all the vessel types used as burial urns were also used as burial gifts. Only shallow bowls ("dish"-shapes) were not used as urns. There is some disparity in the distribution of grave goods, and it appears that not all individuals received them. While goods were not recovered for the badly damaged graves, several well-preserved graves did not have goods (76-B10 and 76-B11, 74-Γ16; see Table 4.2).

4.3.2 Mortuary Practices

The lack of anatomically complete individuals in the burial urns and the incineration procedures provide two important keys for understanding the disposal of the corpse at Zarkou. It is probable that certain bones—such as scapula and other large bone elements—occur in very low frequencies in the graves because they were too large to fit in the burial urns. Instead, these bones became incorporated in the bone scatter found around the crematorium in Trench Γ or were not recovered during excavations. The cremated bones were subjected to high temperatures (higher than at Souphli Magoula). Bones burned to such a state become more brittle and can be broken with a stone or bone tool relatively easily. However, the lack of ash and charcoal in the burial urns and pits suggest that the bones were culled while still in the crematorium and placed in the urn for final burial. These data indicate that the disposal of the dead was *minimally* a four-stage process:

(1) The corpse was first allowed to decompose completely, or nearly so. Since there are many possible methods of accomplishing this, ranging from simple exposure to temporary interment, it is impossible at this stage to say how this portion of the disposal programme was executed.

(2) All (or a portion) of the remaining skeleton was then selected for cremation in the fire-pit located in the cemetery. Live or dead animals, or perhaps just their bones, may have been included in some cremations at this stage.

(3) Certain burnt human bones and some animal bones were then further culled and placed within a specific burial urn.

Finally, the burial urn was placed in a small pit in the cemetery with or without grave goods and burned animal bone. Because numerous graves were found close together, and none were damaged by later burials, it is likely that some type of marker was used to designate the graves.

This reconstruction of the disposal of the corpse indicates that there was only one socially recognised burial type at Zarkou. Further, it appears that the main differences amongst individuals are based on the types of burial urns used and the kinds and quantity of goods. Based upon these criteria, individuals can be ranked into four categories (Table 4.7). The first rank includes only one individual, the adult in grave 76-ΣT27. This person received the greatest number and kinds of burial goods (a black, red, and grey amphora, a figurine, and a flake of white flint).

The second rank is composed of three juveniles, one adult, and three individuals of indeterminate age. These

TABLE 4.7
RANKING OF THE CREMATION BURIALS AT PLATEIA MAGOULA ZARKOU BASED ON THE KINDS
AND QUANTITIES OF BURIAL URNS AND GOODS

| | Grave | Location | Age/Sex | Characteristics of Mortuary Treatment | | |
				Type of Urn	No. of Goods	No. of Types
Rank 1						
	76–ΣT27	NE ditch	Adult	Grey amphora	5	3
Rank 2						
	76–22	SW ditch	Juvenile	Black Larissa ware vessel	2	2
	76–24α	SW ditch	Juvenile	Black zoomorphic vessel	2	2
	74–E 21	NE ditch	Indeterminate	Red amphora	2	2
	76–33	E of wall	Indeterminate	Grey bell-shaped cup	2	2
	76–Δ14	Trench Δ	Indeterminate	Grey bell-shaped cup	2	2
	76–28β	NE ditch	Adult	Single-handled Larissa ware jar	1	1
Rank 3						
	All others except those below	E of wall, 1974 NE ditch, 1976 NE ditch, 1976 SW ditch Trench A, Trench B, Trench Δ, Trench Γ	Adult, Adolescent, Juvenile	Amphora (red, black, grey, and grey single-handled), Bell-shaped cup (grey), Bi-conical bowl (grey), Bowl (red), Conical cup (grey), Handled cup (orange), Handled jar (black), Bowl (red), Skyphos (red)	1	1
Rank 4						
	76–B10	Trench B	Adult	Bell-shaped cup	0	0
	76–B11	Trench B	Adult	Bell-shaped cup	0	0
	76–Γ16	Trench Γ	Adult	Red amphora	0	0
	76–37	1976 SW ditch	Infant	Indeterminate	0	0

high rankings are a result of the exceptional quality of the urns used in these burials, and the presence of two different types of grave goods. Even thought the adult in 76-28β only received one grave good, it was included in this ranking because the remains were placed in a finely-made single handled Larissa ware jar which is uncharacteristic of the lower rankings. The remains of the juvenile in grave 76-22 were recovered from a high quality black Larissa ware vessel, and they were one of the few individuals to receive a single red sherd. The remains of the other juvenile in Grave 76-24α were placed in a unique zoomorphic vessel that had numerous sheep- or goat-like features, and two well-made vessels were placed beside the burial urn. Several burials had remains of indeterminate age. Considering the high-ranking juvenile burials, it is not possible to infer that the other high-ranking burials contained the remains of adults.

The third ranking was made on the basis of individuals receiving only one burial good, and this practice appears to cross-cut the discernable age categories. The fourth, and lowest, rank includes four individuals: the adults buried in Trench B (76-B10 and 76-B11), the adult in Trench Γ (76- Γ16), and the infant remains situated in the SW side of the ditch (76-37). The fact that three adults did not receive any burials gifts is as striking as the presence of children in a high rank, and more so if we consider the only other member of the forth rank is the

cremated remains of an infant that received neither a burial urn nor any grave goods. It is quite possible that social standing may not explain the results of this ranking exercise, and we must look at other dimensions of the mortuary rites at Zarkou to explain these apparent anomalies.

When the distribution of these ranks is examined spatially, the burials tend to cluster around one or more high-ranking burials (Fig. 4.3). There are three clusters along the expanse of the irrigation ditch, and the burial in the trenches are grouped around one individual of high ranking. Cluster 1 includes the burials situated about 2 m apart across the irrigation ditch, which are spatially separated from those to the north by some 3 m. In this cluster there are three persons of high ranking, including 76-ΣT27, 74-E21, and 76-22. The Cluster 2 burials are spatially distinct from those in Cluster 1 and those near the wall. Burials 76-28α and 76-28β are of the highest ranking in Cluster 2. In Cluster 3, near the wall, 76-33 is the person of highest rank. The burials located in the trenches well away from the irrigation ditch are the most obvious spatially discrete cluster. These burials compose Cluster 4 and one burial located near the crematorium, 76-Δ14, is ranked highest. Only Cluster 2 and Cluster 4 have persons belonging to three of the four rank categories. Thus, in each cluster there is at least one individual that received a greater material contribution to their mortuary treatment. Clearly, there are differences

TABLE 4.8
CORRESPONDENCE BETWEEN THE CREMATION TECHNOLOGY AND HANDLING OF THE CORPSE AND
THE SOCIOCULTURAL ASPECTS OF THE FOUR BURIAL CLUSTERS AT ZARKOU

HANDLING OF THE CORPSE

SOCIOCULTURAL ASPECTS

Degree of Bone Incineration

	Cluster 1	Cluster 2	Cluster 3	Cluster 4
Cluster 1	1.00			
Cluster 2	0.99	1.00		
Cluster 3	**0.28**	**0.20**	1.00	
Cluster 4	0.98	0.97	**0.13**	1.00

Grave Goods

	Cluster 1	Cluster 2	Cluster 3	Cluster 4
Cluster 1	1.00			
Cluster 2	0.70	1.00		
Cluster 3	0.90	0.75	1.00	
Cluster 4	0.70	0.88	0.88	1.00

Pre-Cremation Bone condition

	Cluster 1	Cluster 2	Cluster 3	Cluster 4
Cluster 1	1.00			
Cluster 2	1.00	1.00		
Cluster 3	0.82	0.78	1.00	
Cluster 4	0.98	0.99	**0.69**	1.00

Age and Sex Distribution

	Cluster 1	Cluster 2	Cluster 3	Cluster 4
Cluster 1	1.00			
Cluster 2	0.96	1.00		
Cluster 3	0.96	0.89	1.00	
Cluster 4	0.80	0.88	0.77	1.00

Preparation and Treatment Modification Practices

	Cluster 1	Cluster 2	Cluster 3	Cluster 4
Cluster 1	1.0			
Cluster 2	1.0	1.0		
Cluster 3	1.0	1.0	1.0	
Cluster 4	1.0	1.0	1.0	1.0

Distribution of Energy Expenditure Categories

	Cluster 1	Cluster 2	Cluster 3	Cluster 4
Cluster 1	1.00			
Cluster 2	1.00	1.00		
Cluster 3	1.00	1.00	1.00	
Cluster 4	1.00	1.00	1.00	1.00

TABLE 4.9
CORRESPONDENCE BETWEEN THE CREMATION TECHNOLOGY AND HANDLING OF THE CORPSE AND
THE SOCIOCULTURAL ASPECTS OF THE NORTHEAST AND SOUTHEAST GRAVE GROUPS AT ZARKOU

HANDLING OF THE CORPSE

SOCIOCULTURAL ASPECTS

Degree of Bone Incineration

	Group 1	Group 2
Group 1	1.0	
Group 2	0.94	1.0

Grave Goods

	Group 1	Group 2
Group 1	1.0	
Group 2	0.75	1.0

Pre-Cremation Bone Condition

	Group 1	Group 2
Group 1	1.0	
Group 2	0.95	1.0

Age and Sex Distribution

	Group 1	Group 2
Group 1	1.0	
Group 2	0.83	1.0

Preparation and Treatment Modification Practices

	Group 1	Group 2
Group 1	1.0	
Group 2	1.0	1.0

Distribution of Energy Expenditure Categories

	Group 1	Group 2
Group 1	1.0	
Group 2	0.47	1.0

60

LATE NEOLITHIC MORTUARY PRACTICES

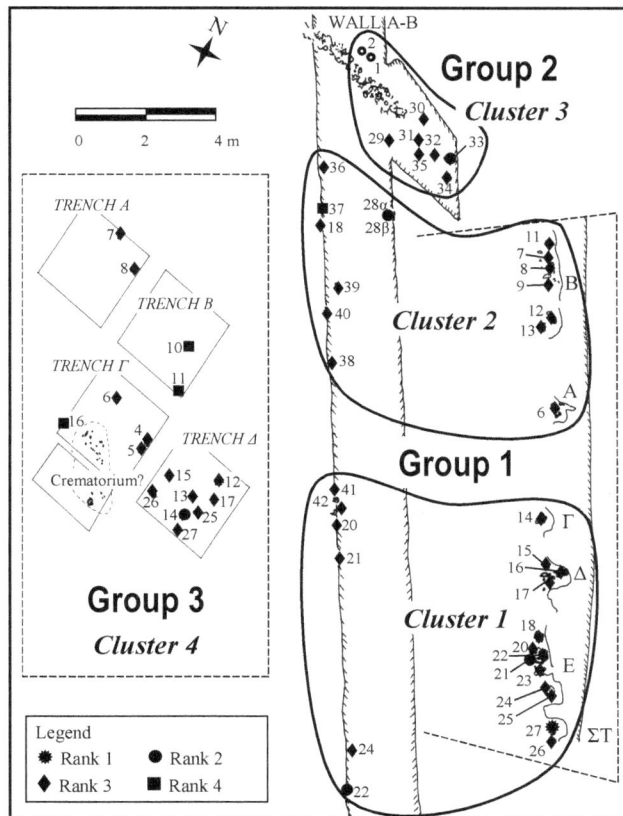

Figure 4.3 Spatial distribution of the cremation burials at Plateia Magoula Zarkou ranked according to the kinds and quantities of burial urns and goods.

amongst *individuals* within these spatially discrete groups. If this ranking mirrors social standing in the community, as Tainter (1978) and others argue, the higher ranking members of each family group would have been the heads of the families that were given greater recognition through mortuary ritual. Such an interpretation must also account for the high ranking of children between the ages of two and twelve years. There are at least two children with much higher energy expenditures than other children, adolescents or adults that were buried near them. If energy expenditure indeed reflects vertical social position in this society, it would follow that these children's burials would represent cases of hereditary status ascription, wherein these children are socially recognised in terms of the relative social standing of their families.

This social interpretation poses two main problems when evaluated against the ethnographic data reviewed in Chapter 2 (Table 2.1). First, we know that overall energy expenditure is equally likely to be determined by horizontal social position. If concerns about either vertical or horizontal social position overrode other potential philosophical-religious determinants of the

disposal programme at Zarkou, then we would expect these social constraints to be clearly expressed amongst individuals and groups through two aspects of the disposal programme: (1) the technical procedures involved in handling of the corpse (the preparation and treatment of the body and the grave), and (2) socio-cultural variables involving the kinds of grave goods, osteo-biological variation, and overall energy expenditure. To examine these constraints at Zarkou, I compared these two sets of variables amongst the burial clusters. To measure inter-group similarity amongst these variables, the Pearson's r correlation coeffecient was employed. Pearson's r determines the linear relationship between variables. In other words, the statistic determines whether large values of one data set are associated with another (positive correlation), whether small values of one set are associated with the large values of another (negative correlation), or whether values in both sets are unrelated (correlation near zero). This method was used to determine the differences and similarities between the data arrays of each grouping.

An assessment of the handling of the corpse was based upon three variables: (1) the degree of bone incineration, (2) the pre-cremation condition of skeletal remains (dry or fleshed); and (3) the overall preparation and treatment practices. These variables take into account the possible the tools used to prepare the body before cremation (leading to the pre-cremated condition of bones) and the cremation method (resulting in the degree of incineration and the final modification of the bone through burning). The assumption is that the pre- and post-condition of the skeletal remains are initially a result of the tools used to prepare the body (if any) and the intensity of fire used in cremation. There is little evidence to suggest substantive bone modification through post-depositional attrition due to the relatively "closed" nature of the burial contexts (see above). This may be largely because the remains were housed in burial vases. Thus, it is reasonable to assume that the most damaging attrition occurred before burial.

The degree of bone incineration, the condition of bone before cremation and the general practices of handling the corpse are similar throughout the cemetery (Table 4.8). However, there are substantial differences in the degree of bone incineration between Clusters 1 and 3 (28% similar), Clusters 2 and 3 (20% similar), and Clusters 3 and 4 (13% similar). While these could reflect real differences in how long the skeletal remains represented in each cluster were subject to fire before final interment, some remains were not classified by the degree of bone incineration or could not be classified according to their condition before cremation (Xirotiris 1982). These mainly affected the bones in Cluster 3, and the scarcity of data from this location is the reason for the lower values in Table 4.8. It is worth mentioning that applying Buikstra and Swegle's (1989) experimental data to these remains indicates that the remains of one individual (76-18) were burnt while articulated. Some of these bones may have not been completely fleshed. This case is unusual, because, as mentioned above, most remains were subjected to high temperatures. Overall, however, the method of handling the corpse is quite homogeneous. Given these results, I reorganized the burials into two larger spatial groups, with Group 1 comprised of the burials located in the northeast (Clusters 1 to 3) and Group 2 including those in Cluster 4 located in the southwest (Fig. 4.3), as there is a substantial distance between the two groups. However, there are no substantial differences between the burials located in the trenches (Group 2) and along the irrigation ditch (Group 1) (Table 4.9).

A second set of variables was used to examine the socially driven aspects of the normative mortuary disposal program in terms of the behaviours governing the material contribution to ritual, which persons are to be included or excluded from the cemetery based upon age, sex, and so forth, and the overall effort expended in mortuary activity. Thus, three sets of cultural data were used to assess the similarities and differences in mortuary practices: (1) the types of grave goods, (2) the distribution of age and sex, and (3) the overall energy expended in the mortuary treatment of the dead as determined from the ranking analysis discussed earlier. The spatial comparison of these socio-cultural variables shows a different pattern than the technological variables.

With the exception of overall energy expenditure, both the clusters (Table 4.8) and northeast and southeast grave groups (Table 4.9) are highly correlated. As noted above, the distribution of the energy expenditure is not uniform throughout the cemetery. The correlation study shows that the energy expenditure ranks are evenly distributed within each cluster, and the pattern is not likely a by-product of the unequal distribution of individuals of different rank *between* the groups. If energy expenditure, as a measure of corporate involvement in mortuary ritual, can be taken as a gauge of social standing then the spatial clusters are not socially differentiated, but the spatial groups are. The main reason for this difference is that there are more people in the fourth rank category in Group 2. Behaviourally, the people buried in Group 2 received a lower degree of corporate involvement in their mortuary treatment than individuals in Group 1. Local grave location tends to be affected equally by vertical and horizontal social determinants as well as cosmology and beliefs about the nature of the soul, its journey to the afterlife, and its affect on the living. There is no firm basis to suggest that the differences between the grave groups are based solely upon social rank. Rather, the source of this variation may have less to do with expressing differences in social personae, than it does with expressing differences in the kinship structure of the community.

A second important problem with the social ranking interpretation is that we also know from ethnography that the source and quantity of grave furniture has a low correlation with vertical hierarchical social position in hunter-gatherer and small-scale farming societies. Instead, the kind of burial goods received by the deceased, not their source or quantity, is more strongly governed by their horizontal social position and/or social personae. Several artefacts and other finds associated with some individuals suggest that such concerns were part of mortuary ritual at Zarkou. The adult buried in Grave 76-ΣT27 and that in 74-E21 are unique in that each received a figurine in their burial assemblage. In a study of figurine imagery dating to the Neolithic, Talalay (1988, 1991) has suggested that the symbolism represented by the figurines does not necessarily have to be linked to religion. Rather, using the example of Kephala, Talalay proposed an intriguing argument based upon the anthropological literature, suggesting that the figures could have otherwise been used as communal social and economic symbols, and representations of ties to the community's ancestral spirits. Talalay suggested that the cemetery "was established to legitimise the villager's control or ownership of the area, and the figurines served as ancestor images which chartered Kephalan ancestral rights to the region" (Talalay 1991:49). Because we do not have comparable data from this cemetery, it is difficult to directly invoke such an explanation for the use of figurines at Zarkou. However, Talalay's proposal that the use of social and economic symbols can be tied to the community's ancestors does open up an intriguing possibility for interpreting the association of figurines, faunal remains, and red-coloured pottery with some burials at Zarkou.

The figurines in the cemetery have an interesting parallel with the spectacular find of a house model containing human figurines and domestic equipment, which were found under a house floor in the settlement (Gallis 1985). The model at Zarkou appears to have more restricted access to the house (one door) and a greater segregation of space within the house for specific activities (Nanoglou 2001). This separation of space is paralleled in the distinction between the living community (the settlement) and the cemetery (the community of the dead). Further, this practice of segregation can be conceptually linked to Hodder's (1984, 1990) proposal that the household was the centre of social and symbolic life. He argued that much of the symbolic behaviour in Neolithic communities was based on distinctions between the domestic or *domos*, the household, and the wild or *agros*, that outside the community, the uncivilized. Symbolic themes built on this distinction are expressed through spatial dichotomies: inside:outside, domestic:wild, male space:female space. A key aspect of this symbolism is the physical incorporation of the dead into spaces used by the living. In this way, the dead remain domesticated; the ancestors are part of the living society. What we are seeing at Zarkou may very well be a different expression of the symbolic theme proposed by Hodder.

The connection between figurines in a mortuary context and the burial of figurines in a household should be viewed as linked processes. In particular, if we follow Talalay's argument that figures may act as ancestor images, the ancestors and the living society were symbolised by the presence of figures under household floors during a time when the actual ancestors were not physically incorporated into spaces used by the living— that is, we have continuity in the symbolic theme expressed by other Neolithic peoples, but a change in how this expressed in practice.

Two further observations point in the same direction. First, there is a change in settlement pattern during this time in Thessaly. Many new, smaller settlements were established, each composed of a smaller number of households. Nanoglou (2001:309-310) sees this trend in settlement pattern as signalling a change in social relationships, wherein people operated in small co-operative webs. Second, this shift in settlement coincides with a change in subsistence practices. Faunal assemblages show a more balanced combination of domesticated animals, which point to a more diversified animal husbandry strategy, built on keeping of smaller, possibly privately owned, herds (Halstead 1992). In the Zarkou cemetery, three individuals (76-2, 76D-15, and 76-G6), two of which are adults, had faunal remains included in their burials urns. Placed in this broader context, these bones may have been included with the corporeal remains of notable herders.

In addition to these trends, special mention should be made of the red-coloured pottery vessels and single red sherds found on top of and/or within several graves (Table 4.4). The colour red, and in particular the use of ochre, has symbolic significance in the mortuary rituals of many cultures. For instance, amongst the Yolngu aborigines of Australia, baskets, digging sticks and ochre are part of the equipment used in the songs, dances, and paintings invoked in ritual performance to aid the soul in its journey to the afterlife (Morphy 1994). Indeed, Gallis (1982:243) has noted that the use of ochre and colour red is often viewed as the colour of life and its renewal. From the ethnographic survey summarised in Chapter 2, we know that the kind of burial goods received by the deceased, not their source or quantity, is strongly governed by social positions (horizontal social position and/or social personae) and a range of philosophical-

religious beliefs surrounding the health/safety of the living, the nature and journey of the deceased to the afterlife, and conceptions of the nature of the afterlife in general (Table 2.1). At this general, cross-cultural level, we may expect that the use of red vessels and sherds at Zarkou has overlapping social and philosophical-religious significance linked to non-hierarchical aspects of social organisation and metaphorical concerns about the destination and journey of the deceased.

It is difficult, if not impossible, to ascribe the same symbolic meaning to the use of red-coloured vessels and sherds during the Neolithic period in Greece. However, it is interesting that the use of red burial urns and sherds cannot be considered part of the normative mortuary programme at Zarkou, as they are found in only 14 graves. If the red burial urns and sherds do indeed express metaphors of death linking the Corpse and Disposal with the Soul and the Dead (Fig. 2.1), not everyone was recognised in the same way. This could imply that the same concerns about the state of the soul were not held for everyone in the community. However, it is more likely that we are seeing the influence of beliefs held about differences in the social personae, which also strongly affects the choice of burial gifts that accompany the dead. This interpretation implicates both social and philosophical-religious factors acting in tandem on the choices and decisions made during the process of disposing the dead, and is further strengthened by the above analysis of the scale of rites at Zarkou—in terms of the material contribution to ritual—implying there were discrete differences in horizontal and not vertical social standing expressed through similarities in the handling of the corpse. Taken together, the procession of rites, the possible metaphors of death, and the scale of rites all suggest an absence, or at least a masking, of social ranking at Zarkou.

4.3.3 Conclusions

Like the cremation burials at Souphli, individuals were not differentiated by the form of burial. There is generally very little variation in the way the body was prepared for burial, although the process itself seems to have been elaborate, and most likely involved a long procession from the settlement to the cemetery for cremation and final interment. The clustering of many burials indicated that the graves were likely marked in some fashion, and perhaps these markers were unique to the cluster of graves identified above. However, mortuary ritual at Zarkou was not used to visibly differentiate groups: the markings of this are subtle and were only arrived at through a consideration of multiple lines of evidence. Mortuary ritual could have been used as a levelling mechanism for most individuals, and perhaps only persons of exceptional ability or potential were recognised in these mortuary practices.

Although the age and sex data available from Zarkou is uneven, it appears that some constraint on the distribution of artefacts was made on the basis of age. Only large open and closed types of vessels were given to adults. Four types of burial gifts are exclusive to adults: amphorae, the bell-shaped jar, skyphos, and the dish. These types are not found with the juveniles or adolescents, and were otherwise found along with the remains of undifferentiated individuals. It is then possible that these individuals are of adult age. Other types, such as single-handled amphora, conical vases, and bell-shaped cups, are found only with juveniles. Other burial gifts run across more than one age category: cups with no handles are found with both adults and juveniles, and single red sherds are found with adults and a juvenile. Other age or sex statuses were impossible to determine based on the variable preservation of the cremated remains. Thus, there is substantial evidence that vertical social positions were not present at Zarkou, but it is difficult to determine how horizontal social differences were expressed through mortuary ritual. The types of grave goods and energy expenditures were the clearest indicators of differences in the scale of mortuary rites, and how the social persona was differentiated.

A study of the method of handling the corpse and other social variable that could have affected the burial directives at Zarkou indicated that mortuary practices were rather homogeneous. However, the presence of high status holders in each burial cluster indicates that the cemetery was used by different groups. Because the mortuary practices are so homogeneous, there is no basis to argue that intra-group differentiation is based upon different corporate group access to or control over resources. If this was the case, we would expect to see clear differences in mortuary treatment between groups (Saxe 1970; Goldstein 1981). It is more probable that the inhabitants of Zarkou belong to the same social group, perhaps a lineage or clan, rather than different ones, and that the discrete areas within the cemetery were used by different descent or "family" groups that share a common heritage. This analysis suggests an absence of social ranking at Zarkou, and, instead, the cremation burials at Zarkou represent several possible alternatives. Socially, mortuary practices may (1) emphasise the non-hierarchical aspects of social organisation of the community, or (2) the relatively homogenous nature of the procession and scale of rites express a denial of the social contradictions that characterised the living community. However, because there are equally plausible non-hierarchical explanations for the differences in the kinds of graves goods and overall energy expenditures, it is quite likely that the material contribution to ritual reflects the horizontal social position of individuals at Zarkou, including age statuses and occupational roles in the community, whilst the procession of rites and the kinds of grave goods reflects concerns about the destination and journey of the deceased. Such practices and their possible determinants parallel many of the mortuary directives at Skoteni Cave and those at Souphli Magoula. They have very little in common with the trends at several other LN cases discussed below and the Final Neolithic, which is the subject of the next chapter.

TABLE 4.10
THE LATE NEOLITHIC 2/FINAL NEOLITHIC MORTUARY REMAINS AT LERNA

F.	Area	MNI	Grave Type	Interment Form	Body Orientation and Posture	Scenario	Age/Sex	Grave Goods	Notes
1	JA-JB	1	pit	inhumation		Single urn burial	infant		Caskey 1957:159
2		1	pit	inhumation	S, left side, flexed	Single, primary	adolescent		Caskey 1957:159
3		1	pit	inhumation	?, ?	?	?		Caskey 1957:159
4	Grave J7	2	pit	inhumation		Double, primary	juvenile		Caskey 1957:159
5	Grave J7		pit	inhumation		Double, primary	infant		Caskey 1957:159
6	Tr. JC	1	pit	inhumation		Single, primary	juvenile		Caskey 1957:159
7		1	pit	inhumation	SW, left	Single, primary	adult	spouted jug, red crusted ware sherds; 2 burnished grey vases at feet	surrounded by stone circle; Caskey (1959:205)
3	Tr. HTN	1	pit	inhumation	E, right, flexed	Single, primary	adult/ adolescent?	stone "pillow," 2 red crusted ware (at shoulder and feet) and one grey-brown burnished bowl	Caskey (1958:136-137)
9					NE, right, flexed	Single, primary	juvenile (~5 yrs.)	black burnished bowl	hands before face

TABLE 4.11
LATE NEOLITHIC MORTUARY PRACTICES

Categories of Observable Mortuary Variation		Late Neolithic Mortuary Sites				
		Skoteni	Lerna	Zarkou	Dimini	Agia Sophia
Preparation & Treatment of the Body						
Preparation	burial & exhumation	●?		?		
	not indicated		●			●
Treatment	inhumation	●	●			●
	cremation			●	●	
Position at burial	flexed	?	●			●
	semi-flexed					
	disarticulated & arranged			●	●	
Orientation at burial	northerly	?	●			●?
	southerly		●			
	not applicable		east	●	●	
Form of disposal	primary		●			●
	secondary	●?		●	●	
Preparation of the Grave						
Grave form	pit grave	●?	●?	●	●	●
	built grave					
	cist grave					
	ossuary					
Number of socially recognised burial types			3	1	2?	>1
Grave Furniture & Goods						
Kinds grave goods	ceramics	?	●	●		
	terracotta	?				
	lithics	?				
	bone					
	shell					
	wood					
Source of goods	local area	?	●	●		
	trade item					
Quantity of goods		?	low	low	?	?
Spatial Location and Designation						
Local location	disposal area in cave	●				
	open-air disposal area		●	●		
	intramural				●	●
Location relative to settlement	spatial separated	●		●		
	incorporated		●		●	●
Graves demarked		no	no	probably	?	?
Intra-cemetery location of burial types	differentiated				?	●?
	not differentiated		?			
	not applicable (1 type)	●		●		
Energy Expenditure						
Levels of energy expenditure		1?	2?	4	2?	2?
Funeral time & duration; secondary funerals				●	?	?
Mourning Ritual						
Funeral dance/games						
Funeral meals/fasting						
Funeral dress and ornamentation						
Grief, bereavement and grave visitation				possible		possible

4.4 OTHER LATE NEOLITHIC MORTUARY REMAINS

In northern Greece, two other sites with mortuary remains date to the later centuries of the Late Neolithic. Much attention has been paid to the intramural cremation burials at Dimini. Eight infants were cremated, placed in pots, and interred under house floors near hearths. Some of the pots do not appear to have had an earlier life-use and could have been made specifically for the burials (Hourmouziadis 1979:33; Halstead 1992). These burials are considerably different from the roughly contemporary cremation burials at Plateia Magoula Zarkou and the earlier cremations at Souphli Magoula.

The two burials of an adult male and a juvenile at Agia Souphli Magoula have also been considered somewhat unusual. They have not been well reported nor clearly dated (Milojĉić et al. 1976). Halstead (1984) has proposed that the two inhumation burials placed within the top two central enclosures of the settlement represent individuals of high status. Halstead interpreted the inclusion of a child in this place as evidence of hereditary status ascription, reflecting the rise of institutional elite during the LN.

Elsehwere on the southern mainland, primary inhumation burials are also found outside of caves. At Lerna, nine individuals were recovered within habitation areas dating to the most recent Neolithic levels, possibly spanning the LN2/FN transition (Table 4.10). The two identified adults (Fr 7, Fr 8) were each interred in single, primary inhumation burials and were given the most burial gifts (up to three ceramic vessels). The adult burials are further notable for the stone circle surrounding one (Fr 7), and the placement of a stone under the head (Fr 8) of the other. An adolescent (Fr 2) was buried like the adults but did not receive any burial goods. Two of the three identified juveniles (Fr 6, Fr 9) were interred in their own grave, and one (Fr 9) received a fine black-burnished bowl. Another juvenile (Fr 4) was found in a double grave along with an infant (Fr 5). The other infant (Fr 1) was buried in an urn. All the burials are extramural primary inhumations found near houses, which may have also acted as specialised activity areas. There are few grave goods, and the juvenile given the black-burnished bowl presents somewhat of anomaly in this mortuary assemblage. There are too few data to determine a general pattern in terms of the orientation and posture of the corpse, but there is clearly an elaboration of graves based on age, with the adults receiving a comparatively large amount of energy expended in their interment and children very little.

4.5 TRENDS IN LATE NEOLITHIC MORTUARY PRACTICES

Variation in mortuary practices during the LN is summarised in Table 4.11. When compared against the earlier EN and MN mortuary practices (Table 3.9), the one notable feature of the LN mortuary practices is the greater number of questions involving the quality of data and inferences that can be derived from them. This largely has to do with the preservation of LN mortuary remains at these sites, which have been variously affected by the scale of excavation and post-depositional disturbance of open-air sites (e.g., Lerna, Zarkou, Dimini) and the reuse of cave sites in later periods (e.g., Skoteni). Nevertheless, the available data from the five major sites with well-preserved mortuary remains are sufficient to comment upon a number of general patterns regarding the procession, scale, form, and symbolism of mortuary rites during the LN.

4.5.1 Procession of Rites

Variation in the treatment of the dead suggests that there were significant physical and conceptual differences in the transformation of the corpse and the social individual amongst the various societies inhabiting the Greek mainland during the LN. Certain of these differences are discernable on a regional basis.

In Thessaly, both cremation and inhumation are practiced. At Plateia Magoula Zarkou, cremation was an elaborate processes, and subtle variations in the preparation and treatment of the corpse and grave goods appear to express social differences amongst the deceased. In stark contrast, cremation at Dimini was used only for infants, who were then placed in pots and interred under house floors. Clearly, the people living at these two settlements had different perceptions of the dead and ways in which they should be related to the living community. This distinction extends to Agia Sophia, just down river from Plateia Magoula Zarkou, where an adult and a child were interred within the two central enclosures of the settlement. A similar practice is not found at Dimini or other sites in Thessaly. While it is enticing to view this kind of rite as being motivated by social directives, we know from ethnographic data that the form of disposal and the location of graves within or near habitation areas are determined almost equally by concerns with the cause of death, classification of the individuals at the time of death, as well as their vertical and/or horizontal social positions. The mortuary data alone do not provide independent evidence of hereditary status ascription and the rise of institutional elite, as Halstead (1984) argues. Rather, the same procession of rites, resulting in the same form of disposal and where it occurs in a settlement, may have been accorded adults and children for different reasons—in recognition of different social positions (not necessarily vertical ones) or causes of death.

While the mortuary data from southern Greece are far more limited, we do also see substantial differences in the mortuary practices at the LN2/FN burials at Lerna and at Tharrounia with the burials in Skoteni Cave. A legitimate case can be made for primary burials in Skoteni Cave, which were disturbed by subsequent activity in the cave. The placement of one skull in a wall niche must have occurred during a later visitation of the burial area. This practice may show some reverence for the dead. The handling of the skull, and any skeletal remains for that matter, more strongly parallels practises in northern Greece than in the south. However, the disposal of the dead in caves continues a southern tradition, seen in earlier phases at Franchthi Cave and Souphli Magoula. Indeed, as is evident during the Final Neolithic as well (explored in the next chapter), the use of caves for burial appears to be a uniquely southern tradition. These transformations of the corpse highlight possible differences concerning the relationship between the disposal of the corpse, the soul, and the community of the dead. As in the EN and MN phases, there is considerable variation in these directives of mortuary practices during the LN. Less apparent are differences in the scale of rites.

4.5.2   Scale of Rites

The scale of mortuary rites according individuals is related to differences in age, gender and social identity. Unlike the EN/MN, social distinctions are most visibly expressed during the LN by the number of socially recognised burial types and the energy expended in mortuary ritual. More than one burial type can be inferred at Dimini and Agia Sophia based on negative evidence; only a small proportion of the mortuary population at each of these sites is represented, including infants at Dimini and the unique mound burials at Agia Sophia, so it is likely that the rest of the dead were treated in at least one different way. The best evidence for more than one burial type comes from Lerna, where there was a single urn burial of an infant in addition to single and double primary burials. Both at Lerna and Agia Sophia, we find infants being treated in significantly different ways than older individuals. I suspect, this likely relates to very young children not being imbued with social responsibilities, which was evident in both the disposal of the corpse and the distribution and types of grave goods at EN/MN Franchthi Cave.

Plateia Magoula Zarkou provides us with an interesting case, because the only significant differences in the disposal of dead involved slight variations in cremation practices and grave goods. The types of grave goods and energy expenditures were the clearest indicators of differences in the scale of mortuary rites, and how the social persona was differentiated. The use of grave goods

to differentiate the dead in social terms is not strongly predicted by ethnographic data (Table 2.1). As well, grave goods are usually utilitarian in nature, but at Plateia Magoula Zarkou they included pottery sherds and animal bones.

While at other sites, the scale of mortuary rites appear to distinguish individuals on the basis of horizontal or 'natural' statuses (age, sex, division of labour), cremation at Zarkou may either emphasise the non-hierarchical aspects of social organisation of the community, or a denial of the social contradictions that characterised the living community. During this time, there are changes in settlement throughout Thessaly, as people aggregated to form larger towns. Zarkou was occupied during this transition, which undoubtedly involved some kind of social changes as people modified their lifestyles to accommodate living in larger settlements. It is unlikely, however, that this change in settlement living spurred on increases in social and economic differences. To accomplish this, people would have had access to greater wealth, which would be evident in differently sized houses and notable differences in their contents. The evidence for families accumulating great wealth, for instance, in livestock or trade items, is not evident during this time in the LN. Given this broader social context, it is plausible that the Zarkou mortuary practices were designed to gloss over social contradictions and differences amongst people in the community. However, these were not 'naturalised' by emphasising age and gender distinctions. Rather, it was suggested above that specific, and rather unassuming, objects (red sherds and animals bones), were used to designate important individuals and members of important families in the community.

4.5.3   Form and Symbolism of Rites

In the previous chapter (Chapter 3), I proposed that the contents as well as the structure of EN/MN mortuary remains captured several symbolic themes related to transformations of the corpse and attitudes towards the ancestors. There is evidence for material culture being used in a metaphorical way at three of the LN phase sites.

In the Classical literature, we are told how caves played an important role in religious life throughout the Greek prehistory. Home to mystery cults and their initiation ceremonies in Classical times, caves were associated with the cosmos (Burkert 1987:83), purity (Burkert 1987:16-17), and sometimes as places of birth or rebirth, analogous to the womb. In some pottery-making societies, pots are also associated with female anatomy and symbolically with the womb (e.g., Aschwanden 1982; David et al 1988). This pot-womb metaphor can not uncritically be applied to all times and places. However, it may go some way to understanding, at least broadly, the meaning of the infant pot burials at Dimini, which were also significantly placed under house floors, presumably near their mothers. Like the covering stones used for the burials at EN-MN Franchthi, this practice may have also been guided by beliefs about the relationship between the dead and the living and the effect they have on each other. Unlike Franchthi, the inhabitants at Dimini may have not believed that their dead children would become malevolent spirits.

A second use of material culture possibly related to the transformation of the corpse and the relationship between the dead and the living involved the use of red sherds and animal bones at Zarkou. As noted earlier, the use of ochre and colour red is often viewed as the colour of life and its renewal, and for Zarkou it was suggested that the use of red vessels and sherds had philosophical-religious significance linked to metaphorical concerns about the destination and journey of the deceased. In contrast, the fauna found in three burials were otherwise interpreted as having social significance, and may be related to these individuals role as livestock owners in a new economic strategy during the LN in Thessaly that was built on keeping of smaller, possibly privately owned, herds. Now, viewed within the broader symbolism of rites at the cemetery, I argue that the use of the animal bones and the red pots and sherds may be conceptually linked to Hodder's (1984, 1990) proposal that the household was the centre of social and symbolic life. At Zarkou, the dead are located in a cemetery outside of the settlement, some burials have symbols possibly related to life and rebirth and the household (red pots and sherds), and a few others contain the bones of domesticated animals. There is a clear domesticated element to this range of funerary gifts. The possible symbolic themes played out in the disposal of the dead contradict the spatial separation of the ancestors from the living community, which is the wild or *agros* opposition referring to that outside the community, the uncivilized. Although the dead are not physically incorporated into spaces used by the living, the dead remain domesticated; the ancestors are part of the living society. This symbolic contradiction actually aligns well with the earlier social interpretation of mortuary practices at the site, which stressed how the disposal of the dead was designed to emphasise the non-hierarchical aspects of social organisation of the community and/or express a denial of the social contradictions that characterised the living community.

The final material culture element that may have held some symbolic significance is the stone 'pillow' used in the funerary rites at Lerna. In one burial (Fr 8), the body of an adult (or possibly an older adolescent) was laid on their right side in a flexed position, their head was laid on a stone, two red crusted ware bowls were placed at either end of the body, one at the shoulder and one at the feet, and beside the body lay one grey-brown burnished bowl (Table 4.10). The use of so-called 'stone pillows' is known elsewhere during the Neolithic in Greece (cf. Jacobsen and Cullen 1981). At Kephala on Kea, for instance (discussed further in Chapter 5), large stones placed under the head of the corpse are associated with both men of women who have little in common except their advanced age. This practice may very well have been reserved for important older individuals in these farming communities. Furthermore, recent analysis of island colonisation sequences in the Aegean suggests an origin for this practice. According to Broodbank (1999:33-34), the south-western islands were first permanently settled by peoples living in present-day Attica as part of a general expansion onto the islands near the mainland peninsulas during the Final Neolithic. Thus, the practice of using stone 'pillows' in the burial of senior members of society likely originated on mainland Attica and subsequently spread to the islands at the end of the Neolithic.

In the analysis of EN-MN burial practices, I suggested that the location of the burials can be seen to symbolise the location of the 'community of the dead,' which reflects beliefs about how ancestors should be integrated into the community of the living. This proposition rests on the assumption that settlements did not expand around the burial areas during the occupation of the settlements masking an earlier separation of burial ground and settlement. Since this did not occur at the Neolithic sites examined thus far, these spatial data suggest that the

dead outside/ ancestors = dissonance : dead inside/ ancestors = solidarity

binary opposition was also in place during the LN phase.

If we apply these concepts to the LN mortuary data, the following relationships are suggested:

LN Skoteni Cave:
cave → outside settlement → place of all ancestors → separate realm

LN2/FN Lerna:
extramural burial near houses → within living areas → place of all ancestors → same realm

LN Zarkou:
cemetery → outside settlement → place of all ancestors → separate realm

LN Dimini:
central enclosure → adjacent to living areas → place of ancestors (only certain adults and juveniles) → same realm

LN Agia Sophia:
intramural burial under houses → within living areas → place of ancestors (only infants)→ same realm

The *outside/inside, ancestors-dissonance/ancestors-solidarity* principle does appear to have continuity from the EN-MN, although it is expressed differently in each of these cases. At this level of analysis, the precise differences in execution of mortuary practices are less important than the possibility that the spatial organisation of the disposal of the dead can be explained by the same principle. Despite the many social, economic, and political transformation that occurred during the time frame considered here, the variety of intramural and extramural burial practices on the mainland indicate very different attitudes towards the dead. Some of these attitudes are contradictory to other organising principles of society, such as an expression of dissonance between the living and the dead at Plateia Magoula Zarkou, during a time when new forms of social solidarity were being established as people began living in larger settlements. Other attitudes align well with what is know about social life during the time, such as at Dimini, Lerna, and Agia Sophia, where the spatial organisation of mortuary practices appear express social solidarity.

4.6   CONCLUSIONS

Unlike the EN-MN, where there were no apparent geographical or temporal relationships between either the mortuary practices or the symbolism expressed through the form of mortuary rites, during the LN we instead find certain similarities in the scale and symbolism of rites at a regional level. The mortuary practices in northern Greece (Plateia Magoula Zarkou, Dimini, Agia Sophia) and in southern Greece (Skoteni Cave and Lerna) have little in common in this regard. While I have tended to emphasize Hodder' *domus:agros* model in exploring symbolic expressions in Neolithic social life, I do not wish to impose this model uncritically on the Neolithic mortuary data. To conclude this chapter, I will briefly discuss the relationship between the elaborate domestic symbolism during the LN and mortuary practices.

In Thessaly, the LN is a time when the household becomes increasingly isolated from others within settlements through the subdivision of villages by walls or ditches and private cooking areas (Halstead 1999). Despite this increasing compartmentalisation, Halstead (1999) has raised the important point that, at the village level, families would still have to deal with uncertain food supplies and an unstable labour force. These uncertainties would have forced them to call upon mutual obligations set up with kin and non-kin. Most importantly, this strategy would have provided both a levelling mechanism on the large accumulation of personal wealth and provided long-term obligations within and between families that promoted social solidarity. Competition would, of course, not be absent in such a situation. Households would have vied to either get rid of their surpluses or debt in any given year while at the same time setting up alliances—through marriage or exchange or both—with other successful households.

We could expect this to be reflected in mortuary practices that emphasized the horizontal social identity of individuals and distinctiveness of family identity. The best example of this is from Zarkou, where the differences amongst individuals were downplayed over the differences amongst (likely) family groups in the cemetery. Such a situation may have also prevailed at Dimini, but the quantity of mortuary data is merely speculative. The mortuary evidence independently supports the contradictory notion of large villages arising by a combination of competition amongst 'isolated' families that are intricately connected by mutually advantageous obligations.

The mortuary practices in the south allow us to consider an entirely different issue—the colonization of the Aegean islands. In the south, there does appear to be some connection with mortuary practices during the LN and later practices during the FN. However, the patterns of mortuary practices may mask the changes in these societies, which contributed towards their colonising nearby islands and developing the distinctly insular societies of the Aegean islands. The mortuary practices merely hint at the origins of these later practices, but belie the differences in identity, ideology, and perhaps theology, that characterise these later insular groups. It is to a more detailed consideration of the latest Neolithic societies that we now turn.

CHAPTER 5
FINAL NEOLITHIC MORTUARY PRACTICES

5.1 FINAL NEOLITHIC CULTURE-HISTORY

The Final Neolithic (FN) phase has only relatively recently been distinguished from the Bronze Age and the Late Neolithic phase. Consequently, the terminology used for the phase remains confusing (Demoule and Perlés 1993: 389-399). This phase has variously been called the 'Late Neolithic' (Treuil et al. 1989), the 'Late Neolithic II'(Sampson 1988; Zachos 1987), the 'Chalcholithic' after the Balkans terminology, the 'Early Bronze Age I' because of the unsure stratigraphy at Pevkakia, and 'Final Neolithic' in southern Greece (Renfrew 1973; Diamant 1974; Phelps 1975). I prefer to use the term Final Neolithic for two reasons. The first, as suggested by Demoule and Perlés (1993), is that the term can be used to encompass settlement occupations dating between ca. 4500-3200 B.C. This time frame subsumes Sitagroi IIIB and C in eastern Greek Macedonia, the Rakhmani Phase in Thessaly, and the Aegina-Attica-Kephala group of the central and southern Greek mainland and Cycladic islands under the same chronological scheme. The second reason is climatic, where the term is used to differentiate between Temperate Europe and the Mediterranean climate of Greece. However, this distinction does not differentiate the Greek Final Neolithic material culture from that of the Balkan Early Chalcolithic (Demoule and Perlés 1993). The archaeological differences and similarities between lands in the modern political boundaries of Greece and to the north of this in the Balkans will be alluded to below.

The FN is a time when very clear differences develop between the societies inhabiting regions on the mainland north and south of the Pindus River. Based on the evidence of ceramic interaction spheres, it is apparent that settlements in the two areas adopt very different relationships with neighbouring groups. In the south and nearby islands, there are distinct cultural zones, intensively interacting. In the north, Macedonia, Thrace, and Thessaly develop a more intense relationship with the cultures of the Balkans. During this phase, Northern Greece is more clearly related to the Balkans and 'north' is used as a proxy for this association. Therefore, intense, spatially differentiated interaction spheres and regional uniqueness characterise the Final Neolithic phase.

5.1.1 Settlement Pattern and Architecture

Within these different regional groups, there are also distinctly different settlement patterns. In the south and in the islands during the first half of the FN, there is an increase in the number of sites occupied. These sites are small, and include an increase in the use of caves (Diamant 1974; Wickens 1986). It is also interesting that most of the new sites identified through surface survey in Boeotia (Bintliff 1977; Bintliff and Snodgrass 1985), Euboea (Sampson 1981), the Berbati-Limnes region of theArgolid (Well et al. 1990 cited in Demoule and Perlés 1993:399), and the southern Argolid (Runnels and van Andel 1987) date to the Final Neolithic. The settlements themselves do not really change in plan from previous periods: small houses predominate and they are spaced very close together (an agglomerative plan). However, they are now commonly scattered across the hillsides (Demoule and Perlés 1993:399), with each house having its own storage pits and hearths. Several authors have argued that this pattern suggests that a seasonal, pastoral economy came to dominate the subsistence strategy (Diamant 1974; Zachos 1987; Wickens 1986). It has also been argued that caves were used as temporary pens for sheep by the transhumant herders. However, the faunal evidence does not support such a hypothesis (Demoule and Perlés 1993:399). Further, Diamant (1974) has observed that access to many of these caves is difficult (i.e., semi-mountainous areas), and some are far from water sources. The use of these sites as shepherd's camps is therefore problematic.

This shift in settlement pattern to small 'farmsteads' or 'hamlets' placed in more marginal agricultural landscapes is thought to be a response to a dramatic increase in population and a continuing trend in the dispersion of settlements (particularly in the Argolid; Runnels and van Andel 1987). A similar pattern is found in the Balkans during this time (Greenfield 1986). Progressive hierarchical differences between settlement size and richness are documented for the Argolid (Runnels and van Andel 1987) from the FN to the Early Bronze Age. This dispersion and disparity between settlements is thought to have been the result of several factors, all linked to agriculture. The results of the Berbati-Limnes survey suggests that this change came when subsistence strategies shifted from spring-fed to rain-fed irrigation techniques (Wells et al. 1990 cited in Demoule and Perlés 1993:399). During the same time, the use of less crops required less nutrient demands have been documented in the south (barley and legumes). Barley dominates crops of this period, especially in the south at Franchthi (Hansen 1991) and the islands (e.g., Zas Cave on Naxos; Zachos 1990). Soil erosion is another factor that has been considered, which may possibly have been caused by the settlement on the hill slopes (e.g., Zangger 1991). It appears that strategies in the south aimed at producing food quickly and independently. The establishment of smaller settlements farther away from a larger, primary settlement would also suggest that a larger catchment area was needed to sustain the growing local population.

The appearance of small, seasonal farming homesteads throughout the countryside is not unprecedented in Greece, and there is growing ethnographic documentation of such strategies in more recent historical periods (Pelapsis and Thompson 1960; Kolodny 1974; McGrew 1985; Sutton 1991, 1994; Fowler in press).[1]

In the north, a different pattern emerges. In Thessaly, there is a dramatic drop in the number of sites occupied during the FN (Gallis 1989; van Andels and Runnels 1995). There are few new sites, and those that are occupied are quite large and unevenly distributed across the region. The precise reason for this is not evident; it could be due to a decrease in population or just a continuing nucleation process where people are rapidly moving into the larger settlements (Demoule and Perlés 1993:401). During historical times, the reasons for the two patterns are clear. During economic prosperity and freedom from crises, there is a dispersed settlement pattern, with small settlements surrounding a larger one (Sutton 1991:401). This seems to be the case in the south and the islands during the FN. On the other hand, during times of economic problems, or some type of socio-political crisis, the outlying settlements are abandoned. People begin congregating in one place, packing into small closely spaced houses, thus creating a larger centre. It has long been suspected that such a situation occurred intensively in Thessaly (Wace and Thompson 1912), as many of the large tell sites inhabited in the first half of the FN are abandoned. While a nucleated settlement pattern appears to be taking place in northern Greece during the FN, this pattern does not appear in eastern Macedonia and the Balkans during the last half of the FN (Greenfield 1986; contra Demoule and Perlès 1993:401).

Further evidence for nucleation of settlements is indicated by the settlement architecture in the north. At the largest sites in the north, Pevkakia in southern Thessaly (Schachermeyr 1976) and Mandalo in western Macedonia (Pilali-Papasterio and Papaevthimiou-Papanthimou 1989) there are massive surrounding walls. At Otzaki, in northern Boeotia, there is also an extensive ditch, some 6 m deep and 4.5 m wide (Milojĉić 1955). These walls and the ditch appear different from those seen earlier at Dimini and Sesklo, simply because of their massive size. They may have been built to separate the inner village from the outer village, distinguishing the main village from the incoming population from the surrounding area. Demoule and Perlés (1993:401) have also noted that there does not seem to be any obvious economic reason for the decrease in site density. Again, there is not a 'secondary products revolution' notable in the FN (Halstead 1987; Hansen 1988; Greenfield and Fowler 2003), and no increase in viniculture (Runnels and Hansen 1986). Demoule and Perlés (1993:403) have suggested that this decrease may be due to some social crises, as Thessaly became weaker in the exchange network during the FN.

Under these circumstances, the nucleation of settlement pattern makes some sense. However, we should also expect that people in these northern settlements expressed broad categories of social differentiation in non-spatial ways as well.

5.1.2   Technology and Crafts

The domestic equipment used in the FN remains abundant and varied. Many sites, such as Rachmani, have numerous areas for grain storage, many coarse pots, grinders, milling stones, celts, flaked stone tools, bone tools, and more spindle whorls (Wace and Thompson 1912). Wild animal skins also are still used at Pevkakia (Hinz 1979), but there is considerably more evidence for weaving and matting during this phase. However, the preservation of textile manufacture is a by-product of ceramic production. Impressions on sherds are far more common in this phase than any other, and some eight sites show that weaving and matting was very commonplace. From Kephala, we find that four techniques were used for matting and weaving: a simple twine, a split twine, a plain weave, and coiled matting. A study by Carrington Smith (1977) has shown that fine grasses were widely used: plant fibre was used as warps, while reeds and grasses were used as weft. There is evidence from both at Tharrounia and Kephala for either fine linen or wool (which is uncertain at this point) and plain woven cloth. Cloth was also built into the walls of coarse pottery found at Kephala, probably as a means of support (Demoule and Perlés 1993: 401). Compared to the pottery of earlier phases, the FN wares seem quite inferior in quality. Coarse wares dominate types throughout Greece during the FN, and, with the exception of Macedonia, painted wares are few and often have sloppy decoration (Demoule and Perlés 1993: 401). With the FN pottery, there is a greater variety of coarse tempering materials being used for vessels. Slips are rarely used in making pottery and most surface treatments were achieved by light burnishing (Diamant 1974; Phelps 1975; Zachos 1987). Several other simple surface decorations are found on FN wares. Like most of eastern and central Europe at this time, crusted ware is produced in Greece, simple painted geometric motifs were used by combining white, reddish, and sometimes black pigments, and large, coarse vessels were seldom decorated with incised lines or applied features (Demoule and Perlés 1993:401).

Different modes of procurement and manufacture have been cited as reasons for similar decline in stone tool production (Demoule and Perlés 1993:401-402). One can infer from this that there was a lack of specialists involved in the procurement and manufacture of lithics during the FN. The most diagnostic stone tools in the FN are the rare, fine, elongated obsidian arrowheads. These are found throughout Greece, but never in large numbers, and since an exact same type is found in the Gulmenitsa and Salcutsa cultures of the Balkans, there is some question if the triangular points were even manufactured in Greece (Demoule and Perlés 1993:402). Copper artefacts are more common than in previous periods, but all metal objects, including the rare gold and silver artefacts, are always found as finished objects. The ongoing excavations at Zas Cave on Naxos (Zachos 1990), have yielded some of the most impressive metal finds of this phase. Still, other sites from around the Aegean, like Kephala (Coleman 1977), Giali (Sampson 1988), and Sitagroi III (Renfrew, Gimbutas, and Elster 1986), all show evidence that indicate smelting may have occurred at these sites. The discovery of ore sources that may have been exploited during the Neolithic (especially silver-rich lead ores; Gropengiesser 1986; Zachos 1990; Coleman 1977), has at least brought attention to the availability of ore for manufacture.

5.1.3   Trade and Exchange

Perlés (1990, 1992; cf. also Perlés and Vitelli 1999) has suggested that two regions in the Aegean acted as principle centres for production and artefact distribution during the FN. Based upon the distribution of artefact types, Perlés has argued that the central region of southern Greece and the islands were key places in the FN exchange system. Most of southern Greece seems to have been neglected in this trade network, and even more so Thessaly, whose position appears quite understated from previous phases (Demoule and Perlés 1993:403). In almost all cases, the Cyclades acted as the main place of production for 'prestige' goods, such as metal objects, jasper points, spondylus ornaments, marbles vases, and figurines. On the mainland, in the south, Lavrion and Siphnos are key places in the production and trade of metal objects during the FN (Perlés 1990). Sites that were once prosperous in trade became less so in the FN economy (Demoule and Perlés 1993:403), and this may have brought about severe social changes, particularly in ways social statuses were symbolised.

5.1.4   Conclusions

The FN was a time when regional differences that began to take during the LN crystallised on the Greek mainland. Changes in settlement pattern, population density, interactions spheres, and circumstantial evidence for periods of economic crisis characterise the north, while in the south hierarchical differences in settlement size and richness and the purposeful exploitation of metal resources appear for the first time, which tend to indicate economic growth and the emergence of new socio-political inequalities. These changes in the south coincide with the initial settlement of many nearby islands during the FN. It is on these islands that a new stone-built tradition of disposing the dead appears, which may very well have influenced patterns of mortuary practice that

occur during the subsequent Early Bronze Age on the Aegean islands (Cosmopoulos 1991; Doumas 1977; Pullen 1985). In the following section, a look at the mortuary practices at several sites in southern Greece and the nearby islands gives us a chance to evaluate the variety of responses to death at both open-air and cave sites used during the twilight of the Neolithic. We will begin by looking first at two important cave sites in the Peloponnese.

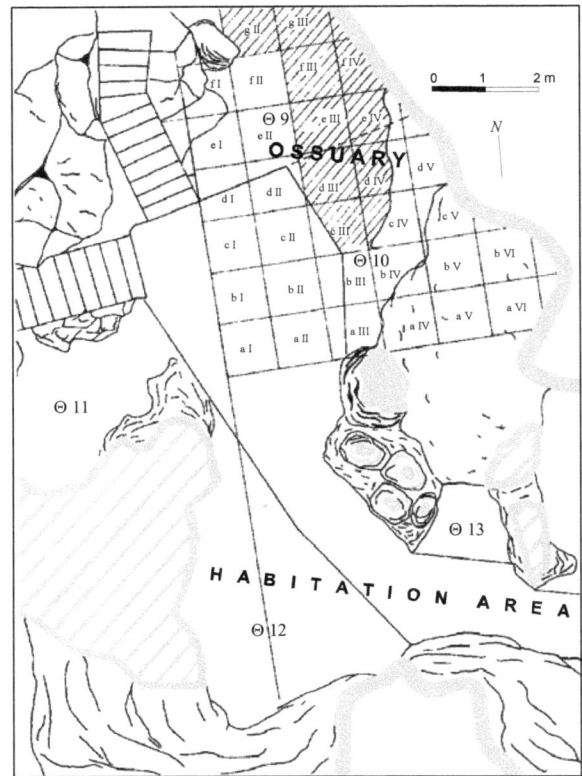

Figure 5.1. Plan of Aleopotrypa Cave showing the ossuary and habitation area (redrawn and modified after Lambert 1972: fig. 5).

5.2   DIROS: ALEOPOTRYPA CAVE

Aleopotrypa Cave is one of the Diros caves located about 2 km to the south of the village of Diros in the district of Mani. G. A. Papathanasopoulos conducted excavations at Diros in the early 1970s (Papathanasopoulos 1971), and the mortuary remains were excavated by N. Lambert in 1971 (Lambert 1972; Duday and Lambert 1981). The Aleopotrypa excavations revealed that certain natural niches deep in the cave were used as habitation areas (Fig. 5.1:12, 13, 14). Two 'rooms' in the southeast section at the back of the cave contained disc-shaped ovens, hearths, and utilitarian pottery (Papathanasopoulos 1971). The material recovered from the cave dates to the latter part of the Late Neolithic phase and can be directly

TABLE 5.1
THE LOCATION AND CONDITION OF LATE NEOLITHIC HUMAN SKELETAL REMAINS AND ASSOCIATED OBJECTS FROM
ALEOPOTRYPA CAVE

| Bone Number | Provenance | | | | Skeletal Remains | | Associated Objects |
	Section	Quadrant	X axis	Y axis	Bone Element, Side and Fragmentation	Age	
Di No. 8	Θ	9	E	3	parietal (right?)	unknown	
71\120	Θ	9	E	3	maxillary	juvenile	
71/199	Θ	9	E	3	femur (left)	juvenile	
71/198	Θ	9	E	3	tibia (left)	juvenile	
71/206	Θ	9	E	3	cuboid (right)	infant	pottery
71/209	Θ	9	E	3	vertebra	unknown	
71/129	Θ	9	E	4	cranium/mandible	adult	
Di No.10	Θ	9	E	4	mandible	adult	
71/149	Θ	9	E	4	péroné (fragment)	adult	
71/145	Θ	9	E	4	humerus (left)	adolescent	
71/148	Θ	9	E	4	femur (left)	juvenile	
Di No.5	Θ	9	E	4	cranium (partial)	unknown	
Di No. 7b	Θ	9	E	4	cranium (partial)	unknown	
71/106	Θ	9	E	4	carpal	unknown	
71/174	Θ	9	E	4	carpal	unknown	
71/188	Θ	9	F	3	cranium/mandible	adult	pottery
71/191	Θ	9	F	3	cranium/mandible	adult	ground stone
71/018	Θ	9	F	3	pubis (partial)	adult	
71/015	Θ	9	F	3	tibia	juvenile	
71/189	Θ	9	G	2	femur (left)	adult	pottery
71/012	Θ	9	G	3	cranium/mandible	adult	stone pounder?
71/011	Θ	9	G	3	vertebra	adult	
71/008	Θ	9	G	3	lumbar vertebra	adult	
71/010	Θ	9	G	3	metatarsal	adult	
71/009	Θ	9	G	3	calcaneum	adult	
71/032	Θ	10	C	3	metatarsal	adult	
71/033	Θ	10	C	3	metatarsal	adult	
71/034	Θ	10	C	3	metatarsal	adult	
71/035	Θ	10	C	3	calcaneum (right)	adult	pottery
71/043	Θ	10	C	3	metatarsal	adolescent	
71/040	Θ	10	C	3	humerus (left)	juvenile	
71/039	Θ	10	C	3	calcaneum (left)	juvenile	
71/048	Θ	10	C	3	pubis (partial)	infant	
71/046	Θ	10	C	3	cuboid	unknown	
71/105	Θ	10	C	3	cuneiform	unknown	
71/201	Θ	10	D	3	parietal (right)/mandible	adult	
71/219	Θ	10	D	3	lumbar vertebra	adult	
71/235	Θ	10	D	3	pubis (right)	adult	
71/126	Θ	10	D	3	cranium/mandible	adult?	
71/215	Θ	10	D	3	pubis (partial, right)	adult?	
71/060	Θ	10	D	3	cuboid (left)	adolescent	
71/082	Θ	10	D	3	cranium/mandible	juvenile	
71/080	Θ	10	D	3	cranium/mandible	juvenile	
71/123	Θ	10	D	3	cranium/mandible	juvenile?	
71/062	Θ	10	D	3	sacrum 1	juvenile	
Di No. 9	Θ	10	D	3	cranium (partial)	unknown	
71/233	Θ	10	D	3	femur (left)	unknown	
71/083	Θ	10	D	3-4	humerus (right)	adolescent	
71/162	Θ	10	D	4	radius (left)	adult	
71/164	Θ	10	D	4	tibia	adult	
71/168	Θ	10	D	4	tarsals	adult	
Di No. 7a	Θ	10	D	4	cranium (partial)	unknown	
71/163	Θ	10	D	4	femur (fragment)	unknown	
71/169	Θ	10	D	4	calcaneum (right)	unknown	
71/221	Θ	10	D4/E4		femur (right)	adult	
71/041	Θ	10	E	3	vertebra	sub-adult	
71/042	Θ	10	E	3	vertebra	sub-adult	
71/044	Θ	10	E	3	vertebra	sub-adult	

Source: Papathanasopoulos (1971) and Lambert (1972).

associated with similar finds at the cave entrance and around the Neolithic acropolis.

5.2.1 Mortuary Remains at Aleopotrypa

The skeletal remains in the Aleopotrypa cave are located deep within the cave near or under a low overhanging rock ledge that runs from Θ10 northeast into Θ9 (Fig. 5.1). This area is distinct from the habitation area, which begins some seven meters to the south and continues east further into the cave. In antiquity, and more recently, several sections of the cave collapsed including the ledge under which the skeletal remains were located. The collapse of this ledge covered many of the skeletons with rocks and boulders of various sizes, affecting their original location and completeness. Upon excavation, the bone elements of many individuals were found mixed together in a large mound. Despite the disturbances in the cave, the disposal area was interpreted as an ossuary (Papathanasopoulos 1971; Lambert 1972; Duday and Lambert 1981). Therefore, formal graves, such as pits, were not used to house the remains of the dead. This implies that secondary burial was practised at Aleopotrypa. However, no suggestions have been made as to the procedures that would have been followed in disposing of the dead, which is one of our primary concerns here.

The skeletal sample consists of 58 different cranial and post- cranial bones. The remains are quite well preserved. Cranial elements are represented by complete, or almost complete, skulls and several isolated cranial elements, such parietals, mandibles, and maxillae, were recovered. A study of the cranial elements suggests that at least 14 individuals were buried in this section of the cave. Most of the post-cranial elements do not occur in the frequencies that one would expect, given the number of individuals estimated from the cranial remains (Table 5.1). Although, the post-cranial bone elements compose over 72% of the overall skeletal sample, the frequencies of long bones, phalanges, carpals, and other small compact bones are comparatively low. While this may be a result of excavation techniques (common if sieves were not used which is not the case here), Papathanasopoulos (1971:296-297) notes that many bones were quite weathered from exposure. He considered these taphonomic properties of the skeletal remains a result of secondary burial practices. The skeletal remains were recovered from specific areas in Θ9 and Θ10. In Θ9, seven individuals are represented in three different locations:

1) four individuals were found in Θ9e (III and IV), one of adult age but the others were not determinable;

2) two adults in Θ9f (III and IV); and

3) in Θ9g (II and III) one adult was identified by a complementary cranium and mandible.

A large hole is apparent in the frontal bone of the skull, and death may not have resulted from natural causes. In area Θ10, only sections Θ10d, Θ10c, and the portion of Θ9eIII that overlaps into section Θ10 held any human skeletal remains:

1) the femur of an adult and several vertebrae also of adult age were recovered in Θ10e;

2) post-cranial bone elements (mainly foot bones) were recovered in Θ10cIII and belong to at least one adult, an adolescent, a juvenile, and part of a pelvis was identified to an infant;

3) in Θ10d III and IV seven skulls, several with associated mandibles, were identified to two adults, three juveniles, and two individuals of indeterminate age.

It is likely these remains are directly associated with those from Θ10cIII (Lambert 1972; Duday and Lambert 1981). Also in this area, a large amount of broken pottery and several stone tools were found. What is unique about this group of remains is that a row of stones was laid out in a circle around them (Lambert 1972). Pottery and stone tools were abundant in the disposal area. It is difficult to determine if any of the items served as burial goods, but several artefacts can be loosely associated with the remains of several individuals (Table 5.1). The area does not have the character of a domestic dumping area, particularly because the range of objects is quite limited (cf. Kent 1999), and there is no mention of organic debris in the area (besides, of course, the human remains). This implies that these objects had some function in the mortuary practices. It may be significant that all of the pottery was quite broken. This practice is repeated at other cave sites where Neolithic mortuary remains are found (e.g., Franchthi, Kitsos, Skoteni).

5.2.2 Mortuary Practices at Aleopotrypa

A reconstruction of mortuary practices at Aleopotrypa necessarily relies upon both positive and negative evidence. There is no indication that formal graves were constructed within the cave. Instead, the disarticulated remains of the dead were placed underneath a rock ledge in the northwest corner of the cave, near but clearly segregated from habitation areas. Interestingly, certain individuals in area Θ10dIII and Θ10dIV were set apart from the others by a stone outline. Excavations revealed that other groups of skeletons were not differentiated in this way.

The bounding of a group of individuals suggests that formal distinctions were made in the disposal area. It is most likely that the dead were place in some location outside the grave after death, perhaps in a pit, and left for several months (depending upon the season) until the body was decomposed. This has certain practical implications. For example, the stench of decomposing corpse within the cave would be considerable, particularly if the cave was inhabited at the same time. After initial burial, the skeletal remains were exhumed, brought into the cave, and placed in a small area marked by a circle of stones. When another death occurred, the process was repeated and the remains in the stone circle were re-deposited further back under the overhang. This burial scenario would go some way to explaining the under-representation of post-cranial bones in the cave, which could have been left elsewhere inadvertently or intentionally. Furthermore, this may also be indicative of the seasonal use of the cave, although this has not been established at Aleopotrypa; such a scenario may have involved the placement of individuals who had died while away from, or *en route* to, the cave when it was reoccupied. This would account for the remains of more than one individual found in the stone circle. These remains would subsequently have been cleared away and deposited farther back in the cave. In either event, the same four stage depositional sequence involving

(1) extramural burial → (2) exhumation → (3) initial ossuary deposition → (4) final ossuary deposition

would have occurred. Such practices are not well-documented during the Neolithic, but this sequence closely resembles that involving cremation burial and a similar process of disposal and clearing at other later Neolithic and Early Bronze Age cave sites (for EBA overview see Cosmopoulos 1991). Also of particular interest are the remains of an adult was found isolated in Θ9gIII, located far back into the cave. The head wound and the location of the body suggests that differential treatment was given this person. The wound is large and appears to have been purposeful. It likely represents a trephination, but does not appear to have healed (although this is difficult to assess from photographs alone), and ultimately may have been the cause of death. Thus, this treatment may be due to the circumstances surrounding the individual's death, regardless of the source of the wound.

5.2.3 Conclusions

In order for burials to be defined as secondary, it must be *clearly* established that some primary treatment was accorded the dead before final interment. The spatial, bio-osteological, and taphonomic evidence, as well as practical considerations, indicates that secondary disposal was used for the treatment of the dead at Aleopotrypa. The burial process supports earlier suggestions that the disposal area in the cave should formally be termed an ossuary. Although secondary burial practices are clear, there is insubstantial evidence to argue that the mandibles of the skull were purposefully removed

(Papathanasopoulos 1971; Lambert 1972; Duday and Lambert 1981; cf. Jacobsen and Cullen 1981:91). If the disposal sequence outlined above holds, then removing the mandibles would clearly have been unnecessary. Furthermore, the pathological evidence does not suggest that the mandibles were removed purposely and/or forcefully before the skeleton had decomposed. The alteration or dislocation of the mandibles could just as likely have resulted from the collapsing ledge.

There is little indication that different levels of energy were expended in the disposal of the dead. This, of course, may be masked due the secondary nature of the mortuary practices. However, the sequence does suggest that individuals may not have been differentiated on the basis of biological criteria. The artefacts found in the ossuary do contradict this statement somewhat. These artefacts are most often associated with domestic activities: pottery and lithics used for food processing (ground stone and possibly a 'pounder'). Although any precise associations between artefacts and individuals are contentious, the artefacts are most abundant around adult remains and may be indicative of adult activities. Thus, any link between the infant remains in Θ9eIII and these artefacts is probably coincidental, resulting instead from later disturbances. More instructive is the abundance of pottery in Θ10dIII, the area of the 'stone circle.' The pottery may have been broken during the early stages of the mortuary treatment or may have occurred when the skeletal remains were brought into the cave. Alternatively, the ceramic containers may have been placed in niches along the ledge of the overhang, which broke and scattered when the ledge collapsed. When the bones were previously cleared from this 'staging area,' they would become intermingled with the remains of earlier burials.

Is this behaviour connected to social statuses, is a ritual practice aimed at symbolizing the transformation of the social personae, or both? Although there is no definitive answer, an understanding of the process of secondary burial can nevertheless more generally indicate when the dead move from the status of 'kin' to one of 'ancestor.' At Aleopotrypa, decarnalisation of the ancestors is a long process that begins immediately after death. The secondary burial practices in the cave show that the skeletal remains and not the body were handled most frequently: perhaps in travel to the cave, after exhumation and disposal in the staging area, then finally as the remains were incorporated into the main ossuary. Therefore, it can be suggested that the decarnalisation of the dead occurred while the corpse of the 'kin' was transformed into the skeleton of an 'ancestor.' Concepts such as these are not often associated with primary inhumation practices. There are exceptions: in Indonesia and Polynesia, for example, where the dead are often kept in communal facilities such as crypts, certain sanctions

TABLE 5.2
THE FINAL NEOLITHIC MORTUARY REMAINS AT FRANCHTHI CAVE

Date	Fr	Location	Grid Location	MNI per Grave	Grave Type	Interment Form	Body Orientation	Body Posture	Pattern of Bone Association	Scenario	Age-Sex	Grave Goods
FN	18	paralia	PQ 6	2?	pit?	inhumation	nw-se	right side	flexed	single	adult female (33)	stones
FN	18A	paralia	PQ 6	1		inhumation		right side	bone scatter	single	adolescent male	
FN	19	paralia	Q5	1	pit?	inhumation		right side	??	single	adult female?	spindle whorl
FN	61	paralia	O5 NE	1		inhumation		right side	disarticulated	multiple	adult female	
FN	62	paralia	O5 NE	1		inhumation		right side	disarticulated	multiple	adult male	
FN	63	paralia	O5 NE	1		inhumation	se-nw	side unknown	disarticulated	single	adult female??	"crusted ware" bowl
FN	69	paralia	?	1	pit?	inhumation		right side	??	single	juvenile male?	
FN	115	paralia	Q6	1		inhumation		right side	disarticulated	single	juvenile	

Source: Jacobsen and Cullen (1981) and Jacobsen (1969).

regarding the handling of the corpse or ancestral remains must be followed by paternal family members. However, at Aleopotrypa, the closeness of the dead to the living areas implies that there may have been fewer sanctions, consequences, and fear of 'spiritual' retribution. In the social sphere, I would suggest these practices express social directives intended to harmonize many of the statuses held during life irrespective of age, gender or ability. Objects in the ossuary may have a functioned in this homogenising process rather than acting as material expressions of socio-economic differences.

5.3   FRANCHTHI CAVE

5.3.1   Mortuary remains

The FN mortuary sample at Franchthi is composed of seven individual interments (Table 5.2) situated south and just west of Wall 3 in the habitation area of the Paralia (Fig. 5.2). As with the burials from previous phases, no graves were detected by the excavators. Therefore, grave type, shape, and dimensions are not listed in Table 5.2. However, the graves were probably simple pits.

While there is little evidence for different grave types as with earlier periods, the location of the burials indicates that there may have been two burial scenarios.

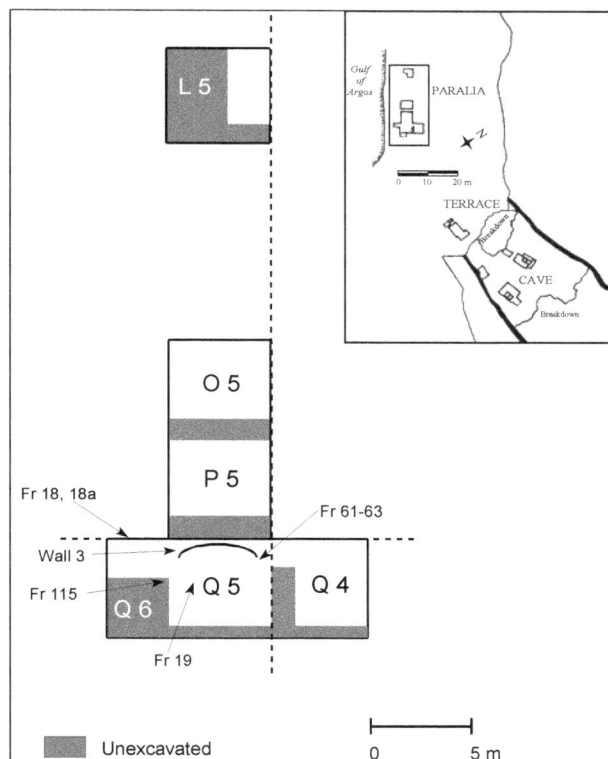

Figure 5.2. Location of the Final Neolithic burials on the Paralia at Franchthi Cave (redrawn and modified after Jacobsen and Farrand 1987: Plate 41).

Five interments appear to be single burials, although some are found close together (e.g., Fr 61, 62, 63). However, Fr 18 and 18a were found together, crosscutting trenches P and Q 6. All bodies were placed on their right side, (except Fr 63 which is questionable), but the remains were disturbed enough that the precise orientation of the body could not be determined. Only the orientation of two bodies (Fr 18 oriented in a north-westerly direction and Fr 63 in a south-easterly direction) was recorded, but the direction is not consistent. These limited data suggest that there is little variation in the preparation and treatment of the body. Despite some disturbance, there is not indication that secondary burial was practised during the FN at Franchthi.

The FN mortuary population at Franchthi is characterised by the complete absence of burials for the very young (neonate and infant). Adults dominate the mortuary population and only one adolescent and two juveniles are present. Females compose over half the mortuary population, while male burials compose less than one third. However, only one of these males is of adult age.

All grave goods are of a utilitarian nature and only females appear to have been given them. One adult, possibly a female (Fr. 19), had a terracotta spindle whorl included in the interment. In another adult female burial (Fr. 63) to the north of Fr.19, a crusted ware vessel was included.

5.3.2   Mortuary practices

There are two burial scenarios at FN Franchthi Cave: single and double inhumation burials. Graves were not elaborate and there appears to have been no modification to the body before interment. This indicates that primary inhumation was the standard practice. The abundance of pottery in the Paralia (Jacobsen 1979) may have had some function in the mortuary ritual and treatment of the dead, but this is speculative. Burial goods are rare in the disposal area, and consist only of locally- made utilitarian items given to adult females. The low frequency of grave goods, and the absence of any trade items in the burial assemblage, is congruent with Perlès' (1990) analysis of trade and exchange during the FN. Many sites in the Argolid were not part of the elaborate trade network during the FN phase. This makes it likely that valued goods (trade or precious items) would represent high social status distinctions. However, grave goods are utilitarian items and probably reflect occupational roles. Therefore, the material contributions to mortuary practices were geared more towards signifying status differences along the horizontal dimension. Skeletal pathologies for women may be indicative of their occupational activities, which may generally have included potting, weaving, and food preparation (Jacobsen and Cullen 1981:94).

The practice of double burial must be considered an alternative mortuary treatment. This is the only case of this grave type during the Neolithic at Franchthi. Particularly interesting is that the burial contained the remains of an adult woman who as probably more than twice the age of the young adolescent male. This particular burial may contain consanguinal pairs given the small population that inhabited Franchthi during the FN (Jacobsen and Cullen 1981). It may also contain unrelated persons who died at the same time, and the double burial may have been used to expedite interment. Because primary inhumation was practised at FN Franchthi, there may have been restrictions on the time permitted between death and final interment. A concern with meeting these restrictions may have overrode the required customary burial form (single interments), and a double burial was used instead as an acceptable alternative within the broader directives of the mortuary practices. While plausible, this scenario is a less likely explanation for the double grave.

The small number of people that make up the FN mortuary population at Franchthi may be a result of the subsistence practices favoured in southern Greece during the FN phase. The lack of any identified neonates or infants probably cannot be taken at face value to suggest a low or insignificant infant mortality rate. As suggested by Jacobsen (1984b), this society was most probably composed of semi-nomadic pastoralists and burials probably took place at other locations within this group's territory of exploitation.

5.3.3 Conclusions

There is variation in the FN burial program at Franchthi. The principle difference is that there were two forms of disposal: single and double primary inhumations. Consequently, it may be suggested that there were two socially recognised burial types. As with earlier mortuary practices at Franchthi, mortuary practices did not create highly visible graves. Instead, burial goods emphasise the links between age, sex and the activities of daily life. The absence of very young individuals may be a product of excavation, but considering the extensive excavation of the area, this is unlikely. Alternatively, very young children may not have been included with other burials on the paralia—which, incidentally, would be a significant departure in the mortuary practices at Franchthi and at other mortuary sites during the Neolithic—or they may have died elsewhere and were buried there.

There are only two discernible levels of energy expended in disposing of the dead: (1) single inhumations with burial gifts, and (2) single or double inhumations without burial gifts. Single and double inhumations are combined here because body posture and positioning does not indicate that the double grave would have been considerably larger than those used for single interment. In this calculation, two adult women (Fr 19 and 63) received the highest amount of energy expenditure and the rest of the mortuary population received lower labour expenditures. There suggests that the mortuary treatment of these adult women may have more to do with socio-economic considerations, although these were expressed along the horizontal dimension of social distinctions. The rest of the mortuary population was not significantly differentiated according to age, sex or other more obvious materialistic criteria. In this instance, mortuary ritual may have been used as a 'levelling' mechanism, conflating status differences held during life (Giddens 1979). Alternatively, the material markers of social identity may simply have been perishable. As during the EN-MN, the FN mortuary remains continue to be incorporated into living areas. We may again consider that this practice was a prescriptive method used to incorporate the dead into the physical realm of the living and symbolise social cohesiveness and continuity. For the EN-MN, it was suggested that such behaviour is also guided by beliefs about the relationship between the dead and the living, the effect they have on each other, and that the use of burial coverings for children could reflect this belief system. During the FN, this same practice was not used, but there are indications that the same objective may have been reached by other means. All of the burials are located behind a boundary created by Wall 3 (Fig. 5.2). While the burials are still integrated within the confines of the settlement area, this practice may represent a desire to segregate the living from the dead. No young children are included in this area. If neonates and infants were purposefully excluded from this burial area, we may be seeing a continuation of earlier practices that underscore perceptions about the differences between the deaths of children and adults. Like the stone coverings during the EN-MN, the stone wall may also have been used to protect the living community, but the practice did not break from the tradition of burying the dead in close proximity to daily activity areas.

5.4 THARROUNIA

A settlement, a cemetery, and storage facilities within Skoteni Cave represent final Neolithic habitation of Tharrounia (Fig. 5.3). In relation to the cave, the settlement is located on a nearby plateau and is just over one hectare in area (Sampson 1993:295). Most finds at the settlement date late in the Final Neolithic, but several scrapers and blades seem to date to a pre-Neolithic context (Sampson 1993:296). Despite severe erosion in the area, FN pottery, obsidian and other stone implements, such as millstones and grinders, were recovered from surface survey of the area (Sampson 1993:295). Stone foundations were discovered around the settlement, and these may represent either buildings or a

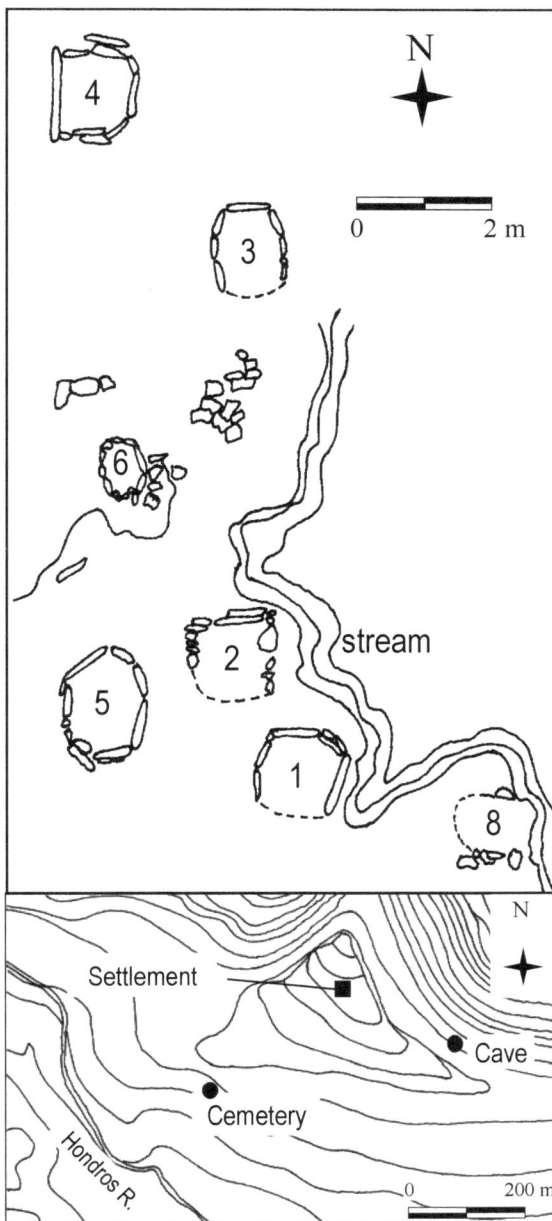

Figure 5.3. Plan of the Final Neolithic cemetery at Tharrounia (redrawn and modified after Sampson 1992: fig. 35). Inset shows the location of the cemetery in relation to the settlement and Skoteni Cave (redrawn and modified after Sampson 1992: fig 2.).

the cave in the LN contrasts to a FN pattern of dense occupation levels in the settlement and infrequent use of the cave.

5.4.1 Mortuary remains

Mortuary remains dating to the FN at Tharrounia occur in two areas: 27 individuals were interred in a cemetery of stone-built graves, and the remains of five individuals were found within Skoteni Cave (Table 5.3). The cemetery occupies a low rise some 400 m to the south-west of the settlement (Fig. 5.3). Regular cultivation and erosion have damaged most of the deposits, contributing to partial, and in some cases, complete destruction of the graves. For example, Grave 7 was located some 15 m away from where the first group of graves were discovered (Sampson 1993:297). This grave belonged to a second group of burials that also probably date to the FN, but have unfortunately almost all been destroyed (illustration of this group remains unpublished and they are therefore not illustrated in Fig. 5.3). It was also noted that slabs from the graves could be noticed in the stone fences that wind throughout the area (Sampson 1993: 296). People were therefore buried in one of two formal cemeteries widely separated from each other. All burials in each cemetery were built graves, roughly circular in shape. There is some variation in the architectural features of the graves. Most walls were constructed of horizontally laid slabs, but there are two other cases where a grave was both slab and stone-lined, or stone-lined on only two sides. It is unknown precisely how Grave 7 in the second cemetery was constructed. However, from the debris, it would be reasonable to suggest a similar architecture. The graves show no substantial treatments of the interior or special features, but one grave had two distinct levels (Grave 6).

While there are differences in the way the graves were constructed, there is substantially greater variation in grave size. Graves 5, 6, and 8 are between 37–85% smaller than the other graves. The smaller size of these graves is significant from a volume standpoint, being at least 0.9 m^3 in volume, which is a cumulative difference of over 3 m^3 when compared to the larger graves. All graves, except Grave 2, were built for multiple interments, but grave size has little concordance with the number of individuals interred. For example, Graves 1 and 2 appear to be the largest graves in the cemetery, but Grave 1 was had three burials and Grave 2 only had the remains of one individual. The moderately sized graves (Graves 3 to 5) held the greatest number of individuals (4 or 5 people), while smaller graves held five (Grave 6) and three (Grave 8) people.

Individuals of various ages and both sexes are found together in the graves. Adult remains are the most abundant and there are comparatively fewer adolescents and infant remains (both n=1). There is no indication that

circuit wall (Sampson 1993:295). Later excavation showed some evidence of structures. A depression made in a rock in Trench A could have served as a post-hole, and two walls, both running east to west in Trench B and Trench D, may have acted as a foundation walls (Sampson 1993:296). Numerous 'domestic' items in Trench B and D, such as bowls, pithoi, obsidian blades, millstones, and grinders, attest to the possibility of these being habitation structures of some sort. Common use of

TABLE 5.3
THE FINAL NEOLITHIC MORTUARY REMAINS FROM THE THARROUNIA CEMETERY AND SKOTENI CAVE

Grave/ Feature Number	Skeleton No.[1]	MNI / Grave	Location	Built Grave Type	Shape	Length	Width	Depth	Burial Form	Pattern of Bone Association	Age and Sex	Pathology	Bone Elements Present[2]	Associated Objects Type	Location
1	1.1	3	cemetery	slab-lined	circular	1.4	1.4	0.65	inhumation disturbed		female	--	C, V, PF	--	--
1	1.2		cemetery	slab-lined	circular	1.4	1.4	0.65	Inhumation disturbed		adult male	arthritis	--	--	--
2	2	1	cemetery	slab/stone lined	circular	1.4	1.4	0.6	Inhumation scatter		--	--	?	spindle-whorl	in grave
3	3.1	5	cemetery	slab-lined	circular	1.25	1.2	--	Inhumation scatter		adult male	arthritis/ osteoporosis	C, L, 2 mand., 2 MX, teeth?	--	--
3	3.2		cemetery	slab-lined	circular	1.25	1.2	--	Inhumation scatter		adult male	arthritis/ osteoporosis	--	--	--
3	3.3		cemetery	slab-lined	circular	1.25	1.2	--	Inhumation scatter		adult female	arthritis/ osteoporosis	--	--	--
3	3.4		cemetery	slab-lined	circular	1.25	1.2	--	Inhumation scatter		adult female	arthritis/ osteoporosis	--	--	--
3	3.5		cemetery	slab-lined	circular	1.25	1.2	--	Inhumation scatter		juvenile	severe porotic hyperstosis	aged 9-11	--	--
4	4.1	5	cemetery	slab-lined	circular	1.15	1	1.25	Inhumation scatter		adult male	advanced arthritis	C, MN, MX, L, V, MC, T, PCF	--	--
4	4.2		cemetery	slab-lined	circular	1.15	1	1.25	Inhumation scatter		adult female	advanced arthritis	--	plain vessel	in grave
4	4.3		cemetery	slab-lined	circular	1.15	1	1.25	inhumation scatter		adult male	advanced arthritis	--	--	--
4	4.4		cemetery	slab-lined	circular	1.15	1	1.25	inhumation scatter		adult male	advanced arthritis	--	quern	in grave
4	4.5		cemetery	slab-lined	circular	1.15	1	1.25	inhumation scatter		adolescent	--	skull # 11	--	--
5	5.1	5	cemetery	slab-lined	circular	1.25	0.95	0.7	inhumation scatter		adult male	arthritis	C, MN, MX, teeth, LF, V, MC, T, U	--	--
5	5.2		cemetery	slab-lined	circular	1.25	0.95	0.7	inhumation scatter		adult female	Arthritis	--	--	--
5	5.3		cemetery	slab-lined	circular	1.25	0.95	0.7	inhumation scatter		adult female	Arthritis	--	--	--
5	5.4		cemetery	slab-lined	circular	1.25	0.95	0.7	inhumation scatter		adult	Arthritis	--	--	--
5	5.5		cemetery	slab-lined	circular	1.25	0.95	0.7	inhumation scatter		juvenile	--	--	--	--
6	6.1	1	cemetery	slab-lined	circular	0.55	0.45	--	inhumation scatter		adult male	--	CF, MN, MX, loose teeth	spondylus on top	--

80

TABLE 5.3 Continued.
THE FINAL NEOLITHIC MORTUARY REMAINS FROM THE THARROUNIA CEMETERY AND SKOTENI CAVE

Grave/ Feature Number	Skeleton Number	MNI In Grave	Location	Grave Construction					Burial Form	Pattern of Bone Association	Age and Sex	Pathology	Bone Elements Present[a]	Associated Objects	
				Built Grave Type	Shape	Length	Width	Depth						Object Type	Object Location
6	6.2	5	cemetery	slab-lined	circular	0.55	0.45	--	inhumation scatter	inhumation scatter	adult female	--	--	--	--
6	6.3	5	cemetery	slab-lined	circular	0.55	0.45	--	inhumation scatter	inhumation scatter	adult	--	--	--	--
6	6.4	5	cemetery	slab-lined	circular	0.55	0.45	--	inhumation scatter	inhumation scatter	juvenile	--	--	--	--
6	6.5	5	cemetery	slab-lined	circular	0.55	0.45	--	inhumation scatter	inhumation scatter	juvenile	--	--	--	--
7	7	?	cemetery	unknown	circular ?	--	--	--	inhumation scatter	inhumation scatter	unknown	--	CF	--	--
8	8.1	3	cemetery	stone-lined (on two sides)	circular	0.14	0.75	--	inhumation scatter	inhumation scatter	adult female	--	CF, MX F	--	--
8	8.2	3	cemetery						inhumation scatter	inhumation scatter	infant	--	--	--	--
8	8.3	3	cemetery						inhumation scatter	inhumation scatter	adult male	--	--	--	--
--	9.1	1?	cave	pit	--	--	--	--	inhumation scatter	inhumation scatter	adult	--	--	--	--
--	9.2	1?	cave	pit	--	--	--	--	inhumation scatter	inhumation scatter	infant	--	--	--	--
--	9.3	1?	cave	pit	--	--	--	--	inhumation scatter	inhumation scatter	infant	--	--	--	--
--	9.4	1?	cave	pit	--	--	--	--	inhumation scatter	inhumation scatter	adult female	--	--	--	--
--	9.5	1?	cave	pit	--	--	--	--	inhumation scatter	inhumation scatter	juvenile	--	--	--	--

[1] These skeleton number are used in the text to reference to individual remains. They were arbitrarily assigned because field record numbers for skeletal remains were not reported by Stravopodi (1992).

[2] Abbreviations: C=cranial, F=bone fragments, P=post-cranial, MX=maxilla, MN=mandible, V=vertebrae, L=long bones, MT=metatarsals, T=tarsals, C=carpals, MC=metacarpalsm U=unidentified.

Source: Sampson (1992) and Stravopodi (1992).

certain age or sex groups were excluded from the cemetery. It should be noted that the remains of one infant found in the cemetery contrasts with two found in the cave. It is a possibility that the partial skeleton of the infant was interred in the cemetery and the delicate remains were not recovered because of poor preservation due to the factors discussed above (see also discussion in Sampson 1993:296). Cases of arthritis, advanced osteoarthritis, and a combination of arthritis and osteoporosis dominate the pathological specimens. All of these cases involve adult men and women. The nature of the pathologies suggests only that they developed as a result of occupational stresses (Stravopodi 1993:386). However, one juvenile shows signs of porotic hyperstosis (No. 3.5), a classic osteological marker for anaemia of any aetiology. Angel (1964, 1966, 1967, 1975, 1978, 1984) has suggested that these abnormal alterations in the bony structure of the skeleton were a result of thalassemia or sickle-cell anaemia that developed in resistance to endemic malaria. Stravopodi (1993), however, points out that the characteristic pitting of the cranial vault can also result from low iron levels caused by menstruation, pregnancy and lactation, an iron-deficient diet, prolonged diarrhoea, or parasitic infection. The present data suggest that these latter aetiologies are less likely because porotic hyperstosis is not present in any other individuals in the mortuary population, particularly juveniles. Thus, the anaemia may be genetically based and this young person was a recessive homozygote for thalassemia or sickle-cell anaemia endemic in Mediterranean Neolithic populations.

There are few artefacts represented in the FN graves at Tharrounia. According to Sampson (1993:296-297) only four objects can be considered as grave goods. Each grave good is a different material and all were manufactured or collected locally: a terracotta spindle-whorl was found in Grave 2; a stone quern and a plain pottery vessel were recovered from Grave 4; and a spondylus ornamental shell found on top of Grave 6.

Although the shell was not found in Grave 6, Sampson (1993:297) has noted that the shell could represent an offering to someone in that grave. Sampson (1993:297) also notes that the lack of burial gifts cannot suggest poverty. Rather, this is a characteristic noted at Kephala (see below) and observed at Yali, Nissiros (Sampson 1993:297). Due to the practice of using multiple interments, it is difficult to assign any of these grave goods to a particular individual, save the person buried in Grave 2. However, neither the sex nor age of this person could be determined.

5.4.2 Mortuary practices

All the burials at Tharrounia were inhumations. The remains were likely disturbed by later interments, but the latest burials were not oriented in a particular direction nor did they have particular posture (Sampson 1993: 297). From these data alone, it is difficult to tell if these were primary interments. However, the remains found in the cave shed some light on this issue. In the cave, post-depositional processes have has claimed the outline of any graves if, indeed, they once existed. The skeletal remains in the cemetery and the cave are anatomically incomplete, and, comparatively, the remains in the cave are much less complete than those in cemetery even though they include finer bone elements that more easily decompose (e.g., cranial fragments). Generally, fragmentary bone elements found in the cave are found in the cemetery, but many bone elements found in the cemetery are not present in the cave. Because there is also no physical evidence that the bones had been modified in any physical way, such as cut marks to sever tendons, this pattern suggests selective bone disposal characteristic of secondary interment. In this situation, the ritual practice of exhumation and reburial seems a likely candidate for the method of preparing the body. After death, individuals were buried in the cave until their remains had decomposed. Because there are no cut marks or other forms of bone modification, decomposition was likely complete. The remains were then gathered and placed in one of the communal built tombs in the cemetery at the bottom of the hill slope.

It is therefore likely that the disposal of the corpse at Tharrounia was achieved through a process of secondary burial. The same procedure appears to have been used for all members of the society regardless of their age or the circumstances surrounding their death. There are differences in mortuary treatment, however, and these differences are found primarily in the way graves were constructed. While there was only one type of grave in the cemetery, their construction is different and this implies that different levels of labour were put into building the graves. Graves 1, 3, 4 and 5 exhibit the highest levels of labour expenditure. Considerable effort was put into acquiring, moving, and arranging the massive stone slabs in making these graves. The graves made of small rocks and stone slabs (Grave 2), or with a combination of slabs and moderate sized stones (Grave 6 and 8) can be ranked lower. Grave 8 is the most poorly preserved, but is somewhat larger than Grave 6, which was constructed with small to moderate sized stones. It is clearly the smallest grave despite containing the remains of five individuals. From what can be determined of Grave 7, the size and labour expenditures would probably not be that different from Grave 6. Thus, graves were built in three ways at Tharrounia:

1) large graves built of large, heavy stone slabs with smaller stones used to fill in gaps (Graves 1, 3-5);

2) moderate sized graves built with a combination of small slabs and stones (Grave 2); and

3) small graves primarily constructed of moderate-sized stones and a few small slabs (Graves 6-8).

Therefore, at least three different levels of energy were expended in building the graves, but there was only one socially recognised burial type in the cemeteries.

The spatial separation of the two cemeteries is consistent with the segregation of groups on social and/or economic bases (Saxe 1970, 1971; Goldstein 1981). There are two possible interpretations for this pattern. First, the two distinct disposal areas correspond to the exclusive disposal areas of corporate groups, (Group 1 graves representing one group, and Group 2 the other), who occupied the settlement at the same time. Second, the two disposal areas represent the disposal areas of two social groups who occupied the area during different seasons. Sampson (1992) has suggested that Tharrounia was a seasonal settlement, and that the inhabitants were semi-nomadic pastoralists.

Grave goods are uncommon in the cemetery and no objects were associated with the human remains in the cave. The shell that was found above Grave 6 cannot be associated with any individual in this multiple grave. In his report, Sampson states that the quern found in Grave 4 could not 'have served to support...the dead man's head' (Sampson 1993: 296), suggesting it was found near one of the adult males in the grave. However, querns are used in food preparation, which is often considered to fall into the sphere of female activities. A simplistic interpretation is that this object was a grave good for the adult woman in Grave 4, and represents the domestic activities of women. Regardless of the possible gender association of the quern, it was clearly not used as a stone 'pillow,' and therefore does not parallel the practices at other Neolithic sites, including Nea Nikomedia, Franchthi Cave, and Kephala. The pottery vessel also found in this grave may also be associated with the woman. The only other grave good is a spindle whorl found in Grave 2. The age and sex of the person in this grave could not be determined. Livestock were a key feature of the FN economy at Tharrounia (Sampson 1992), and it is not surprising to find a spindle whorl in this grave. Spindle whorls were used for making linen or wool, which also may have been associated with women, although such an association is far from universal. It is clear, however, that these objects are associated with women, and, on the face of it, the material contribution to mortuary ritual can be seen to emphasise female occupational roles. This may mean that this society did not express men's statuses in material ways, or the objects associated with men were more perishable and have not been preserved. The grave goods do not indicate that wealth was not a differentiating factor at Tharrounia. Therefore, this suggests that social identity was achieved in this society, and not ascribed to individuals.

5.4.3 Conclusions

The Tharrounia cemetery is a true cemetery in the sense that it is located some distance from the contemporary settlement. The location of Grave 7 and the other graves found destroyed around it, suggest that there were two distinct formal disposal areas at Tharrounia. The precise architectural features of the second group of graves are not known, but they were built graves. All individuals during the FN received burial in irregularly shaped built graves, which appear to have been constructed in three different ways. The two disposal areas may be one contemporary cemetery divided into two parts, or two cemeteries constructed to house the remains of two different corporate groups. The skeletal data show that there was little variation in how the body was prepared for burial. Minimally, all individuals received a two-stage process of secondary interment defined by burial in the cave, exhumation, and reburial in the cemetery.

The use of multiple graves and the type of grave goods at Tharrounia indicate that individual and group social differentiation was based upon biological criteria, kinship, and occupational roles. There is no evidence for vertical stratification based upon wealth or power in this society. It is probable that each grave was used for the interment of family members. Only Grave 2 had the remains of one individual, but this grave is large and was probably also constructed for the final burial of members of that family. The site may simply have been abandoned, or shifted elsewhere, before further use of the grave could be made.

The FN cemetery at Tharrounia has been compared to the FN cemetery at Kephala, although the two cemeteries differ fundamentally in many ways (Sampson 1993: 296). There are some similarities between the two settlements and certain objects, such as the so-called 'scoops' found in the Tharrounia settlement, (Sampson 1993:293) are analogous with the finds at Kephala, and it is to this cemetery that we now turn.

5.5   KEPHALA

The site of Kephala is located on a headland on the north-west coast of the Cycladic island of Keos (Fig. 5.4), and is one of a group of more or less contemporaneous sites on the island (including Paoura, Sykamia, and Ayia Irini). Although the temporal placement of these sites has not been resolved (Davis 1992), Kephala represents the best evidence for initial settlement of the island during the second major southward colonisation of the Aegean late in the Neolithic (3300-3200 B.C.). Considered unique enough to be a distinct archaeological 'culture,' the Kephala Culture has numerous connections with sites in Attica (Athens, Thorikos, Kitsos Cave) and the Saronic Gulf (Kolonna on Aegina).

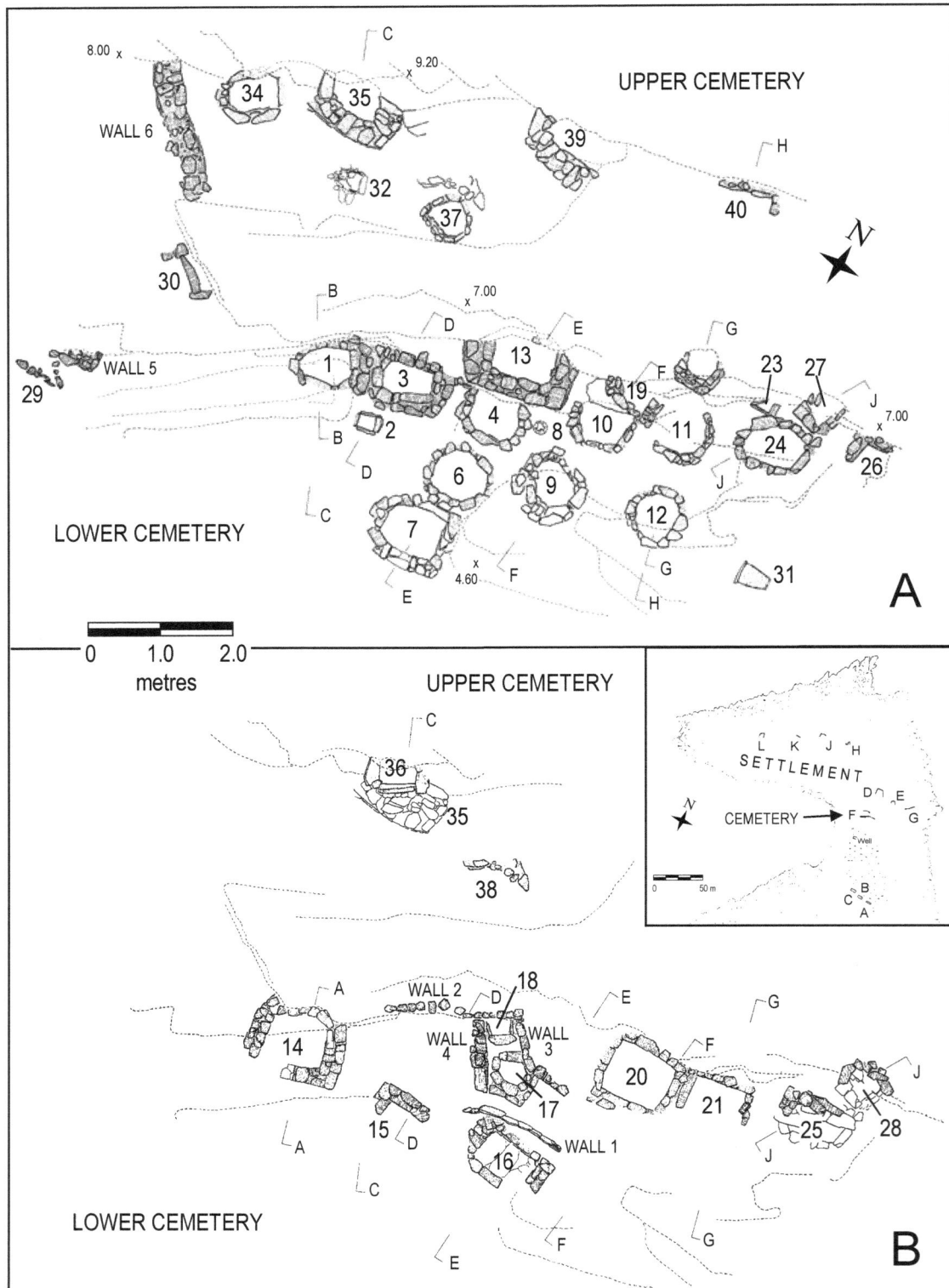

Figure 5.4. Plan of the (A) lower and (B) uppermost graves in the Kephala cemetery. Inset shows the location of the cemetery (F) in relation to the settlement structures (A, B, C, D, E, G, H, K, L) (redrawn and modified after Coleman 1977: Plates 8 [A], 9 [B], and 1 [inset]).

TABLE 5.4

THE LOCATION AND CONSTRUCTION FEATURES OF THE FINAL NEOLITHIC GRAVES AT KEPHALA

Grave No.	Location	Construction Phasing[1]	MNI	Grave Type	Shape	L	W	D	Vol.	Floor	Special Features	Platform	Bounded by Walls
1	Lower	1A	6	built	circular	1.05	0.75	0.60	0.47	pebbles		?	
2	Lower	1A	1	cist	rectangular	0.32	0.30	0.20	0.02	earth/gravel fill		?	
3	Lower	1A	3	built	rectangular	1.00	0.65	0.85	0.55	pebbles		P7	
4	Lower	1A	1	built	circular	1.00	0.80	0.50	0.40	earth/gravel fill		P6	
5	Lower	1B	1	built	rectangular (irregular)	0.80	0.70	--	--	earth/gravel fill			
6	Lower	1A	1	built	circular	1.08	0.96	0.45	0.47	earth/gravel fill			
7	Lower	1A	13	built	rectangular	1.13	0.97	0.75	0.82	sand	doorway	?	
8	Lower	1A	1	pit	circular	--	--	--	--	earth/gravel fill			
9	Lower	1A	2	built	circular	0.96	0.72	0.45	0.31	earth/gravel fill		P3	
10	Lower	1A	1	built	rectangular (irregular)	1.04	0.76	0.50	0.40	earth/gravel fill		P1	
11	Lower	1A	1	built	circular	1.00	--	0.50	--	earth/gravel fill			
12	Lower	1B	2	built	circular	0.93	--	0.30	--	earth/gravel fill		P2	
13	Lower	1C	2	built	rectangular	1.23	0.70	0.48	0.41	earth/gravel fill		P5	
14	Lower	2A	6	built	rectangular	1.22	1.05	1.00	1.28	pebbles	doorway?, plaster	?	
15	Lower	2A	1	built	rectangular?	1.23	--	--	--	pebbles		?	
16	Lower	2A	4	built	rectangular	1.14	0.70	--	--	earth/gravel fill	doorway?	?	yes
17	Lower	2A	1	built	circular	0.57	0.49	0.35	0.10	earth/gravel fill		?	yes
18	Lower	2A	1	built	rectangular (irregular)	0.46	0.35	0.42	0.07	earth/gravel fill		?	yes
19	Lower	2A	1	built	circular	0.67	0.36	0.20	0.05	earth/gravel fill			
20	Lower	2B	9	built	rectangular	0.14	0.11	0.35	0.01	pebbles	plaster	?	
21	Lower	2B	1	built	rectangular?	1.05	--	--	--	earth/gravel fill		?	
22	Lower	2C	1	built	circular	0.42	--	--	--	earth/gravel fill			
23	Lower	2A	1	cist	triangular	0.42	0.29	0.25	0.03	pebbles			
24	Lower	2B	1	built	circular	0.12	0.80	0.45	0.04	earth/gravel fill			
25	Lower	2C	1	built	rectangular?	--		--	--	earth/gravel fill		?	
26	Lower	2C	1	built	rectangular?	--	--	--	--	slabs/foundation		?	
27	Lower	2B	1	built	rectangular	0.50	0.30	0.15	0.02	pebbles			
28	Lower	2C	1	built	?	--	--	--	--	earth/gravel fill		?	
29	Lower	--	1	built	?	--	--	--	--	earth/gravel fill		?	yes
30	Lower	--	1	built	rectangular?	0.72	--	--	--	earth/gravel fill		?	
31	Lower	--	2	pit	depression	--	--	--	--	earth/gravel fill		?	
32	Upper	3A	1	pit	depression	--	--	--	--	pebbles			yes
33	Upper	3B	1	built	?	--	--	--	--	--		?	
34	Upper	--	1	built	rectangular	0.97	0.65	--	--	earth/gravel fill		?	yes
35	Upper	3B	1	built	circular	1.05	0.72	0.40	0.30	earth/gravel fill		P9?	yes
36	Upper	3C	1	cist	rectangular	0.73	0.53	0.45	0.17	earth/gravel fill		P8	yes
37	Upper	3A	1	built	circular	0.79	0.69	0.50	0.27	earth/gravel fill			yes
38	Upper	3B	1	built	circular?	0.12	--	--	--	earth/gravel fill		?	yes
39	Upper	3A	1	built	circular	1.58	0.60	0.60	0.57	earth/gravel fill			yes
40	Upper	--	1	built	rectangular?	--	--	--	--	earth/gravel fill		?	yes

[1] These data are based upon the relative dating of grave construction on stratigraphic grounds (Coleman 1977: tables 5 to 7 and plates 12 to 17).
Abbreviations: MNI = minimum number of individuals present in grave, L = length, W = width, D = depth. *Source*: Coleman (1977).

During the 1960s, the University of Cincinnati excavations at Kephala revealed a Final Neolithic settlement and cemetery on the headland (Caskey 1964). John Coleman (Coleman 1977) completed these excavations in the 1970s. The cemetery at Kephala is located on a south-facing slope at the narrow entrance to the headland overlooking the sea. This is considered the first highly organised, built cemetery known in the Aegean Islands, and is therefore of considerable importance. The remains of over 60 individuals represent the largest and best-preserved sample known from the Neolithic period in Greece, with the exception of the Early Neolithic site of Nea Nikomedia discussed earlier. The settlement itself is set in behind the cemetery on the rocky expanse of the headland and consists of small, poorly preserved buildings composed of one or more rectangular rooms. As one approaches the settlement, one must pass the cemetery to the left (Area F) and the remains of houses to the right (Areas D, E and G). The settlement was short-lived, occupied for perhaps no more than a century, and was small, probably having no more than 50 people at any one time.

5.5.1 Mortuary Remains

The graves at Kephala are located on two different natural terraces on the hill slope: the graves higher on the slope have been termed the 'Upper Cemetery' and those on the lower level of the slope the 'Lower Cemetery' (Coleman 1977; see Fig. 5.3). The number of graves in each area is uneven. The Lower Cemetery has the most graves, while the Upper Cemetery has very few. The location of the Kephala cemetery makes it highly visible both from land and from the sea and its placement on the hillside may have served as a way to open up arable land in the past. However, this strategy has led to the severe destruction of some of the uppermost graves and those on the periphery of the cemetery. Many of the graves and skeletons were disturbed to a greater or lesser degree. There was little damage to the graves because of later burials, but wind and water erosion have acted as the major post-depositional effects at the cemetery because it is located on the steep hillside (Coleman 1977: 44).

5.5.1.1 Architecture

There are three types of grave at Kephala: (1) built graves made with moderate to large stones, (2) *cist* or slab-lined pit graves, and (3) graves formed around small pit depressions (Table 5.4). Forty graves were recovered in total, and all were originally covered with stone slabs of varying sizes. The size of the covering stones is congruent with grave size. Graves are irregularly shaped, but are generally rectangular or circular. In Table 5.3, graves of oval or circular shape have been standardised as being circular. In questionable cases, the excavators could not discern the precise shape of these graves and they are often listed as circular-oval (Coleman 1977: table 2).

Overall, it appears the graves were differentiated on broad categories of shape (rounded or rectangular) and oval-shaped graves simply represent a variation of round-shaped graves. There is also one example of a triangular built structure (Grave 23), where two large stone slabs were cornered against two previously constructed graves to form a facility. There is also considerable variation in the size of the graves: the largest grave is 1.28 m³ and the smallest is less than 0.1 m³, as it is only a depression in the bedrock.

There is no correlation between the size of the grave and the number of persons interred in it. Most graves were used for single inhumations (n=21, 68%), while substantially fewer graves were used for multiple (more than three; n=6, 20%), or double burials (n=4, 12%). In the multiple graves with more than two people, corpses were organised by separating them with successive layers of pebbled or earthen/gravel floors. The interior of two graves was sealed by covering the walls with a clay-plaster (Grave 14 and 20), but it likely that this practice was more common.

Stone slab platforms were constructed above eight graves (Fig. 5.5; Graves 3, 4, 9, 10, 12, 13, 35, and 36). All except one is found in the Lower Cemetery, and these are confined to the central group of graves. Two other platforms were built over Graves 34 and 35 in the Upper Cemetery. Except for the graves in the Upper Cemetery, all the platforms were placed over the lowest graves and must have been constructed early in the use of the cemetery. The platforms are not always built over the largest graves or those with the most burials. Half were built over graves with single inhumations (Graves 4, 10, 35, 36) and the other half contained only two (Graves 9, 12, 13) or three persons (Grave 3). None of the graves with high numbers of multiple interments had any discernible platforms. Interestingly, one other platform (P4) did not cover any grave. Instead, it was built between three other graves with platforms (Graves 9, 10, and 12).

Another unique feature of the Kephala cemetery is the six low walls that were placed around or beside the graves (Fig. 5.4). The walls are of three types: stacked (Walls 5 and 6), stood vertical in the earth (Wall 1), or laid flat in a circuit around graves (Walls 2-4). Five walls are located in the Lower Cemetery, and one large wall is in the Upper Cemetery. Most of the walls are associated with the uppermost graves in the crowded central area of the Lower Cemetery, and probably date late in the use of the cemetery. The walls could have had a limited number of functions. Several may have acted to segregate certain groups of graves from others. For example, the walls in the Lower Cemetery appear to separate four graves from the others: Walls 2, 3 and 4 surround Graves 18 and 17, and Wall 1 appears to distinguish Grave 16 (and Grave 6

TABLE 5.5
THE FINAL NEOLITHIC SKELETAL REMAINS AND ASSOCIATED OBJECTS AT KEPHALA

Grave No.	Angel No.	MNI per Grave	Burial Scenario	Body Position	Body Posture	Body Orientation	Age/Sex	Pathology	Types of Burial Goods	Objects Associated with Burials (found near or above grave)
1	32 KeK	6	multiple	?	disturbed	?	adult female			
1	32A KeK			?	disturbed	?	adolescent female			
1	31 KeK			?	disturbed	?	adult female			
1	31A KeK			?	disturbed	?	adult		wooden? box	
1	34 KeK			right	flexed	W-E	adult male	tooth lesions		
1	33 KeK			?	Legs bent underneath?	?	adult male			
2	39 KeK	1	single	left	flexed	NE-SW	infant		1 crucible	
3	--	3	multiple	?	disturbed	?	--			
3	30 KeK			right	flexed	SW-NE	adult female	vertebral arthritis	1 stone "pillow"	
3	30A KeK			?	disturbed	?	adult			
4	36 KeK	1	single	right	flexed	W-E	adult male	teeth lesions	1 large jar	1 female figurine, 1 perforated figurine "necklace"
5	--	1	single	?	disturbed	unknown	--			
6	16 KeK	1	single	?	disturbed	?	adult male	separated jaw during life		
7	29 KeK	13	multiple	?	disturbed	?	adult male			
7	28KeK			?	disturbed	?	adult male			
7	27 KeK			?	disturbed	?	adult male			
7	26 KeK			?	disturbed	?	infant			
7	25 KeK			?	disturbed	?	adult male	only skull?		
7	27A KeK			?	disturbed	?	adult female			
7	24 KeK			?	disturbed	?	adult female			
7	23B KeK			?	disturbed	?	infant			
7	23 KeK			?	disturbed	?	adult male			
7	23A KeK			?	disturbed	?	adult female			
7	24A KeK			?	disturbed	?	adult female			
7	22 KeK			?	disturbed	?	adult female			
7	21 KeK			?	disturbed	?	adult female			
8	29A KeK	1	single	?	disturbed	?	Infant		1 large Type B2 jar (burial urn)	
9	18 KeK	2	double	right	flexed	NW-SE	Adult female			
9	18A KeK			?	disturbed	?	Adult female		1 incised scoop handle (Type C1), at knees	
10	20 KeK	1	single	?	disturbed	?	adult female		1 stone "pillow"?, 1 Type A1 bowl, near skull	

TABLE 5.5 CONTINUED.
THE FINAL NEOLITHIC SKELETAL REMAINS AND ASSOCIATED OBJECTS AT KEPHALA

Grave No.	Angel No.	MNI per Grave	Burial Scenario	Body Position	Body Posture	Body Orientation	Age/Sex	Pathology	Types of Burial Goods	Objects Associated with Burials (found near or above grave)
11	1 / KeK	1	single	?	disturbed	?	adult male	piercing head wound; post-mortem holes in both parietals		3 Type 1A obsidian blades
12	19 KeK	2	double	?	disturbed	?	adolescent female		1 Type 1B obsidian blade	1 Type 3 obsidian scraper
12	19A KeK			?	disturbed	?	infant			
13	35 KeK	2	double	?	disturbed	?	adult female		1 Type B1 obsidian blade	1 Type A1 obsidian blade
13	--			?	disturbed	?	adult? male?			1 obsidian blade
14	1 KeK	6	multiple	?	disturbed	?	adult male			
14	4 KeK			?	disturbed	?	adult male			
14	4A KeK			?	disturbed	?	adult male			
14	4B KeK			?	disturbed	?	adult male			
14	2 KeK			?	disturbed	?	adult female	bowed humerus		
14	3 KeK			?	disturbed	?	adult female		1 Type C1 incised scoop?	1 crucible?, 1 Type 1A obsidian blade
15	--			?	--	--	--			
16	15 KeK	4	multiple	?	disturbed	?	adult male	vertebral arthritis		
16	14 KeK			?	disturbed	?	adolescent female			
16	15A KeK			?	disturbed	?	juvenile			
16	15B KeK			?	disturbed	?	juvenile male?			
17	--	1?		?	--	--	--			
18	--	1	single	?	disturbed	?	juvenile?			
19	--	1	single	?	disturbed	?	juvenile?			
20	9 KeK	9	multiple	?	disturbed	?	adult male	severe wear of ankle flexion facets	1 marble rhyton, under floor	Burial goods found in Grave 20, but cannot be linked with any individual: - 1 Type A1 bowl, - 1 Type B2 jar, - 1 Type C2 cylindrical vessel, - 1Type 6 obsidian tool, - 1 flint tool
20	10 KeK			?	disturbed	?	adult male	no teeth		
20	12 KeK			?	disturbed	?	adult male	right stephanion has oval hole, acquired post-mortem		
20	7 KeK			?	disturbed	?	adult female			
20	8 KeK			?	disturbed	?	adult female			
20	11 KeK			?	disturbed	?	adult female			
20	13 KeK			?	disturbed	?	adult female			
20	13A KeK			?	disturbed	?	adult			
20	12A KeK			?	disturbed	?	juvenile			
21	--	1?		?	--	--	--			
22	40 KeK	1	single	?	disturbed	?	juvenile			

TABLE 5.5 CONTINUED
THE FINAL NEOLITHIC SKELETAL REMAINS AND ASSOCIATED OBJECTS AT KEPHALA

Grave No.	Angel No.	MNI per Grave	Burial Scenario	Body Position	Body Posture	Body Orientation	Age/Sex	Pathology	Types of Burial Goods	Objects Associated with Burials (found near or above grave)
23	41 KeK	1	single	?	disturbed	unknown	Infant		1 Type B2 large jar (burial urn)	
24	38 KeK	1	single	?	disturbed	?	adult female			4 Type A1 obsidian blades
25	37 KeK	1	single	?	disturbed	S-N	adult male			
26	6 KeK	1	single	?	disturbed	E-W	adult male	vertebral arthritis		
27	--	1	single	?	disturbed	unknown	Juvenile		1 small oval bowl, crusted red-on-white decoration	1 flake tool; 1 waste obsidian
28	--	1?		?	--	--	Indeterminate			
29	--	1?		?	--	--	Indeterminate			
30	--	1?		?	--	--	(adult?; >1?)			
31	5 KeK	2	double	?	disturbed	unknown	Infant	hemolytic anemia?	1 large Type B2 jar (burial urn)	
31	5A KeK			?	disturbed	unknown	Infant	porotic hyperostosis; hemolytic anemia	1 large Type B2 jar (burial urn)	
32	69 KeK	1	single	?	disturbed	unknown	Infant		1 large type B2 jar (burial urn)	2 female figurines
34	43 KeK	1	single	?	disturbed	?	adult female		1 marble bowl, below head	1 Type 1A obsidian blade, 1 Type 6 obsidian tool
35	71 KeK	1	single	front	legs flexed	W-E	adult male	ankle wound	1 flint tri-scraper, beneath legs	
36	70 KeK	1	single	left	flexed	W-E	adult female	trace porotic hyperostosis	1 Type C1 incised scoop, beside legs	
37	42 KeK	1	single	left	semi-flexed	W-E	juvenile male			1 perforated figurine "necklace," 1 crucible
38	--	1?		?	--	--	infant??			
39	68 KeK	1	single	back	one flexed, one semi-flexed	W-E	adult male	growth arrest lines on teeth	1 stone "pillow," beneath head	1 Type 1A obsidian blade, 1 Type 6 obsidian tool, 1 bone tool (ovicaprid metaphalange)
40	--	?	?	?	--	--	--	--	--	

[1] Those individuals that are classified to an age and/or sex category but do not have a field record number, were assigned according to Angel's observations discussed in Appendix 5 (Angel 1977:133-141). The age and/or sex of these skeletons are designed by a (?) following the classification.

Source: Coleman (1977).

below it) from the graves to the north and west of it. In this sense, they may have acted as grave markers, identifying common groups of individuals. Only one wall seems to have been constructed to impede access into the cemetery. This wall, built in the Upper Cemetery (Wall 6), is the largest (2.0 m long by 0.5 m wide). If the Upper Cemetery holds the most recent burials, this may have been built to divert foot traffic while the cemetery was still in use, or enclose the disposal area when the site was abandoned.

5.5.1.2 Human Remains

Of the forty observed facilities, only 31 (or 78%) had preserved skeletal material (Table 5.4 and 5.5). It is assumed that at least one individual was interred in the grave for badly damaged graves that contained no skeletal remains. This calculation predicts that a minimum of 79 individuals were buried at Kephala, although the actual number is likely higher. Seven of the most damaged graves with poorly preserved or no skeletal remains are omitted from discussions about the association of artefacts with individuals (Graves 5, 15, 17, 21, 28, 29, and 40). Therefore, the MNI used for these calculations totalled 72, even if age and sex were indeterminate. However, the indeterminate cases are included in discussions regarding demographics. It should also be noted that the most fragmented human skeletal remains, often of children, were not assessed by Angel (1977:133-134) in his two-week study of the Kephala burials and were not considered in this analysis.

Due to the nature of the remains and the conditions surrounding their study, only 64% of the sample was ascribed a sex with certainty, and undifferentiated individuals compose the largest single category in the sample (35.9%). Probably due to the number of uncertain cases, males and females occur in equal frequencies (n=25; 32%). Most individuals buried in the cemetery are of adult age (n=48; 62%). Few adolescents are represented in this population (n=3; 4%). Juveniles (n=8; 10%), infants (n=9; 12%) and indeterminate individuals (n=10; 13%) make up the remainder of the sample. These low levels of identifiability are likely related, at least in part, to the short time the skeletal remains were studied.

A small range of skeletal pathologies was observed in this sample (Table 5.5), which, again, may be a result of the superficial osteological analysis that focused on metric and non-metric racial traits (especially of the cranium) rather than palaeopathological markers. Nevertheless, several of the more obvious pathologies were observed. The most common by far are arthritic conditions, particularly on the vertebral column. Several cases of lesions or growth arrest lines were noticed on teeth. Another case that may also relate to health and nutrition at Kephala, was a bowed humerus of a young adult female. Several adult males show signs of stress and wear

on ankle facets, likely related to repeated squatting or moving about in rough terrain. Perhaps the most interesting cases are those involving wounds and cranial deformation. One adult male appears to have suffered from a head wound, likely caused by a blade of some sort. This individual also has two post-mortem holes drilled into both parietal bones. The reason for this is uncertain.

Other cranial deformities were also noticed by Angel, which he identified as porotic hyperostosis. Malaria was common in the circum-Mediterranean, and is often contracted by populations in close proximity to marshy areas. The headland that makes up Kephala does have a low-lying area to the south, which was certainly breeding ground for mosquitoes (south of Trenches A, B, and C, Fig. 5.4). However, the presence of this disease in the infant suggests it was a recessive homozygote. On the other hand, for adult female, it is more likely that another aetiology of low iron levels, such as menstruation, pregnancy and lactation, an iron-deficient diet, diarrheal disease, or parasitic infection may have contributed to the presence of porotic hyperostosis (see discussion above, pp. 49–50). Without proper study of the post-cranial skeleton, discussion of the precise vectors of the disease will remain speculative.

5.5.1.3 Burial Gifts

The majority of burial gifts were made using local resources. However, there are objects, such as obsidian, that must have been acquired from sources further away in the central Aegean. Long distance trade in obsidian and other materials is well documented for the Neolithic and earlier periods (Renfrew 1973; Perlès 1992). It is apparent, however, that the obsidian was worked locally rather than imported as a finish product. Most goods were intended for practical everyday usage. All the objects found in graves or around the cemetery have parallels in the settlement and none seems to have been intended specifically for mortuary ritual. Many artefacts could be ascribed to certain individuals because of the careful organisation of the bodies into layers.

5.5.2 Mortuary Practices

5.5.2.1 Construction of the Cemetery

It has been suggested that all the graves at Kephala were in contemporary use, and that this uneven pattern is likely a result of the Upper Cemetery being a later addition to compensate for over-crowding in the Lower Cemetery (Coleman, 1977:45). Based upon the stratigraphic relationships of the graves, Coleman suggested that the first thirteen graves were built earliest and Graves 14 to 28 were built before Graves 30 to 40 in the Upper Cemetery (Table 5.4). Thus, the first graves were built on the broadest portion of the hillside, and building then later expanded to open areas east and south of the central

TABLE 5.6
THE TEMPORAL DISTRIBUTION OF SOCIALLY RECOGNIZED BURIAL FORMS AT KEPHALA

| | Age Category | | | | | | | | | | | |
| | Adult | | Adolescent | | Juvenile | | Infant | | Indeterminate | | Total | |
	n	%	*n*	%	*n*	%	*n*	%	*n*	%	*n*	%
Burial Scenario												
Single	11	23%				62%	4	44%	5	46%	25	32%
Multiple (≥2)	37	77%	3	100%	3	38%	5	56%	2	18%	50	63%
Indeterminate									4	36%	4	5%
Relative Temporal Placement												
Phase I	28	58%	2	67%	2	25%	8	89%	2	18%	42	54%
Phase II	19	40%	1	33%	6	75%	1	11%	4	36%	31	39%
Phase III	1	2%							1	9%	2	3%
Indeterminate									4	36%	3	4%
Total Frequency	48	100%	3	100%	8	100%	9	100%	11	100%	79	100%

area. Graves were then constructed on top of earlier burials and finally placed along the upper terrace. This chronological ordering is somewhat supported by the platforms built over the lowest graves in the Lower Cemetery. All of the graves with platforms butted up against the hillside had graves built over top of them. However, five other graves were built over that did not have platforms. Also, Upper Cemetery graves with platforms stand out (Graves 34 and 35) because they were constructed late in the use of the cemetery. Platform 4 is also unusual because it contained no human remains or burials gifts. Its function in not apparent: while it may have functioned in some ritual capacity, it may also have been used as a cenotaph burial, or, just as likely, it was never used.

If the sequence of grave construction proposed for Kephala is reasonable accurate, despite being logical, then this provides some basis for exploring the relationship between age, burial location, burial type, and the temporal placement of graves in the cemetery (Table 5.6). This analysis shows several interesting trends regarding grave construction and mortuary demography, which are displayed graphically in Figure 5.6.

First, in terms of grave construction, single graves outnumber double and multiple graves in each phase of construction, but the number of graves constructed is almost the same during the first (n=13) and second (n=15) phases. There is a notable increase in the construction of graves for single interments during the second phase of tomb building at Kephala (Fig. 5.6a). As well, a large number of graves continued to be used during the first and second phases of cemetery use and most burials occurred in graves designed for multiple interments (Fig. 5.6b).

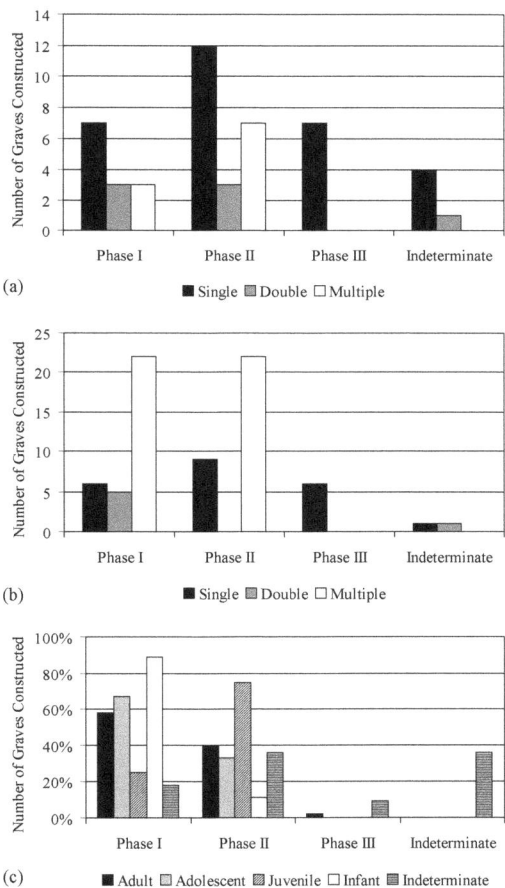

Figure 5.5. The distribution of (a) grave types, (b) interments, and (c) age categories during the three possible phases of cemetery use at Kephala.

While there is evidence for substantial forethought and effort put into the disposal of the corpse throughout the Neolithic, the cemetery at Kephala is perhaps the earliest example of the complex logistics and energy expenditures that appear more commonly during the subsequent EBA. It is possible that high mortality rates during the early phase of occupation stimulated the construction of burials that could be used for multiple interments. However, single burials are another form of accepted burial at Kephala regardless of the type of grave used. Additionally, there are no apparent restrictions placed upon who was buried in single or group tombs. Therefore, there were three socially recognised burial types at Kephala used for five different burial scenarios: built graves used for single or multiple (>2) interments; cist graves used for single interments; and pit graves used for single or double interments.

Mortuary demography also yields an interesting pattern. Most adults, adolescents, and infants were buried in multiple graves that date early in the use of the cemetery (Fig. 5.6b). In contrast, only one infant (Grave 32) and a large number of juveniles were interred in single graves in later phases. These data suggest that adult (Phase I = 58%), adolescent (Phase I = 67%) and infant morbidity (Phase I = 89%) was high when Kephala was first settled

and decreased over the time the headland was occupied and the cemetery was used. The juvenile mortality rate, on the other hand, increased during the later occupation at Kephala, as 75% of all juvenile deaths occurred during Phase II. Adults and infants were more often buried in multiple graves and adolescents were always buried in multiple graves. In contrast, 62% of juveniles were interred in single graves. There is a shift, then, from interring juveniles in single graves to either single or multiple graves in later burials.

5.5.2.2 The Disposal of the Corpse

From the interments recovered intact, it seems most individuals were laid in a flexed position on their right side, facing west, or towards the sea (Table 5.5). This consistent orientation may have some relation to the importance of the sea. Standardised burial orientation can also relate to pointing the dead in the direction of ancestors or a homeland. In this case, it is the Greek mainland. This pattern is not surprising for two reasons. First, the islands near the mainland were first inhabited during this period (Davis 1992; Broodbank 1999), and second, there are strong archaeological affinities with these settlements to those on the mainland, particularly those in Attica (Broodbank 1999; Coleman 1977:98-108; Pullen 1985).

TABLE 5.7
THE DISTRIBUTION OF BURIAL GOODS IN THE AGE AND SEX CATEGORIES REPRESENTED AT KEPHALA

Age	Sex		
	Male	Female	Indeterminate
Adult	flint tri-scraper •	marble bowl •	bowl (Type A1)
	marble "rhyton" •	incised scoop •	incised scoop (likely female)
	bone tool •	flint tool •?	obsidian tool (Type 6)
	ithyphallic figurine •		obsidian blade (Type 1A)
	figurine "necklace" •	stone "pillow" †	wooden box
		Type A1 bowl †	flint tool
	stone "pillow" †	obsidian tool Type 6 †	
	bowl (Type A1) †?	obsidian blade (1A) †	
	obsidian blade Type 1 †		
	obsidian tool Type 6 †	obsidian blade 1B ‡	
	female figurine §		
	large jar (Type B2) §		
Adolescent		obsidian scraper •	
		obsidian blade 1B ‡	
Juvenile			small decorated oval bowl •
Infant			crucible-sized vessel •
			large jar (Type B2) §
			female figurine §
Indeterminate			female figurine (adult male? or infant?)
			large jar (Type B2) (adult? or infant?)
			crucible (?)
			cylindrical vessel (?)

† Object constrained by age.   ‡ Object constrained by sex.   • Object constrained to age/sex category.   § Object not likely constrained by age/sex.

Burial goods and objects associated with funeral ritual were primarily ascribed to adults (Table 5.7). Several objects are found specifically with adult men (flint tri-scraper, marble rhyton, bone tool, ithyphallic figurine, figurine "necklace") and women (marble bowl, incised scoop, and possibly a flint tool), but several types appear constrained by age alone (stone pillow, Type A1 bowl, Type 1 obsidian blade, Type 6 obsidian tool). Based upon this pattern, several other objects found with adults of indeterminate sex can be tentatively ascribed to women (an incised scoop and a flint tool). The remaining objects may belong to either men or women. Only one object (obsidian blade 1B) was found exclusively with women, an adult and adolescent. An obsidian scraper was characteristic of only the adolescent female burial goods. Other objects are only constrained by age. A small decorated oval bowl and a waste piece of obsidian was found with a juvenile, and a crucible- sized vessel was found with an infant. Two types of objects, the female figurines and Type B2 large jars, are found with an adult male, an infant, and an individual of indeterminate age or sex. Two other objects, a crucible and a cylindrical vessel cannot be associated with any confidence to an individual of known age or sex.

Most grave goods appear to be assigned on the basis of age and or sex. Only adult women were given artefacts based upon a combination of their age and sex. These goods are mainly utilitarian items, such as obsidian blades and scrapers, and ceramic objects. There were a small number of women given ceramic scoops as part of their grave assemblage. Three adult women were given Type C1 scoops. The precise function of these objects is unsure, but they may have been used in food preparation. Only one female (Grave 36) was buried alone in small grave in the Upper Cemetery. Six other women were also associated with obsidian and flint tools of various types. While these objects likely relate to age-based statuses, they also reflect the sphere of activities undertaken by these women. It is clear that the occupational statuses or group membership of women is far more visible in this mortuary record than it is for men (Cullen and Talalay 1995).

The disposal practices for infants are clearer. Infants buried alone were placed in a large jar, then interred in a pit, and were not given burial gifts. Alternatively, infants were interred in communal graves without grave goods. The exclusion or certain infant burials in the cemetery reflect a prohibitive ritual practice, and there is some relationship between these exclusionary practices, and infant pathology. In one instance, two infants were buried in an isolated grave (Grave 31) without accompanying burial gifts. This grave lies isolated to the south-east of all others in the Lower Cemetery, quite segregated from the rest of the burials. One of these infants may have had sickle-cell anaemia or thalassemia, a condition that is fatal. Although infants were treated differently than the rest of the mortuary population, this particular case is clearly a non-normative treatment. It appears these infants were purposefully buried in this location due to the circumstances surrounding their sickness and death.

A study of the energy expended on the preparation and treatment of the body and the grave and the quantity and types of burial furniture associated with each individual indicate four levels of labour expenditure at Kephala (Fig. 5-7). Several interesting observations can be made regarding this pattern. First, it is notable that almost as many females belong to the first category as males. This suggests that both males and females could receive similar degrees of corporate involvement in their mortuary treatment. From a purely social perspective, one might suggest that there was unrestricted access to status in this society, and both men and women could exercise authority. While this may be an overly simplistic interpretation, high levels of energy expenditure in mortuary treatment do often reflect elevated social positions in a community (Tainter 1975; O'Shea 1984; McGuire 1992; Carr 1995).

Second, it is also significant that the quantity of grave goods does not correspond with overall energy expenditure. That is, the number of grave goods does not correlate with the labour expenditure ranking. This suggests that it is the type of grave goods rather than their quantity held greater significance in the mortuary treatment at Kephala. This observation is supported by ethnographic studies showing that the quantity of grave goods often does not relate to vertical social position either in terms of rank of status (Tainter 1975; Carr 1995). On the contrary, the different types of burial furniture used in mortuary ritual usually have a symbolic connection to philosophic-religious beliefs (Carr 1995). Thus, the quantity of grave goods does not indicate that vertical stratification existed at Kephala.

Third, another interesting observation is that there is no association between an absence of pathology and energy expenditure. For example, even in individuals with high labour expenditure rank, there is evidence of growth arrests during childhood (teeth lesions). This suggests that there were several instances when nutritional intake was not optimal when these individuals were children. These children and their families did not have preferential access to resources, yet upon their death, they received comparatively elaborate burials.

Taken together, these data do not indicate rank grading at Kephala. In social terms, it appears that status was largely a result of individual achievement (i.e., achieved status). While individual achievement may account for many status positions at Kephala, young individuals with high energy expenditures is often taken as evidence of the contrary - the social ascription of status (Tainter 1977;

Peebles and Kus 1977; McGuire 1992). At Kephala, the high amount of energy expended in the treatment of the young person in Grave 27 (juvenile?) and an adolescent female (19 KeK) in Grave 20, reveals that these individuals were treated differently than others of the same or similar age. The high amount of energy expended in these burials cannot be directly correlated to a cause of death or other special circumstances to explain the peculiar pattern. However, the presence of young individuals in high rank categories does not have to be a result of status ascription. Of course, our conceptions of 'young' individuals or 'children'—which physical anthropologists categorise by small, incremental age groupings—may not necessarily translate to the prehistoric record, and it is dangerous to assume that age is valued the same cross-culturally and trans-temporally.

At Kephala, older juveniles and adolescents may have taken on many of the responsibilities of an adult. While we may perceive them as children, in this particular society they could have been treated as adults, with all or many of the associated rights and responsibilities. In a society where status was based upon biological differences and individual achievement, it should not be surprising to find exceptional individuals. Thus, the high energy expended in the mortuary treatment of these two young persons was motivated by the social responsibilities they held, corporate recognition of their status, potential and achievements, and a reaction to the devastating loss of their presence from the small community.

5.5.2.3 Non-normative Mortuary Practices

There are several other anomalies to the general pattern of disposing the corpse. The burial of several adult males contradicts the normative pattern. One man was laid on his front with his leg flexed towards is head (Grave 35), and the other man was found on his back with his legs bent under his body (Grave 39). Both positions are reminiscent of the body simply being dropped in the grave. In order to have the bodies assume and hold this position, burial must have occurred soon after death, likely within 12 hours. Rigor mortis usually sets in 12 hours post-mortem and disappears around 36 hours, after which the body usually begins to bloat and putrefy making body positioning difficult. These individuals are otherwise similar in their age, sex and the later date of burial in the life-use of the cemetery, and there is no apparent pathological origin for this behaviour.

The adult male in Grave 4 also does not conform to the treatment given adults. The grave is in the centre of the cemetery, which might indicate some prestige, and it seems that obvious measures were taken to not disturb this grave (no graves built above it) and mark it off from the others (building short walls around it). Another interesting aspect is the link between the large jar given

this individual and the same type being used as burial urns for infants in the cemetery. It appears that this is an individual was subtly segregated and symbolically associated with infants. Also, a female figurine (possibly a symbol of fertility, growth, and/or rebirth) and a figurine necklace (which may have acted as an 'amulet' of some sort) were found above this individual's grave. If the ithyphallic figurine was once associated with this grave, one could include a symbol of male power/authority, fertility or male potency to this list. This represents a somewhat contradictory set of symbols, combining both elements of inclusion and distinction. In many societies, individuals who hold positions of ritual or spiritual significance, such as shamans, are accorded special distinction with the community. However, they are also often treated as "outsiders" because they deal mainly with the unknown and the aspects of life that others in the community know little of—what they revere, but also fear. Long-standing or repeated sickness in childhood is also a common characteristic of shamans and other ritual healers. Some sort of sickness is evidenced by repeated interruptions in tooth enamel growth during childhood. This is a trait only shared with two other adult males. The relatively modest mortuary treatment of this man, and the artefacts associated with him, could signify his importance in the community as well as his exclusiveness. As a whole, this contradictory symbolic package may have symbolised his socio-economic and religious importance in the community.

The adolescent female and an infant found in Grave 12 also present an anomaly. Angel had suggested that both individuals could have died during or shortly after childbirth (Angel 1977:135). While there is no medical evidence to the contrary, this particular mortuary treatment contrasts other interments at Kephala. This is the only case of double burial at Kephala apart from the two infants in Grave 31. This connection does suggest that double burials at Kephala only occurred when the circumstances of death overrode other directives of the mortuary program. Another interesting case is presented with the juvenile interred in Grave 37. This juvenile is one of many other juveniles buried during the later use of the cemetery. The loose association of this particular juvenile with a figurine is unique. The death of this individual may have provoked the use of powerful protective amulets. Besides having protective functions, it is also possible that these figures were used to purify the dead in the hope of preventing further deaths of young people.

5.5.2.4 Ancestor Worship at Kephala?

The presence of figures in the Kephala cemetery presents a useful case for inferring figure function during the Greek Neolithic. In a study of figurine imagery dating to the Neolithic, Talalay (1987, 1991, 1993) has suggested that the symbolism represented by the figurines does not necessarily have to be linked to religion, especially the practice of 'goddess' worship. Rather, Talalay proposed an intriguing argument based upon the anthropological literature. For this cemetery, she suggested that the figures could have otherwise been used as communal social and economic symbols, and representations of ties to the community's ancestral spirits. Talalay suggested that the cemetery 'was established to legitimise the villager's control or ownership of the area, and the figurines served as ancestor images which chartered Kephalan ancestral rights to the region' (Talalay 1991: 49).

It appears that a number of graves may potentially be associated with figurine function at Kephala (potentially, Graves 4, 17 or 18, 32, 37, and 38). As discussed above, even considering the post-depositional effects at Kephala, several figurines can be loosely associated with a single grave: the figures above Grave 4, Grave 32, and Grave 37. The location of the other figures is likely the result of post-depositional displacement, and they can be discussed in little detail. Most interesting is *who* is associated with figurines—not only in relation to each other, but also to everyone else in the Kephalan cemetery.

These figurines correlate to a temporal shift in the mortuary treatment of younger individuals in the cemetery. This shift is also manifest in other practices, such as the building of walls around Grave 17 and 18, and the building Grave 22 backed into the slope of the hill. The earlier practice of interring juveniles and infants in communal graves continues, as shown by Graves 16 and 20. These changes in mortuary practice appear to relate to an increase in juvenile deaths and the decrease in infant mortality.

Despite the evidence for economic and subsistence prosperity at the settlement (Coleman 1977), it appears that improved health and nutrition did not contribute greatly to preventing the death of young individuals, although they did not die within the first five years (Angel 1975, 1984). Genetic predisposition to anaemia in this population may have also contributed to the death of the young at Kephala. Regardless of the aetiology, it is very likely that this increase in the mortality of juveniles contributed in some way to the abandonment of the settlement. While none of these factors explains why figurines were associated with younger individuals, their distribution in space, time and to specific individuals do de-emphasise the possibility of their functioning solely as calling cards to the ancestral spirits.

The presence of figurines within a cemetery alone does not necessarily support ancestor worship. Ancestor worship in many cultures also tends to focus ritual on prominent individuals in the lineage and these persons may be recognised in mortuary ritual (Douglas 1973).

This may be the case with the man in Grave 4. However, the association of figurines with non-normative burials also implies they had other functions, perhaps as protective devices both for the dead and for the living. Thus, the figurines could have had multiple functions in mortuary ritual at Kephala. For instance, they may have been used to represent individual socio-economic and possibly philosophical-religious classification at the time of death. As part of the belief system, where mortuary ritual was a means to promote and legitimise group solidarity, the figurines could be used to ensure the continuity of the community by acting as devices to protect the dead and the living. Perhaps this is why they occur more often when child mortality was so high.

5.5.2.5 Corporate Group Structure at Kephala

The notion that residence patterns reflect different types of social groupings has been drawn from ethnographic studies of kinship and descent groups. When anthropologists talk of a 'corporate group' they are generally speaking of a kinship or descent group that collectively has access to certain valued assets and rights, including both economic and non-economic holdings (Murphy 1989: 118). It becomes increasingly necessary for the group to establish rules stating who has exclusive rights to the corporately held assets, be they land, resources, or even other people. The extended family moves from being an *ad hoc* group defining themselves by a residence preference to being 'a formally defined, continuing group with rules of membership and exclusion' (Murphy 1989: 118). A corporate group is a very general term, and may be used to designate one or more types of descent groups. The largest descent group unit is identified as a lineage, or a clan, which utilises a common ancestor to symbolise the social unity and identity of its members, usefully distinguishing them from other groups. If members of a particular descent group live the same area, such as the same village, they are known as a local descent group. However, within a community, there may be a situation where two descent groups exist, and this is known as a moiety.

The corporate group has also been recognised as a valuable archaeological unit of study (Saxe 1970; Hayden and Cannon 1982; Pullen 1985: 37-42). This was considered an important advance mainly because it allowed archaeologists to infer the type of social group(s) (lineage, clan, moieties, etc.) that make up a society's structure. As Goldstein (1981: 60-61) has shown, the corporate group can be identified through the mortuary record. Goldstein's work focused on the restructuring of Saxe's original hypothesis. This hypothesis states that corporate groups, which control crucial and restricted resources through lineal descent, will maintain discrete formal cemeteries (Saxe 1970: 119). However, not all cultures will symbolise their social system in such a way, and Saxe's hypothesis failed in testing. In reaction to this, modifications have been made to Saxe's original hypothesis that take symbolic (Goldstein 1981), economic and more precise spatial variability into account (Charles and Buikstra 1983). As such, five criteria must be met in order to identify the presence of one or more corporate group(s) when using mortuary data:

1) 'Within the larger society, corporate groups will be distinguished by inclusion in separate cemeteries or in spatially distinct areas within a single cemetery. Inclusion of individuals in the cemetery implies inclusion of those individuals in the corporate group' (Charles and Buikstra 1983: 120).

2) '[A] corporate group…has rights over the use and/or control of crucial but restricted resources' (Goldstein 1981: 61).

3) 'corporate control is most likely to be attained and/or legitimized by means of lineal descent from the dead, either in terms of actual lineage or in the form of a strong, established tradition of critical resource passing from parent to offspring' (Goldstein 1981: 61).

4) 'The degree of spatial structuring present in the mortuary domain will correlate with the degree of competition among groups for crucial resources' (Charles and Buikstra 1983: 120).

5) 'Utilization of formal cemetery areas will correlate with sedentary subsistence strategies employed by the group(s) using the cemetery" (Charles and Buikstra 1983: 120).

Because Kephala is one of the few formal cemeteries dating to the Greek Neolithic, it has often been considered one of the best candidates for identifying the presence of corporate group structure. Corporate groups at Kephala has previously been suggested because the cemetery is highly organised (Pullen 1985). It has also been proposed that certain resources were important to the economy at Kephala (Talalay 1988), indicating there were exclusive rights to an control over these resources. However, the presence of corporate group structure cannot be based upon these two criteria alone. Instead, the five criteria outlined above must be identified to propose the presence of one or more corporate groups.

The arbitrary spatial distinctions drawn between the graves have provided the circumstantial evidence of multiple corporate groups being represented in the cemetery (Coleman 1977): a western group and a central group in the Lower Cemetery, and the Upper Cemetery. The first problem with proposing multiple corporate groups is the estimated size of the population at Kephala.

The settlement is small, and likely had a population of around 50 people at any one time. If more than one corporate group were present at this settlement, we would expect the population to be much larger (Binford 1964; Goldstein 1981).

Second, intra-cemetery variability at Kephala shows that, as whole, the preparation and treatment of the body and grave is relatively homogeneous in spatial terms. While there is significant variability in mortuary practices at Kephala, it is not attributable to certain spatially distinct sub-groups in the cemetery. The multiple graves indicate that certain groups desired to be buried together, and these communal graves may have belonged to specific families. Only certain infants were spatially segregated, and this was likely a result of the circumstances surrounding their deaths. The walls placed around the cemetery do suggest that certain graves were spatially distinguished. However, the walls do not separate different types of graves, mark different burial practices, or distinguish individuals on socio-economic criteria. Instead, they separate later graves in the Lower and Upper Cemetery. Thus, the walls were probably constructed to mark different family groups and/or generations as the cemetery eventually became overcrowded.

1) In reference to resource rights and control, Talalay (1988) had suggested that the harbour, marble resources, and copper production could all have been considered vital, restricted and valuable resources at Kephala. While it can be assumed that the harbour, and the sea for that matter, were valuable resources, the mortuary data do not indicate that certain individuals or groups had preferential access to these resources:

2) The pathological data indicate that persons of higher status were not in better health than any other individuals, and therefore did not have restricted access to certain food resources.

3) There is no evidence that marble-working or copper production was a more highly valued craft over any others. If this was the case, it was not recognised in mortuary ritual. Only a juvenile received a pot with copper smelting residue and is unlikely that this young person specialised in copper-production.

4) There is no indication that status was based upon wealth or power deriving from economic sanctions.

Thus, individual socio-economic differences at Kephala were not based upon preferential access to certain resources. Instead, the community as a whole had rights to and control over these resources. Therefore, at Kephala corporate control of resources was probably legitimised more broadly by identifying common lineal descent from the dead, and not by transferring resource control through individual familial lines.

This is directly linked to the third criterion that requires evidence for resource continuity between generations must be shown. Status ascription is often considered a mechanism for the passing of critical resources from parents to offspring (Goldstein 1981). The evidence for this practice is weak and unconvincing, and there is no substantial evidence to suggest ascribed status at Kephala. However, this criterion assumes that of resources were privately owned and controlled and passed through familial kinship lines. With the absence of evidence for this at Kephala, it can be proposed that resources were treated as generally being under the control of the larger kinship group. However, the production and distribution of goods may have been the responsibility of individuals or smaller groups distinguished on the basis of age, gender, and ability.

Fourth, it is necessary to show that there was resource competition on Keos during the Final Neolithic. There is some indication that a proportion of the economy was based upon the production, trade, and exchange of valued (e.g., metals, marble, etc.) and possibly some non-valued, utilitarian goods (e.g., flint, chert, etc., objects). It is possible that the people of Kephala could have been in competition for certain resources, but it simply cannot be determined with whom this would have been. To demonstrate clearly territorial socio-political legitimisation of behaviour in the archaeological record, one must first understand the relationship of settlements on a regional scale. Until this is better understood for Kea, we remain limited to discussing Kephala in isolation. Lastly, the sedentary subsistence strategies practised at Kephala supports the presence of corporate group structure.

TABLE 5.8

CORRELATION BETWEEN THE CRITERIA FOR ESTABLISHING THE PRESENCE OF CORPORATE GROUPS USING MORTUARY REMAINS AND THE MORTUARY PRACTICES AT KEPHALA

Corporate Group Criteria	Correlation
1. Presence of valued resources	+
2. Spatial segregation and differentiation between groups	-
3. Preferential access to resources/ resource control	-
4. Resource continuity	-
5. Resource competition	+?
6. Sedentary subsistence strategies	+

The highly structured mortuary behaviour in this cemetery suggests that a corporate group was present at Kephala. This analysis supports earlier quantitative suggestions that a corporate group structure was present at Kephala. However, the mortuary data only match two of the six criteria for this hypothesis (Table 5.8) and only one corporate group can be confidently defined. Biological affinity tests using non-metric traits or DNA analyses may go some way to understanding the details of lineage associations and kinship structure at Kephala.

5.5.3   Conclusions

There was substantial forethought put into the construction and maintenance of the cemetery at Kephala. This may indicate that the relationship between the living and the deceased was deeply imbedded within daily life at Kephala and that this relationship was a core feature of this community's belief system. While the cemetery was spatially separated from the community, it was highly visible both from the settlement and from the sea. The unique location of the settlement and the evidence for long-distance trade and exchange shows that the community at Kephala was involved in a broader sphere of interaction. The prominent location of the cemetery may have been used to identify this community within this socio- economic framework.

The procedure for disposing of the corpse shows that transformation of the social individual was not a long process and individuals appear to have been interred very soon after death. The use of figurines in mortuary ritual at Kephala may have been used a mediation device between the living and the dead as a means of recognising the communities ancestral heritage while simultaneously marking differences in social personae. Differences in grave construction indicate that there were three socially recognised burial types at Kephala. The different grave types and the number of individuals interred in them reflect status differences and the circumstances of death. Several single adult burials possibly represent the remains of prominent individuals in the community, who received special treatment based on this status. Other single burials were intended to distinguish individuals who had died very young in life. The communal graves indicate the use of the same tomb, possibly by the same family, for more than one generation. Floors were carefully laid to separate earlier from later interments. It was suggested that this practice has practical significance, which can be linked to high mortality when Kephala was first settled.

The mortuary evidence indicates that there was a complex kin- based social structure at Kephala. There is no evidence that social status was based upon wealth or power. Instead, mortuary differentiation indicates that social stratification was horizontal and based upon biological differences, kinship ties and ability. The most telling evidence for this conclusion is that the key criteria for identifying vertical social stratification using mortuary and settlement data are not met:

1) there is no indication that settlement architecture was differentiated (although house Y is somewhat larger), or was organized according to principles characteristic of hierarchical differentiation (Wason 1994), and

2) the quantity of burial goods does not correlate with energy expenditure (Peebles and Kus 1977).

5.6 OTHER FINAL NEOLITHIC MORTUARY REMAINS

The evidence for mortuary activity during the Final Neolithic also comes from a variety of other caves and open-air sites. At many of the cave sites (e.g., Kitsos, Tharrounia, Ayia Triada, Marathon, Agios Petrochoros, Fournospilia, Hagios Nikolaos, Kalythies, etc.) disarticulated and friable human remains have been found incorporated with faunal remains, pottery sherds, and lithics.

At Kitsos Cave, for example, the remains of at least 18 individuals were found scattered about Sondage 2 and 3 (Lambert 1981; Duday and Lambert 1981). While the remains were probably disturbed during the Classical period when the cave was used as a sanctuary (Duday and Lambert 1981:559), this does not explain why much of skeletal anatomy is underrepresented. The 474 human bone elements recovered only compose about 16 per cent of the anatomy that should be represented by 18 individuals.

Two other taphonomic processes also affected the human remains. First, in Sondage 2 a small number of bones (n=20 or 4%) have a scorched (reddish) appearance, suggesting that they had some contact with fire. The low frequency of burnt human bone makes it unlikely that individuals were cremated at Kitsos. However, mineral staining resulting from water percolation or leeching in the cave has not been ruled out as a cause for the colouring of these bones. Second, portions of the post-cranium (femurs, ulnae, and tibiae) have cutmarks (Duday and Lambert 1981: 562, 564, and fig. 346). While anthrophagy has been introduced as one possible interpretation, the cutmarks probably represent a technique used to disarticulate the skeleton for secondary interment elsewhere or to bind the body into contracted positions (e.g., Binford 1963, 1971), such as is known during EBA (Cosmopoulos 1991). However, at Kitsos, the preservation of bone under these conditions is not optimal, and it would be hazardous to suggest that low representativeness of the skeleton alone indicates secondary burial practices. The fact that all of the most durable elements of the cranial and post-cranial skeleton are present in the cave may suggest otherwise.

A good example of a contrary situation is found at Kalythies cave on Rhodes (Halstead and Jones 1987). Secondary burial has proposed at Kalythies because only bones of the feet, hands, and teeth were found in the cave. Secondary disposal was only used for juvenile and adult burials, and infants were instead given final interment in the cave. Elsewhere on the southern mainland, primary inhumation burials outside of caves are found.

At Lerna, nine individuals were recovered within habitation areas dating to the most recent Neolithic levels. Adults were interred in single, primary inhumation burials and were given the most burial gifts (up to three ceramic vessels). Only one black-burnished bowl was found with a juvenile. One adolescent was buried in the same way as adults, but did not receive any burial goods. Juveniles were more often interred in their own grave, but one is found in a double grave. One infant was given an urn burial and another was found in the double grave. All burials are extramural, primary inhumation burials found near houses, or perhaps more specialised activity areas. There are few grave goods, and the juvenile given the black burnished bowl may present somewhat of an anomaly. There is one site in northern Greece with mortuary remains dating to the FN phase that deserves mention. One house at Pefkakia contained several small pits, storage vessels, and a large rectangular pit lined with mudbrick and filled with ash was found below the floor. Also under the floor, near the rectangular pit, was an adult inhumation burial containing two obsidian cores. The practice of interring the dead under house floors (intramural burial) is only documented in northern Greece during the Neolithic. Other sites with intramural burials include the eight infant cremation burials discussed earlier at Dhimini and Agia Sophia.

5.7 TRENDS IN FINAL NEOLITHIC MORTUARY PRACTICES

The case studies of FN mortuary practice reveal that very different approaches were taken in the procession, form and symbolism, and scale of rites (Table 5.9). Mortuary practices that occur in caves during the FN are quite similar (Kitsos, Aleopotrypa, etc.), although the precise details are not available from most cave sites because of the severe affect later use of the caves had on Neolithic deposits. The open-air cemeteries are also more similar in contrast to the funerary deposits in cave, but, as discussed next, they also present a wide-variety of practices. This is particularly surprising because three of the four case studies analysed in this chapter belong to the Aegina-Attica-Kephala culture group. Pevkakia, in Thessaly, stands out from this southern group of sites, particularly because intramural burial was used. This links the site more closely with the later LN practices observed at Dimini and Agia Sophia.

TABLE 5.9
FINAL NEOLITHIC MORTUARY PRACTICES

Categories of Observable Mortuary Variation		Final Neolithic Mortuary Sites		
		Franchthi Cave	Kephala	Tharrounia
Preparation & Treatment of the Body				
Preparation	extramural burial and exhumation			●
	not indicated	●	●	
Treatment	inhumation	●	●	●
	cremation			
Position at burial	flexed	●	●	
	semi-flexed		●	
	disarticulated and arranged			●
Orientation at burial	northerly	●	●	
	southerly	●	●	
	not applicable			●
Form of disposal	primary	●	●	
	secondary			●
Preparation of the Grave				
Grave form	pit grave	●?	●	
	built		●	●
	cist		●	
Number of socially recognised burial types		1?	3	1
Grave Furniture & Goods				
Kinds of grave furniture	ceramics	●	●	●
	terracotta	●	●	●
	lithics		●	●
	bone			
	shell			●
	wood			
Source of grave furniture	local area	●	●	●
	extra-local trade item		●?	
Quantity of grave furniture		low	low	low
Spatial Location and Designation				
Local grave location	disposal area in cave			● (primary)
	open-air disposal area	●	●	● (secondary)
Regional location of disposal area relative to settlement	spatial separated		●	●
	incorporated	●		
Grave formally demarked			● (some)	
Intra-cemetery grave location of burial types	differentiated			
	not differentiated		●	
Energy Expenditure				
Levels of energy expenditure		1?	4	3
Funeral time & duration; secondary funerals		?	●	●?
Mourning Ritual				
Funeral dance/games				
Funeral meals/fasting			?	
Funeral dress and ornamentation				
Grief, bereavement and grave visitation			●	

A study of the procession of rites shows that Tharrounia and Kephala are similar in two ways. The built graves were probably made in much the same way and the cemeteries lay outside the settlements. However, this is where the similarities end. A case was presented for secondary burial at Tharrounia, a practice out of line with Kephala. Also, the types of grave goods used at Kephala indicate that they were used both as markers of the social personae and as ritual equipment linked to beliefs about the dead in general and more specifically their effect on the living. The separation of the cemetery from the settlement at Tharrounia may indicate similar beliefs, but burial goods and other objects were not intended to have served such a function. Furthermore, the inhabitants of Kephala made use of three different burial types and short walls to differentiate individuals according their social status, probably their kinship affiliation, and the circumstances of death. Social status at Tharrounia, on the other hand, appears to have only been expressed along familial lines and the subsistence obligations of women. Representing the social personae through mortuary ritual practices does not seem to have been of primary concern.

Mortuary practices at Franchthi, by comparison, are somewhat simpler and are reminiscent of earlier practices at the site. However, burials are no longer located in the cave and most burials occur in the same general area within the settlement. Also unlike earlier phases, there is less noticeable variation between the mortuary treatment of children and adults. The handling of the corpse is also different at these FN sites. If the disposal of the corpse was used to express metaphors of death during the FN, it is clear that substantial differences in beliefs about the dead, the state of the soul, and cosmology can be entertained at each of these places.

There is also an overwhelming difference in the scale of rites. Interestingly, the scale is not substantially different within each cemetery or disposal area, but varies considerably from one site to the next. Most notable is the degree of time and labour invested in constructing the graves at Kephala and Tharrounia in comparison to the practices at Franchthi. Individual families may have undertaken the construction of the graves at Kephala and Tharrounia, but it is more likely that this aspect of the funerary practices involved broader corporate involvement. The mortuary remains at Franchthi do not indicate such large-scale labour investment. These practices suggest that the size and social structure of the groups in these places was substantially different and that they were likely organised according to very different principles. These differences may have their roots in the subsistence practises at these sites: Tharrounia and Franchthi have more of a focus upon livestock-keeping, whereas subsistence at Kephala was more diversified, drawing on resources from both land and sea. However,

this does not explain the differences between the mortuary practices at Franchthi and Tharrounia. The similarity in material culture between these settlements indicates they belong within a well-defined interaction sphere. However, the mortuary practices indicate very different cultural practises and beliefs systems were in operation at these settlements.

The placement of the dead within the settlement at Pefkakia is similar to the practices at Franchthi, but the adult burial at Pefkakia is intramural. This indicates that some very deep association existed between the dead and living at this and other earlier (LN) sites in Thessaly. It also suggests that the disposal of the corpse was solely the responsibility of the family, a practise not expressed in southern Greece during the FN. Thus, even though comparisons with the north are very limited, there is some indication at least that the cultural differences between FN settlements in northern and southern Greece also seem to be expressed in mortuary ritual.

5.8   NOTES

[1] Historically, there are three main settlement patterns typical of Greece. There is often a move from upland to lowland villages (Wagstaff 1968:175; McNeill 1978:50-64; Sutton 1991:401); there is a move from inland villages to coastal villages (Kolodny 1974:259-266; Sutton 1991); and, under certain economic conditions, there is commonly a nucleated or dispersed settlement pattern (Sutton 1991:401). A study of settlement and land use in Greece has shown these patterns to be typical of the settlement dispersal that occurred recently in the Kalmos region in northeastern Attica (Fowler in press).

CHAPTER 6
TRENDS AND IMPLICATIONS

6.1   INTRODUCTION

While the number of cases considered in this analysis is small, they are situated at key times in Neolithic. The nature of the mortuary data from most of these sites, and their placement in time, has the potential to provide a different perspective on several significant issues, particularly those raised by Jacobsen and Cullen (1981), whose study remains the keystone of mortuary analysis in Greece. In their survey of Greek Neolithic mortuary practices, and specifically of the mortuary remains at Francthi, Jacobsen and Cullen concluded that Neolithic mortuary treatment is diverse, but there is no emphasis on the visibility of the dead. Further, their review suggested that there is little indication for elaborate mortuary ritual during the Neolithic, and equally scant evidence for social inequality. Based on the preceding analyses, in this final chapter, I present a variety of evidence that is ambiguous or contradictory to these points.

6.2   DIVERSITY OF MORTUARY PRACTICES

As shown in Table 6.1, this analysis confirms Jacobsen and Cullen's finding that Neolithic mortuary practices are diverse. During the EN, there are some superficial similarities between Prosymna and Souphli and Franchthi and Nea Nikomedia. The details of the mortuary practices differ, but as suggested in Chapter 3, there may also be common symbolic themes expressed in the mortuary practices at each of the two groups of settlements.

Mortuary practices in the LN become even more diverse. At sites often considered to fall under the same sphere of influence, like Plateia Magoula Zarkou, Dimini, and Agia Sophia, we find that the form and symbolism of mortuary practices is quite different. Zarkou and Dimini may be considered more similar in terms of the social differentiation expressed through the scale of rites, but both contrast what is known about the mortuary practices at Agia Sophia. During the FN, there is again little similarity in mortuary practices.

Settlements belonging to the Aegina-Attica-Kephala group (Franchthi, Kitsos, Tharrounia, Kephala) have many similarities in material culture, but the mortuary practices are very different. Burials at Kitsos and Aleopotrypa probably occurred both inside and outside caves, whereas that practice is no longer followed at Franchthi as in earlier phases. Burial at Tharrounia and Kephala is in formally built graves outside of the settlement, but secondary burial was probably used at Tharrounia. Also, the frequency and types of grave goods at Kephala are unlike any other site. The closest parallels to this aspect of mortuary treatment are at LN Zarkou and

later Early Cycladic burials. The use of intramural burial at Pevkakia is not documented in the south during the FN, but does show some continuity with Dimini and Agia Sophia.

The range and diversity in Neolithic mortuary practices in Greece has been explicitly or inexplicity under-emphasised and, I would suspect, probably in many cases unappreciated. This has prompted statements suggesting that in the Early and Late Neolithic there are no 'obvious differences in ritual or funerary deposits' (Demoule and Perlés 1993: 396), despite evidence for greater diversity in mortuary ritual, the so-called ritual equipment found at settlements, and the evidence for increasing status differences within Late Neolithic groups, particularly in Thessaly.

Despite a rigorous attempt to find some keys or markers that could be used to define common clusters of mortuary practices within or between the various phases of the Neolithic, both quantitative (Fowler 1997) and non-quantitative (this volume) efforts have fallen short. This suggests that, for the present at least, the diversity of Neolithic mortuary practices should itself be made a detailed subject of study.

6.3   VISIBILITY OF THE DEAD

The lack of visibility of the dead noted by Jacobsen and Cullen can be approached in two complementary ways: first, the physical visibility of the dead, and second, the visibility of the directives of disposal.

There is a variety of evidence contradictory to the first point. A consideration of the spatial structure and stratigraphic relationships of the Neolithic cemeteries and disposal areas indicates that contemporary burials were only disturbed by burials dating to later periods, usually much later, and by other later activities unrelated to mortuary practices. Several examples support this conclusion. For instance, at Souphli and Zarkou, where urn cremations were placed at least over half a meter under the surface, there is not one instance where a later urn burial disturbed an earlier one. In fact, at Zarkou there is one instance when an urn was later placed directly on top of an earlier burial (Urn 28b on top of Urn 28a). This behaviour implies that these graves were marked in some way.

As well, the two burials found in the mound at Agia Sophia suggest that the location of interment, but probably not the burials, was highly visible. At Franchthi too, some graves have stone coverings, or paving stones, placed over top of them. Distinguishing the stones that were originally placed on top of the graves and those that

TABLE 6.1
THE MORTUARY PRACTICES OBSERVED AT FIFTEEN GREEK NEOLITHIC SITES

Categories of Observable Mortuary Variation		Early and Middle Mortuary Sites				Late Neolithic Mortuary Sites					Final Neolithic Mortuary Sites					
		Prosymna	Franchthi	Souphli Magoula	Nea Nikomedia	Skoteni	Lerna	Zarkou	Dimini	Agia Sophia	Pevkakia	Kitsos	Aleopotrypa	Franchthi	Tharrounia	Kephala
Preparation & Treatment of the Body																
Preparation	burial & exhumation	•				•?					•					
	not indicated		•	•		•					•	•?	•	•	•	•
Treatment	inhumation	•	•	•	•		•			•	•	•			•	•
	cremation			•	•		•	?	•	•						
Position at burial	flexed	•	•	•	•	?	•	•	•	•			•	•	•	•
	semi-flexed		•		•											•
	disarticulated & arranged									?						
Orientation at burial	northerly	•	•	•	?	?	•	•	•			•?		•	•	•
	southerly		•		?		• east					1?		•	•	•
	not applicable															
Form of disposal	primary	•	•	•	•	•?	•	•	•	•	•		•			
	secondary	•		•					•				•	•		•
Preparation of the Grave																
Grave form	pit grave	•	•	•	•	•?	•?	•	•	•	•	•?	•	•?	•	•
	built grave															•
	cist grave												•			•
	ossuary											1?				
Number of socially recognised burial types		1	2	1	2		2?	1	2?	>1	2?		1	1	1	3
Grave Furniture & Goods																
Kinds grave goods	ceramics	•	•	•	•	?	•	•	•	•		•?	?	•	•	•
	terracotta	•		•	•	?	•					•?	?	•	•	•
	lithics	•		•	•	?					•	•?	?		•	•
	bone		•												•	
	shell		•													
	wood															
Source of goods	local area	•	•	•	•	?	•	•	?	•		•	•	•	•	•?
	trade item	•	•													•?
Quantity of goods		low	low	low	none	?	low	low	?	?	low	?	?	low	low	low

TABLE 6.1 CONTINUED
THE MORTUARY PRACTICES OBSERVED AT FIFTEEN GREEK NEOLITHIC SITES

Categories of Observable Mortuary Variation	Early and Middle Mortuary Sites				Late Neolithic Mortuary Sites					Final Neolithic Mortuary Sites					
	Prosymna	Franchthi	Souphli	Nea Nikomedia	Skoteni	Lerna	Zarkou	Dimini	Agia Sophia	Pevkakia	Kitsos	Aleopotrypa	Franchthi	Tharrounia	Kephala
Spatial Location and Designation															
Local location — disposal area in cave	•	•			•						?	•	•	primary	•
Local location — open-air disposal area		•	•	•		•	•	•	•	•	?			secondary	
Local location — intramural															
Location relative to settlement — spatial separated															
Location relative to settlement — incorporated	•	•	•	•	•	•	•	•	•	•		•		•	•
Graves demarked	no	no	probably	no	no	no	probably	?	?	no	likely	yes	?	yes	some
Intra-cemetery location of burial types — differentiated									? •						
Intra-cemetery location of burial types — not differentiated		•	•			?		?		?					•
Intra-cemetery location of burial types — not applicable (1 type)	•			•	•		•					•			
Energy Expenditure															
Number of levels	2	2	4	1?	1?	2?	4	2?	2?	?	?	1?	1?	3	4
Funeral time & duration; secondary funerals	•		•	•		2?	•	?	2?	?	?	•	•		
Mourning Ritual															
Funeral dance/games															
Funeral meals/fasting	?		?										?		
Funeral dress and ornamentation			•												
Grief, bereavement and grave visitation	•						possible		possible					likely	

TABLE 6.2
THE ARCHAEOLOGICAL VISIBILITY OF THE SOCIAL AND PHILOSOPHICAL-RELIGIOUS DIMENSIONS OF MORTUARY PRACTICES DURING THE GREEK NEOLITHIC

	Early and Middle Neolithic				Late Neolithic					Final Neolithic					
	Prosymna	Souphli	Franchthi	Nea Nikomedia	Skoteni	Lerna	Zarkou	Dimini	Agia Sophia	Aleopotrypa	Kitsos	Pevkakia	Franchthi	Tharrounia	Kephala
Cause of Death		•			•										•
Social Position of the Deceased															
Social classification at death				•?					•?		•?		•		•
Vertical Social Position															
Horizontal Social Position															
corporate group membership	•?						•	•		•?		•	•	•	•
age and/or sex status	•	•	•	•			•	•	•?	•	•?	•?	•	•	•
utilitarian duties		•	•			•	•						•	•	•
special duties based on ability		•	•			•?	•					•?	•	•	•
ritual duties			•?	•?			•?								
Indicator of social personae	•	•	•	•			•	•	•	•			•	•	•
Philosophical-Religious Beliefs															
Cause of death		•	•		•	•				•	•				
Health/safety of living	•	•	•	•			•	•?	•?	•	•?	•?	•	•	•
Beliefs about the afterlife	•	•	•	•			•	•?	•?	•	•?	•?	•	•	•
Beliefs about the soul: soul's nature, journey, and its effect on the living	•	•	•	•			•	•?	•?	•	•?	•?	•	•	•
Universal orders, mythology	•	•	•	•			•		•?	•	•?		•		•

104

resulted from later cave-ins or other activity was difficult. However, because contemporary burials or even later ones did not disturb each other, there is distinct possibility that the paving stones were used as grave markers.

As a final and more obvious example, the built graves at Tharrounia and Kephala were highly visible, and the cemeteries themselves probably served as markers. At Tharrounia the graves may have been signals of territorial claims. At Kephala, the cemetery is clearly visible from the sea and it could have functioned in some navigational capacity. It may also have been a territorial marker, but because the relationships between Final Neolithic settlements on Keos are poorly understood, such a function can only be assumed.

The second point can be addressed by considering the visibility of the possible social and philosophical-religious determinants of mortuary practices (Table 6.2). There is less convincing evidence that mortuary practices were used to express vertical social distinctions during the Neolithic; that is, acting as markers of social ranking. This will be taken up in more detail below. As well, often as many philosophical religious directives of mortuary practices could be inferred as social ones. This later observation has two important implications.

First, most of the Neolithic mortuary assemblages showed some evidence that the differences in the physical disposal of the dead involved

1) a conceptual transformation of the social personae guided by a set of philosophical and religious beliefs,

2) that the preparation and treatment of the body was guided by these beliefs and also influenced by the circumstances of the persons death, and

3) that social organisational factors could be expressed indirectly through the belief system, and visa versa—in numerous cases the same behaviour may be indelibly linked to both sets of factors.

Second, these observations suggest that the form and meaning of Neolithic mortuary behaviour is non-arbitrary in each particular historical context (Hodder 1982b:9), and we should be able to isolate those aspects of a belief system that are constructed through structural oppositions. There are three highly visible structural oppositions displayed in these mortuary practices.

'Natural' oppositions: These have their basis in "natural" statuses, like age, sex, and ability (Giddens 1979). Most notable are the male: female and adult: child distinctions expressed through a variety of mortuary behaviour such as grave goods (or the absence of them), the spatial location of burials, or the handling of the corpse. Some

occupational duties are also reflected in the osteo-biological data. Also, a study of energy expenditure, as a measure of the overall corporate involvement in the mortuary rites of individuals, indicates that *high:low* status distinctions are more subtly expressed through discrete differences in the sequence of adult funerary preparation.

Cause of death oppositions: Mortuary practices were also used to express a *normal:abnormal* opposition relating to the circumstances of death. For example, the infants in the double at Kephala were generally treated much the same way as other infants, but were placed in an uncommon grave type and spatially segregated from the rest of the cemetery.

Segregation oppositions: Lastly, there is a common *inclusion:exclusion* dichotomy expressed through the placement of burials within or outside of the confines of the settlement or habitation areas in caves. This dichotomy generally expresses the nature of the relationship between the dead and the living society.

6.4   RITUAL COMPLEXITY

Another problematic issue is the suggestion that disposal practices during the Greek Neolithic are uncomplicated (Gallis 1982; Demoule and Perlés 1993), or unelaborate (Jacobsen and Cullen 1981: 95; Orphianidis-Georgiadis 1981). I believe this analysis has shown that the cremation and inhumation practices during the Neolithic cannot be characterised as uncomplicated or devoid of elaborate ritual.

In regard to the complexity issue, it has been assumed that cremation was a quick and more effective means of disposing the dead (Gallis 1982). In fact, cremation during the Neolithic was a time-consuming procedure involving elaborate planning and effort, and by no means was it an entirely effective means of reducing human remains to ash. At Souphli, often the entire individual was not given final interment, partly because of the incineration procedures, and specific bones of the burnt remains had to be culled and perhaps broken so they would fit in the burial urns. Later, at Zarkou, the degree of bone incineration is much higher, and the more delicate bones were not preserved. Yet, it is likely that some the skeletal remains still had to be broken up in order to place them in the urns. In another instance, the bones of one infant—the one buried in the zoomorphic vessel—were so fragile they had to be bundled in some type of cloth so they could be placed in the burial urn.

Most inhumations were also not simple, especially secondary burials. In many cases, the digging of grave pits alone would have taken a considerable amount of time, considering the topography and rocky soils at some of these sites (e.g., Kephala and the cave sites). The complexity of the problems involved in these practical aspects of disposal are also reflected in the elaboration of rites. Even limiting our consideration to only the procession of rites, some burials, such as those at Souphli and Zarkou, can be considered very elaborate. However, it was the *process* of disposing the dead that was elaborated and not the 'product'. The same situation probably also existed at Aleopotrypa and Kitsos. At Aleopotrypa, a long, elaborate multi-stage mortuary ritual involved burying and exhuming the dead, placing the remains in a special area encircled by stones in front of the ossuary, and then later incorporating the skeletal remains into the ossuary once the mortuary rites for someone else began. Similarly, the cut-marks on the human bones from Kitsos may indicate some time-consuming pre-interment treatment used to either disarticulate the corpse, or prepare it for binding in contracted positions.

In contrast, Tharrounia and Kephala had elaborate stone-built graves, which can properly be termed tombs. The amount of effort to build the tombs was considerable. At Kephala there are also traces that the graves were covered with plaster, and many of the dividing floors within the tombs were carefully laid down using small pebbles. However, there is little indication that the bodies of the dead underwent any pre-interment treatment and preparation procedures, and all of the burials at Kephala probably occurred very soon after death. Therefore, at Kephala, we see the elaborateness of mortuary ritual being expressed in the product rather than the process of disposing the dead. Alternatively, the evidence for secondary burial at Tharrounia indicates that considerable effort was invested in both aspects of mortuary ritual.

6.5   IDEOLOGICAL ORGANISATION

One other important issue surrounds the private or public nature of mortuary ritual practices and how these relate to Neolithic social and economic organisation. It has been proposed that the evidence provided by funerary ritual and the 'ritual equipment' found in settlements (e.g., figurines, models, etc.) indicate that ritual activities occurred within the context of the family and did not integrate the wider community (Demoule and Perlés 1993: 385-386). Thus, the performance of ritual falls within the domestic sphere of activities, and the control over ideological organisation was the responsibility of each household. Such an interpretation falls in line with Chapman's (1989) conclusion that the ideological focus of Neolithic society was on the village group and not a wider network of communities, and Hodder's (1984, 1990) view that the household was the centre of Neolithic life.

The Neolithic mortuary practices are ambiguous on this issue. At some sites, the location of graves near houses or

habitation areas (Franchthi, Nea Nikomedia, Lerna, Dimini, Agia Sophia, and Pevkakia) may indicate more direct connections with family of the dead. The intramural burials at Dimini and Agia Sophia provide better direct evidence that mortuary practices were a family responsibility. Similarly, the burial urn clusters noted at Zarkou may be organised according to genealogy, while the broader division of grave clusters into two groups may have been used to represent lineal associations. Alternatively, the tombs at Tharrounia and Kephala were probably built and used by families, but mortuary ritual incorporated the entire community. However, the mortuary rites conducted in caves (Aleopotrypa and perhaps Kitsos) appear to be more communal, continuing a pattern already seen in the LN at Skoteni.

We are left with several problems. Clearly, genetic analysis of Neolithic mortuary remains would help resolve the issues of tomb use. Also, there is no chronological pattern to this phenomenon: there is no apparent relationship between the elaborateness and locus of mortuary remains to patterns of increasing or decreasing population, resource competition, or settlement pattern. With the present data, it is a leap to conclude that individual families were responsible for mortuary treatment, had control over ritual practices, and that the wider community had no influence over the procession or scale of rites. It is difficult to imagine that rituals were not used as a means to express solidarity and identity in these small communities, or that rites were not performed in both domestic and communal loci. Only certain rites may have been performed in the house (e.g., those having to do with ancestors), while other rites requiring consensus of the broader community would have taken place in communal settings (legitimisation of status, like puberty or age-set rituals).

6.6   SOCIAL DIFFERENTIATION AND
INEQUALITY

Another area of considerable importance is the evidence for social differentiation expressed through mortuary activity. It has been suggested that there is a distinct lack of evidence for social inequality during the Neolithic. In this sample, only horizontal social differentiation was detected. In particular, key markers of vertical stratification were not obviously expressed in any of the mortuary samples.

For example, at Kephala there was the lack of correlation between the quantity of burial goods and energy expenditure. This indicates that social differentiation was not based upon vertical social stratification (Peebles and Kus 1977; Wason 1994). This pattern differs from that observed during the EBA, with which Kephala has been compared (Pullen 1985). While Kephala and some EBA

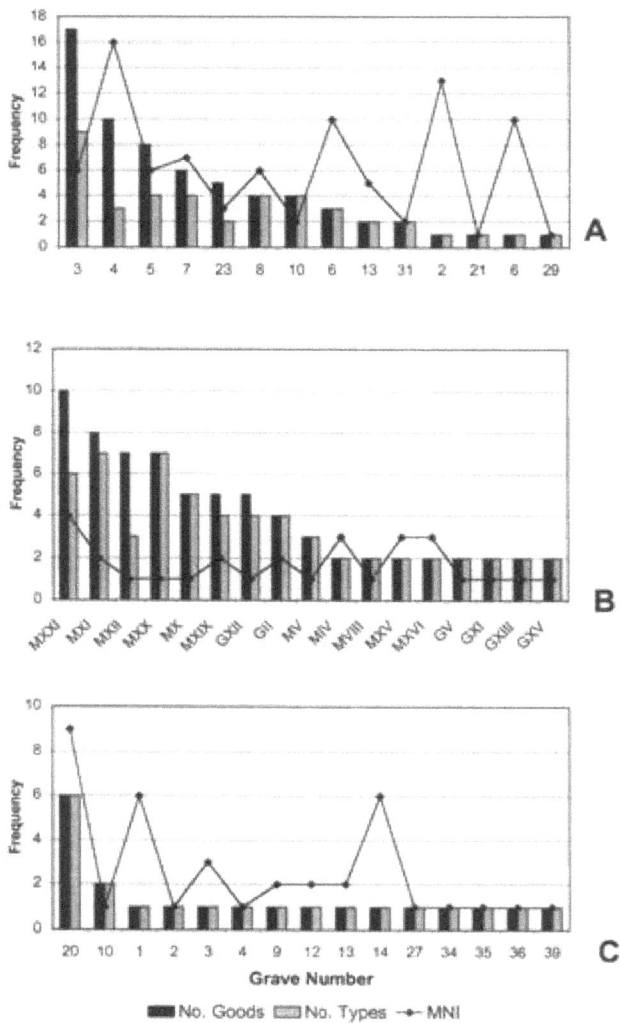

Figure 6.1. The number and types of grave goods in relation to the number of individuals in the graves at the Early Bronze Age sites of (A) Agios Kosmos and (B) Manika compared to (C) Final Neolithic Kephala. (EBA data from from Cosmopoulos 1991).

burials, in particular those in the Cyclades, have many of the same construction features in common, researchers have also differentiated these burials on the frequency of gifts given individuals (Doumas 1977; Renfrew 1972; Cosmopoulos 1991). Single burials in the EBA had more grave goods than multiple burials (Doumas 1977: 55-60), and many of the objects were domestic items (including jewellery and weapons in the EBA) not made specifically for inclusion in tombs (Cosmopoulos 1991, 1995). It has been argued that this aspect of EBA burial practices represents different wealth categories (Renfew 1977). If one compares the number different types of burial goods

in EBA tombs against the raw frequency of goods, the distribution of goods is not significantly different.

At Agios Kosmos (Fig. 6.1, A), for example, the graves with the most individuals do not always have the most goods or the highest diversity of artefacts when compared to single graves. At Manika (Fig. 6.1, B), the graves with the most people have lower numbers of goods and less diversity of artefact types than single graves, except for one grave (MXXI). The situation at Kephala is considerably different (Fig. 6.1, C). The grave with the most individuals (Grave 20) has the largest number of goods and greatest diversity of types, and single graves have the lowest diversity of artefact types. However, it not surprising to find more goods in multiple graves than in single ones simply because more people were interred there. A similar pattern was also reflected in the expenditure analysis. Clearly, wealth was either not a differentiating factor at Kephala (which is unlikely), or was not expressed in the disposal of the dead. Instead, Neolithic mortuary ritual tends to emphasise horizontal social positions that differentiate male versus female statuses, utilitarian or subsistence duties, and the social personae.

Also interesting is the evidence for single corporate groups during the Neolithic. Measured against the modifications to the Saxe-Goldstein hypotheses (Brown 1995), the mortuary complex at Prosymna, Aleopotrypa, Kitsos, Tharrounia, and Kephala met the null hypothesis that at least one corporate group occupied the site. Only at Tharrounia is there any secure evidence that the site was used by more than one corporate group.

Also significant is the possibility that ritual duties were expressed in the mortuary ritual at Franchthi and Kephala. The mortuary assemblage of one woman at EN-MN Franchthi suggests she may have been a potter, and following Vitelli's (1989, 1999) intriguing hypothesis, potting may be associated with shamanistic duties. At Kephala, the unusual mortuary complex of one adult man in the Lower Cemetery suggests he received a suite of symbols often associated with infants. The burial can also be associated with a female and ithyphallic figurine and a figurine 'necklace,' all of which may have had some ritual or symbolic importance (Talalay 1993). These data point towards the likelihood that both men and women held important ritual positions in Neolithic society.

These findings tend to support Cullen and Talalay's (1995) research indicating that men and women received considerably different treatments and males are not as visible in funerary samples as women. However, differentiation was not based upon the three distinctions they suggested: the location of their graves, their proximity to children's graves, and the type of grave goods they received. The first two distinctions actually combine one difference, the location of graves. In this sample, male:female distinctions were not based upon spatial location, although women were buried with children in a few of cases. However, this custom cannot be considered pervasive or common. Male:female differences are most visible in the types and quantity of grave goods received. Men seldom received any grave goods, and they only appear during the FN as prestige items (spondylus shell at FN Tharrounia?; a marble rhyton at Kephala), or as lithic and bone tools only associated with men. Women, in contrast, commonly received grave goods, which may generally reflect duties associated with women, such as potting textile-making, food-preparation), although we should keep in mind, however, there is no one-to-one correlation between these activities and women cross-culturally, and this may certainly be oversimplifying Neolithic reality. However, there are rather important exceptions on a case by case basis. As one example, at Kephala a women received a stone 'pillow' possibly symbolising her high status, while another woman can be directly associated with a rare marble bowl.

In contrast to these findings, it has been proposed that the mortuary practices at Agia Sophia represent individuals of high status, reflecting the rise of institutional elite during the LN (Halstead 1984). As further support of this idea, Halstead suggested that a child burial under a central structure provided evidence of hereditary status ascription. Clearly, the adult and child burials are considered in complete isolation from any other burial practices at the site, mainly because none has been found. The fact that these are intramural burials does not go against other mortuary practices known of the 'Dimini Culture' at this time. It is also possible to interpret this unusual mortuary complex from a non-hierarchical perspective, and I will limit this critique to three pertinent points.

First, societies without vertical stratification can also produce elaborate burials, with the reverse also being true (Carr 1995; O'Shea 1984). Second, interpretations like that of Agia Sophia ignore their intellectual roots in the Durkheimian enterprise where complexity is equated with hierarchy, privileging the search for vertical differentiation. These explanations stress that social complexity must ultimately be based upon the control over labour provided by a control over surplus, overlooking alternative explanations. Given the socio-economic and cultural-historical context of the 'Dimini Culture', it may also be useful to consider a variety of models that explore horizontal complexity (e.g., Arnold 1996; Blanton et al. 1995; Ehrenreich et al. 1996; McIntosh 1999a, 1999b; Morris 1997; Nelson 1994; Price and Feinman 1995; Stone 1997; Yoffe 1993). As one example, the elaborate burial of the Igbo Ukwu in West Africa—a man buried with elephant tusks, a copper crown, breastplate, anklets and staff, and over 100,000

imported glass and carnelian beads—may represent a high status title-holder within a non-hierarchically organised society (Shaw 1970).

Also, the pivotal role that belief systems play in the formation of new social groupings should be considered, especially when addressing periods of change during the Late Neolithic in Thessaly and the colonisation of the Cyclades in the Final Neolithic. Netting (1972:233), for example, argues that the new social groupings

> must be united, not by kinship or territory alone, but by belief, by the infinite extensibility of common symbols, shared cosmology, and the overarching unity of fears and hopes made visible in ritual. A leader who can mobilize these sentiments, who can lend concrete form to an amorphous moral community, is thereby freed from complete identification with his village or age group or lineage.

Yet, it is unknown how similar Dimini Culture burial practices are, and the limited data from Dimini and Agia Sophi provide little help. I believe that exploring these alternative explanations is one direction that future analyses of mortuary practices during the Neolithic in Greece must take. Practically, however, the quantity of Neolithic mortuary data and untapped potential of the osteological data must be made a priority.

6.7   CONCLUDING REMARKS

In this book, I have attempted to apply general observations arrived at through ethnographic studies of mortuary practices to archaeological case studies. These observations provided a framework within which to assess the plausibility that certain social directives and/or beliefs were driving mortuary behaviours at specific places in specific cultural-historical contexts during the Greek Neolithic. Rather than provide concrete answers to the motivations behind Neolithic mortuary practices, the procedure instead suggested a variety of alternative, but often complementary, explanations for these mortuary behaviours. I hope to have shown that grounding in the anthropological and sociological literature can give direction to the study of Greek Neolithic mortuary practices as a distinct line of inquiry in and of itself, but not, of course, one that should be undertaken in isolation. I also hoped to show that a detailed study of even poorly preserved or reported mortuary assemblages can have broader implications and can provide insights into a variety of cultural-historical, theoretical, and methodological issues. If this study instigates more detailed research of this potentially rich mortuary record than has been previously undertaken, then it has served its purpose. At the end, I return to paraphrase the quote that began this book: life during the Neolithic certainly continues to be full of riddles, but sometimes the dead do have answers.

REFERENCES CITED

Aschwadnden, H. (1982). *Symbols of Life: An Analysis of the Conciousness of the Karanaga*, Mamba Press, Gweru.

Allen, W.L., Richardson, J.B. (1971). The reconstruction of kinship from archaeological data: the concepts, the methods, and the feasibility. *American Antiquity* **36**: 41–53.

Alekshin, V.A. (1983). Burials customs as an archaeological source. *Current Anthropology* **24**: 137–150.

Ambrose, S.H. and M.A. Katzenberg (2001) (Eds.). *Biogeochemical Approaches to Paleodietary Analysis*, Kluwer Academic/Plenum Press, New York.

Andreou, S., Fotiadis, M., and Kotsakis, K. (1996). Review of Aegean Prehistory V: The Neolithic and Early Bronze Age of Northern Greece. *American Journal of Archaeology* **100**: 537–597.

Angel, J.L. (1950). Skeletons. *Archaeology* **3**: 233–241.

_____(1964). Osteoporosis: Thalassemia? *American Journal of Physical Anthropology* **22**:369–374.

_____(1966). Porotic hyperstosis, anemia, malarias and marshes in the prehistoric eastern Mediterranean. *Science* **153**:760–763.

_____(1967). Porotic hyperstosis or osteoporosis symmetrica, In Brothwell, D., and Sandison, A.T. (Eds.), *Diseases in Antiquity: A Survey of the Diseases, Injuries and Surgery of Early Populations*, Thomas, Springfield, pp. 378–389.

_____(1969). Appendix II. Human skeletal material from Franchthi Cave. *Hesperia* **38**:380–381.

_____(1972). Appendix B. Late Bronze Age Cypriotes from Bamboula: the skeletal remains. In Benson, J. (Ed.), *Bamboula at Kourion: The Necropolis and the Finds*, University of Pennsylvania Press, Philadelphia, pp. 148–158.

_____(1973). Neolithic human remains (Franchthi Cave). *Hesperia* **42**:277–282.

_____(1975). Palaeoecology, palaeodemography and health, In Plogar, S., (Ed.), *Population Ecology and Social Evolution*, Mouton, The Hague, pp. 167–190.

_____(1977). Appendix 5: Human skeletons. In Coleman, J.E., *Kephala. A Late Neolithic Settlement and Cemetery*, American School of Classical Studies, Princeton, N.J., pp. 133–156.

_____(1978). Porotic hyperstosis in the eastern Mediterranean. *Medical College of Virginia Quarterly* **14**:10–16.

_____(1984). Health as a crucial factor in the changes from hunting to developed farming in the eastern Mediterranean. In Cohen, M.N., and Armelgos, G.J. (Eds.), *Palaeopathology at the Origins of Agriculture*, Academic Press, Orlando, pp. 51–70.

Arnold, P. (1985). *Ceramic Theory and Cultural Process*, Cambridge University Press, Cambridge.

Arnold, J. (1996). (Ed.). *Emergent Complexity: The Evolution of Intermediate Societies*, International Monographs in Prehistory, Archaeological Series 9, Ann Arbor.

Beck, L.A. (1995) (Ed.). *Regional Approaches to Mortuary Analysis*. New York/London: Plenum Press.

Binford, L.R. (1962). *Archaeological investigations in the Carlyle Reservoir, Clinton County, Illinois*. Archaeological Salvage Report No. 17, Southwestern Illinois University Museum.

_____(1964). *Archaeological investigation on Wassam Ridge*. Archaeological Salvage Report 19, Southwestern Illinois University Museum.

_____(1971). Mortuary practices: their study and their potential. In Brown, J.A., (Ed.), *Approaches to the Social Dimensions of Mortuary Practices*, Memoirs of the Society for American Archaeology 25, Washington D.C., pp. 6–29.

_____(1972). *An archaeological perspective*. New York: Seminar Press.

Bintliff, J.L. (1977) *Natural Environment and Human Settlement in Prehistoric Greece, Based on Original Fieldwork*, British Archaeological Reports S28, Oxford.

Bintliff, J.L. and Snodgrass, A.M. (1985). The Cambridge/Bradford Boeotian Expedition: The first four years. *Journal of Field Archaeology* **12**:123–161.

Blanton, R., Feinman, G., Kowalewski, S., and Peregrine, P. (1996). A dual-processual theory for the evolution of Mesoamerican civilization. *Current Anthropology* **37**: 1–14.

Blegen, C.W. (1937). *Prosymna, the Helladic Settlement Preceding the Argive Heraeum*. Cambridge: Cambridge University Press.

Bloch, M. (1981). Tombs and states. In Humphreys, S.C. and King, H. (Eds), *Mortality and Immortality: The Anthropology and Archaeology of Death*, Acadmic Press, London/New York, pp. 137–147.

Boessneck, J. (1955). *Zu den Tierknochen aus neolithischen Siedlungen Thessaliens*. Bericht der Römisch–Germanischen Kommission 36:1–51.

_____(1962). Die Tierreste aus der Argissa–Maula vom präkeramischen Neolithikum bis zur mittlere Bronzeit. In Milojcic, V., Boessneck J., and Hopf, M. (Eds.), *Die deutschen Ausgrabungen auf der Argissa–Magula in Thessalien, I.* Das präkeramische Neolthikum sowie die Tier- und Pflanzenresete, pp. 27–99.

Bökönyi, S. (1986). Faunal remains. In Renfrew, C., Gimbutas, M., and Elster, E. (eds.), *Excavations at Sitagroi. A Prehistoric Village in Northeast Greece, Vol. 1*, Monumenta Archaeologica 13, UCLA, Institute of Archaeology, Los Angeles, pp. 63–96.

Bottema, S. (1990). Holocene environment of the Southern Argolid: a pollen core from Kiladha Bay. In T.J. Wilkinson and S. Duhon (Eds.), *Franchthi Paralia, The Sediments, Stratigraphy, and Offshore Investigations*, Excavations at Franchthi Cave, Greece, Facsimile 6, Indiana University Press, Bloomington/Indianapolis, pp. 117–138.

_____(1994). The prehistoric environment of Greece: a review of the palynological record. In Kardulias, P. Nick (ed.), *Beyond the Site: Regional Studies in the Aegean Area*, University Press of America, New York, pp. 45–68.

Braun D. (1979). Illinois Hopewell burial practices and social organization: A reexamination of the Klunk–Gibson mound group. In Brose, D., and Greber, N. (Eds.), *Hopewell Archaeology, the Chillicothe Conference*, Kent State University Press, Kent, Ohio, , pp. 66–79.

Broodbark, C. (1999). Colonization and configuration in the Insular Neolithic of the Aegean. In Halstead, P. (Ed.), *Neolithic Society in Greece*, Sheffield Studies in Archaeology 2, Sheffield Academic Press, Sheffield, pp. 15–41.

Broodbark, C. and Th. F. Strasser 1991. Migrant farmers and the Neolithic colonization of Crete. *Antiquity* 65:233–245.

Brown, J.A. (1971a). The dimensions of status in the burials at Spiro. In *Approaches to the Social Dimensions of Mortuary Practices*, Brown, J.A. (Ed.), Memoirs of the Society for American Archaeology 25, Washington D.C., pp. 92–112.

_____(1995). On mortuary analysis—with special reference to the Saxe-Binford Research program. In Beck, L.A. (ed.), *Regional Approaches to Mortuary Analysis*, Plenum Press, London/New York, pp, 3-26.

Buckley, H.R. (2000). Subadult health and disease in prehistoric Tonga, Polynesia. *American Journal of Physical Anthropology* 113:481–505.

Buikstra, J.E. (1977). Biocultual dimensions of archaeological study: A regional perspective. *Southern Anthropological Society, Proceedings 11.*

Buikstra, J.E. and Mark Swegle (1989). Bone modification due to burning: experimental evidence. In Bonnichsen, R., and Sorg, M.H. (Eds.), *Bone Modification*, Peopling of the Americas Publications Series, University of Maine, Orondo, Maine, pp. 247–258.

Burkert, W. (1987). *Ancient Mystery Cults*, Harvard University Press, Cambridge, Mass.

Cannon, Aubrey (1989). The historical dimension in mortuary expressions of status and sentiment. *Current Anthropology* 30:437–458.

Carr, C. (1995). Mortuary practices: Their social, philosophical-religious, circumstantial, and physical determinants. *Journal of Archaeological Method and Theory* 2:105–200.

Carr, C. and Maslowski, R. (1995). Cordage and fabrics: Relating form, technology, and social processes. In Carr, C., and Neitzel, J.E. (Eds.), *Style Society, and Person*, Plenum Press, New York, pp. 297–343.

Carrington Smith, J. (1977). Appendix 2: Cloth and mat impressions. In Coleman, J.D., *Keos I. Kephala*, American School of Classical Studies, Princeton, N.J., pp. 114–125.

Caskey, J.L. (1957). Excavations at Lerna, 1956. *Hesperia* 26:142–162.

_____(1958). Excavations at Lerna, 1957. *Hesperia* 27:125–144.

_____(1959). Activities at Lerna, 1958–1959. *Hesperia* 28:125–144.

_____(1964). Investigations in Keos, 1963. *Hesperia* 33:314–335.

Cauvin, J. (1992). A propos de l'ouvrage de C. Renfrew: L'énigme indoeuropéenne. Le modèle oriental de la diffusion néolithique. *Topoi. Orient–Occident* 2:91–106.

Chapman, R. (1981). The emergence of formal disposal areas and the 'problem' of megalithic tombs in Europe. In Chapman, R., Kinnes, I., and Randsborg, K. (Eds.), *The Archaeology of Death*, Cambridge University Press, Cambridge, pp. 71–81.

_____(1982). Autonomy, ranking and resources in Iberian prehistory. In Renfrew, C., and Shennan, S.J. (Eds.), *Ranking, Resource and Exchange*, Cambridge University Press, Cambridge, pp. 46–51.

_____(1989). The early Balkan village. In Bökönyi, S. (Ed.), *Neolithic of SE Europe and its Eastern Connections*, Varia Archaeologica Hungarica II, Budapest, pp. 33–53.

Chapman, R. and Randsborg, K. (1981). Approaches to the archaeology of death In Chapman, R., Kinnes, I., and Randsborg, K. (Eds.), *The Archaeology of Death*, Cambridge University Press, Cambridge, pp. 1–24.

Charles, D.K., and Buikstra, J.E. (1983). Archaic mortuary sites in the Central Mississippi Drainage: Distribution, structure, and behavioral implications. In: Phillips, J.L., and Brown, J.A. (Eds.), *Archaic Hunters and Gatherers in the American Midwest*, Academic Press, New York, pp. 117–145.

Cherry, J.F. (1981). Pattern and process in the earliest colonization of the Mediterranean islands. *Proceedings of the Prehistoric Society* 47:41–68.

_____(1990). The first colonization of the Mediterranean islands: a review of recent research. *Journal of Mediterranean Archaeology* 3:145–221.

Cherry, J.F., Davis, J.L., Demitrack, A., Mantzourani, E., Strasser, Th., and Talalay, L. (1988). Archeological survey in an artifact–rich landscape: a Middle Neolithic example from Nemea, Greece. *American Journal of Archaeology* 92:159–176.

Coleman, J.E. (1977). *Keos I. Kephala, A Late Neolithic Settlement and Cemetery*, American School of Classical Studies, Princeton, N.J.

Cosmopoulos, M.B. (1991). *The Early Bronze 2 in the Aegean*, Studies in Mediterranean Archaeology XCVIII, Paul Åströms Förlag, Jonsered.

Cosmopoulos, M.B. (1995). Social and political organization in the Early Bronze 2 Aegean. In Laffineur, R. and Niemeier, W-D. (Eds.), *Politeia: Society and State in the Aegan Bronze Age, Aegeum* 12: 23–32.

Cresswell, R. 1976. Avant-propos. *Techniques et Culture* 1: 5–6.

Cullen, Tracy (1985a). *A Measure of Interaction among Neolithic Communities: Design Elements of the Greek Urfinis Pottery*. Doctoral dissertation, Program in Classical Archaeology, University of Indiana, Bloomington.

_____(1985b). Social implications of ceramic style in the Neolithic Peloponnese. In Kingery, W.E. (Ed.), *Ancient Technology to Modern Science*, The American Ceramic Society, Columbus, pp. 77–100.

_____(1995). Mesolithic mortuary ritual at Franchthi Cave, Greece. *Antiquity* 69: 270–289.

Cullen, Tracy and Lauren Talalay 1995: Recovering gender in the Greek Neolithic: a viable goal? *American Journal of Archaeology* 99:333 [Abstract].

Cummings, M.R. (1991). *Human Heredity: Principles and Issues*, Second Edition, West Publishing Company, New York.

Darcque, P. (1990). Pour l'abandon du terme "megaron." In. Darque, P., and Treuil, R. (Eds.), *L'habitat égée préhistorique*, Ecole Française d'Athénes, de Boccard, Paris, pp. 21–31.

David, N. (1992a). The archaeology of ideology: Mortuary practices in the Central Mandara Highlands, Northern Cameroon. In Sterner, J., and David, N. (Eds.), *An African Commitment. Papers in Honour of Peter Lewis Shinnie*, University of Calgary Press, Calgary, pp. 181–210.

_____(1992b). Integrating ethnoarchaeology: A subtle realist perspective. *Journal of Anthropological Archaeology* 11: 330-59.

David, N., Sterner, J., and Gavua, K. (1988). Why pots are decorated. *Current Anthropology* 29:365–389.

Davis, J.L. (1992). Review of Aegean prehistory I: The islands of the Aegean. *American Journal of Archaeology* 96:699–756.

Demoule, J.-P., Gallis, K., and Manolakakis, L. (1988). Transition entre les cultures nèolithiques de Sesklo et de Dimin; les catégories céramiques. *Bulletin Correspondance Hellénique* 112:1–58.

Demoule, J–P. and Perlès, C. (1993). The Greek Neolithic: a new review. *Journal of World Prehistory* 7:355–416.

Diamant, S.R. (1974). The Later Village Farming State in Southern Greece. Unpublished doctoral dissertation. Department of Anthropology, University of Pennsylvania, Philadelphia.

Dickinson, O.T.P.K. (1994). *The Aegean Bronze Age*, Cambridge University Press, Cambridge.

Doumas, C.G. (1977). *Early Bronze Age Burial Habits in the Cyclades*, Studies in Mediterranean Archaeology 48, Paul Åströms Förlag, Göteborg.

Duday, H. and Lambert, N. (1981). *La Grotte Préhistorique de Kitsos (Attique), missions 1968–1978*, ADPF–Ecole Français d'Athèns, Paris.

Ehrenreich, R., Crumley, C., Levy, J. (1995) (Eds.) *Heterarchy and the Analysis of Complex Socieities*, Archaeological Papers of the American Anthropological Association 6, Washington, D.C.

Elia, R.J. (1982). *A Study of the Neolithic Architecture of Thessaly, Greece*. Doctoral dissertation, Department of Archaeology, Boston University, Boston.

Elster, E. (1989). The chipped stone industries. In Gimbutas, M, Winn, Sh., and Shimabuku, D., (Eds.), *Achilleion, A Neolithic Settlement in Thessaly, Greece, 6,400–5,600 B.C.*, UCLA Monumenta Archaeologica 14, Los Angeles, pp. 273–306.

Emerson, T.E. (1989). Water, serpents, and the underworld: An exploration into Cahokian symbolism. In: Galloway, P. (Ed.), *Southern Ceremonial Complex: Artifacts and Analysis: The Cottonlandia Conference*, University of Nebraska Press, Lincoln, pp. 45–92.

Evans, J.D. and Colin Renfrew (1968). *Excavations at Saliagos near Antiparos*. The British School at Athens, Supplementary Volume 5, Thames and Hudson, Oxford.

Flannery, K.V. and Marcus, J. (1996). Cognitive archaeology. In Preucel, R.W., and Hodder, I. (Eds.), *Contemporary Archaeology in Theory: A Reader*, Blackwell, Oxford, pp. 350–363.

Fotiadis, M. (1987). Kitrini Limni, Momou Kozanis, 1987. Proistoriki erevna. *To Archaiologiko Ergo sti Makedonia kai Thraki*, 1, Thessaloniki, pp. 51–61.

_____(1988). Proistoriki erevna stin Kitrini Limni, N. Kozanis, 1988. Mia syntomi ekthesi. *To Archaiologiko Ergo sti Makedonia kai Thraki*, 2, Thessaloniki, pp. 41–51.

Fowler, K.D. (1997). *Status and Society during the Greek Neolithic: A Multi-dimensional Approach to the Study of Mortuary Remains*. MA Thesis, Department of Anthropology, Winnipeg.

_____(2002). Monitoring mortuary ritual: a multi-dimensional approach to mortuary differentiation and social distinctions. In Lesick, C., Kulle, B., Cluney, C., Peuramaki-Brown, M., (Eds.), *Eureka! The Archaeology of Innovation and Science*, Proceedings of the 27th Annual Chacmool Conference, The Archaeological Association of the University of Calgary, Calgary, pp. 378–391.

_____. (In press). Late historic settlement pattern and agricultural land use in Kalamos, Attica, Greece: implications for anthropological and archaeological research. In Fossey, J. (Ed.), *Proceedings of the Ninth International Conference on Boiotian Antiquities, Winnipeg, Manitoba, October 1998*, Ares Press, Chicago.

French, D. (1972). Notes on prehistoric pottery groups from Central Greece. Manuscript on file at the British School of Archaeology, Athens.

Frierman, J. (1969). Appendix II. The Balkan Graphite ware. In Renfrew, C. (Ed.), The autonomy of the South–East European Copper Age, *Proceedings of the Prehistoric Society 35*, pp. 42–44.

Gallis, K. (1975). Karseis necron apo tin archaioteran neolithikin epohin eis tin Thessalian. *Athens Annals of Archaeology* **8**:241–258.

_____(1979). Cremation burials from the Early Neolithic in Thessaly. In Decourt, J.-C., Helly, B., and Gallis, K. (eds.), *La Thessalie: Actes de la Table–Ronde, 21–24 Juillet 1975, Lyon*, Collection de la maison de l'Orient Méditerranéen No.6, Série Archéologique 5, Maison de L'Orient, Paris, pp. 65–79.

_____(1982). *Kafseis Nekron apo tin Neolithiki Epochi sti Thessalia*. Ekdosi Tameiou archaeiologikon poron ka apallotrioseon, Athens.

_____(1985). A Late Neolithic foundation offering from Thessaly. *Antiquity* **59**:20–24.

_____(1989). Atlas proistorikon oikismon tis anatolikis thessalikis pediadas. *Thessaliko Imerologio* **16**:6–144.

Giddens, A. (1979). *Central Problems in Social Theory: Action, Structure and Contradiction in Social Analysis*, Allen and Unwin, London.

Gifford, J.A. (1990). Analysis of submarine sediments off Paralia, in Wilkinson, T.J., and Duhon, S. (eds.), *Franchthi Paralia, The Sediments, Stratigraphy, and Offshore Investigations*, Excavations at Franchthi Cave, Greece 6, Indiana University Press, Bloomington/Indianapolis, pp. 85–116.

Gimbutas, M. (1989). Figurines and cult equipment: their role in the reconstruction of Neolithic religion. In Gimbutas, M., Winn, Sh., and Shimabuku, D. (Eds.), *Achilleion, A Neolithic Settlement in Thessaly, Greece, 6,400–5,600 B.C.*, UCLA Monumenta Archaeologica 14, Los Angeles, pp. 251–258.

Gimbutas, M., Winn, Sh., and Shimabuku, D. (1989). *Achilleion, A Neolithic Settlement in Thessaly, Greece, 6,400–5,600 B.C.*, UCLA, Monumenta Archaeologica 14, Los Angeles.

Goldstein, L.G. (1976). *Spatial Structure and Social Organization: Regional Manifestations of Mississippian Society*. Doctoral dissertation, Department of Anthropology, Northwestern University. Ann Arbor: University Microfilms.

_____(1980). *Mississippian Mortuary Practices: A Case Study of Two Cemeteries in the Lower Illinois Valley*. Evanston, Illinois: Northwestern Archaeological Program.

_____(1981). One–dimensional archaeology and multi–dimensional people: spatial organization and mortuary analysis. In Chapman, R., Kinnes, I., and Randsborg, K. (Eds.), *The Archaeology of Death*, Cambridge University Press, Cambridge, pp. 53–69.

Greenfield, H.J. (1986). *The Palaeoeconomy of the Central Balkans (Serbia): An zooarchaeological perspective on the Late Neolithic and Bronze Age (4500–1000 B.C.)*. British Archaeological Reports International Series 304, Oxford.

_____(1991). A kula ring in prehistoric Europe? A consideration of local and interregional exchange during the Late Neolithic of the central Balkans. In Gregg, S.A. (Ed.), *Between Bands and States*, Centre for Archaeological Investigations, Occasional Paper No. 9, Carbondale, pp. 287–308.

Greenfield, H.J. and K.D. Fowler (2003). Megalo Nisi Galanis and the secondary products revolution in Macedonia. In Kotjabopoulou, E., Hamilakis, Y., Halstead, P., Gamble, C., and Elefanti, P. (Eds.), *Zooarchaeology in Greece: Recent Advances*, British School at Athens Studies 9, pp. 133-144.

Gropengiesser. H. 1986. Siphnos, Kap Agios Sostis: Keramische prähistoriche Zeugnisse aus dem Grube– und Hüttenrevier. *Athenische Mitteilungen* 101:1–39.

Gruber, J.W. (1971). Patterning in death in a late prehistoric Village in Pennsylvania. *American Antiquity* **36**: 64–76.

Hall, R.L. (1979). In search of the ideology of the Adena-Hopewell Climax. In: Brose, D.S., and Breber, N. (Eds.), *Hopewell Archaeology: The Chllicoth Conference*, Kent State University Press, Kent, OH, pp. 258–265.

_____(1983). A pan-continental perspective on Red Ochre and Glacial Kame cremonialism. In Dunnell, R.C., and Grayson, D.K. (Eds.), *Lulu Linear Punctates: Essays in Honor of George Irving Quimby*, Anthropological Papers 72, University of Michigan Museum of Anthropology, Ann Arbor, pp. 74–107.

Halstead, P. (1981). Counting sheep in Neolithic and Bronze Age Greece. In Hodder, I, Issac, G., and Hammond, N. (Eds.), *Patterns of the Past. Studies in Honor of David Clarke*, Cambridge University Press, Cambridge, pp. 307–339.

_____(1984). *Strategies for Survival: An Ecological Approach to Social and Economic Change in Early Farming Communities of Thessaly, Northern Greece.* Doctoral dissertation, University of Cambridge, Cambridge.

_____(1987). Man and other animals in later Greek prehistory. *Annual of the British School in Athens* **82**:71–83.

_____(1989). The economy has a normal surplus: economic stability and social change among early farming communities of Thessaly, Greece. In Halstead, P, O'Shea, J. (Eds.), *Bad Year Economics: Cultural Responses to Risk and Uncertainty*, Cambridge University Press, Cambridge, pp. 68–80.

_____(1992). Dimini and the DMP: faunal remains and animal exploitation in Late Neolithic Thessaly. *Annual of the British School in Athens* **87**:44–55.

_____(1999a). Neighbours from Hell? The household in Neolithic Greece. In Halstead, P. (Ed.), *Neolithic Society in Greece*, Sheffield Studies in Archaeology 2, Sheffield Academic Press, pp. 77–95.

_____1999b. (Ed.) *Neolithic Society in Greece*, Sheffield Studies in Archaeology 2, Sheffield Academic Press.

Halstead, P. and G. Jones (1987). Bioarchaeological remains from Kalythies Cave, Rhodes. In Sampson, A. (Ed.), *I Neolithiki Periodos sta Dodekanisa*, Ekdosi tou Tameiou Arhaiologikon poron kai appallotrioseon, Athens, pp. 135–145.

Hansen, J.M. (1988). Agriculture in the prehistoric Aegean: data versus speculation. *American Journal of Archaeology* **92**:39–52.

_____(1991). *The Palaeoethnobotany of Franchthi Cave*, Excavations at Franchthi Cave, Greece 7, Indiana University Press, Bloomington.

_____(1994). Palaeoethnobotany in a regional perspective. In Kardulas, P.N. (Ed.), *Beyond the Site: Regional Studies in the Aegean Area*, University Press of America, New York, pp. 173–190.

Hauptmann, H. (1981). *Die deutschen Ausgrabungen auf der Otzaki-Magula in Thessalien. III. Das späte Neolithikum und das Chalkolithikum*, Beiträge zur ur–und frügeschichtlichen Archaeologie des Mittelmeer–Kulturraumes 9, Rudolf Habelt, Bonn.

Hauptmann, H. and V. Milojĉić (1969). *Die Funder der frühen Dimini–Zeit aus der Arapi–Magula, Thessalien*, Beiträge zur ur–und frügeschichtlichen Archaeologie des Mittelmeer–Kulturraumes 9, Rudolf Habelt, Bonn.

Hayden, B. (2001). Funerals as feasts: Why are they so important? Paper presented at the 2001 SAA Annual Meetings, New Orleans. Report on-line at www2.sfu.ca/archaeology/dept/fac_bio/hayden/reports/faf.pdf. Accessed 22.04.04.

Hayden, B. and Cannon, A. (1982). The corporate group as an archaeological unit. *Journal of Anthropological Archaeology* **1**: 132–158.

Hershkovitz, I., Rothschild, B.M., Latimer, B., Dutour, O., Léonetti, Greenwald, C.M., Rothschild, C. Jellema, L.M. (1997). Recognition of sickle cell anemia in skeletal remains of children. *American Journal of Physical Anthropology* **104**:213–226.

Hertz, R. (1907). Contribution a une étude sur la representation collective de la mort. *Année Sociologique* **10**: 48–137.

_____(1960). *Death and the right hand.* Translated by R. Needham and C. Needham. Glencoe, Ill.: Free Press.

Hinz, G. 1979. *Neue Tierknochenfunde aus der Magula Pevkakia in Thessalien. I: Die Nichtweiderkäuer.* Doctoral dissertation, Munich.

Hodder, Ian (1982b). *The Present Past: An Introduction to Anthropology for Archaeologists*, Batsford, London.

_____(1982c). *Symbolic and Structural Archaeology*, Cambridge University Press, Cambridge.

_____(1984). Burials, houses, women and men in the European Neolithic. In Miller, D., and Tilley, C. (Eds.), *Ideology, power and prehistory*, Cambridge University Press, Cambridge, pp. 51–68.

_____(1986). *Reading the Past: Current Approaches to Interpretation in Archaeology*, Second Edition, Cambridge University Press, Cambridge.

_____(1990). *The Domestication of Europe*, Blackwell, Oxford.

Holland, T.D. and O'Brien, M.J. (1997). Parasites, porotic hyperostosis, and the implications of changing perspectives. *American Antiqutiy* 62: 183–193.

Hourmouziadis, G.A. (1971). Dio neai egkatastaseis tis archaiotera Neolithikis eis tin dytikin Thessalian. *Athens Annals of Archaeology* 4: 164–175.

_____(1973). Burial customs. In Theocharis, D.R. (Ed.), *Neolithic Greece*, National Bank of Greece, Athens, pp. 210–212.

_____(1974). *I Anthpomorphi Eidoloplakstiki tis Neolithikis Thessalias*, Etaireia Thessalikon Erevnon, Athens.

_____(1977). Ena eidikevmeno ergstirio kerameikis sto neolithiki Dimini. *Athens Annals of Archaeology* 10:207–226.

_____(1979). *To Neolithiko Dimini*, Etairia Thessalikon Erevnon, Volos.

Huntington, R. and P. Metcalf (1979). *Celebrations of Death*, Cambridge University Press, Cambridge.

Huss-Ashmore, R., Goodman, A.H., and Armelagos, G. (1982). Nutritional inference from paleopathology. *Advances in Archaeological Method and Theory* 5: 395–473.

Jackes, M. (1988). Demographic change at the Mesolithic–Neolithic transition: evidence from Portugal. *Rivista di Antropologia* (Roma), Supplemento del Vol. LXVI, pp. 141–158.

Jacobsen, T.W. (1969). Excavations at Proto Cheli and vicinity, preliminary report II: the Franchthi Cave, 1967–1968. *Hesperia* 38:343–381.

_____(1973a). Excavation in the Franchthi Cave, 1969–1971, part I. *Hesperia* 42:45–88.

_____(1973b). Excavations in the Franchthi Cave, 1968–1971, part II. *Hesperia* 42:253–283.

_____(1976). 17,000 years of Greek prehistory. *Scientific American* 234:76–87.

_____(1979). Excavations at Franchthi Cave, 1973–1974. *Archaeologikon Deltion* (Chronika) 29:268–82

_____(1981). Franchthi Cave and the beginning of settled village life in Greece. *Hesperia* 50:303–319.

_____(1984a). Investigations at Franchthi Cave. *Archaeologikon Deltion* (Chronika) 31:75–78.

_____(1984b). Seasonal pastoralism in Southern Greece: A consideration of the ecology of Neolithic Urfirnis pottery. In Rice, P.M. (Ed.), *Pots and Potters: Current Approaches in Ceramic Archaeology*, UCLA Institute of Archaeology, Monograph 24, Los Angeles, pp. 27–43.

Jacobsen, T.W. and Cullen, T. (1981). A consideration of mortuary practices in Neolithic Greece: burials from Franchthi Cave. In Humphyreys, S.C. and Kingery, H. (Eds.), *Mortality and Immortality: The Anthropology and Archaeology of Death*, Academic Press, London, pp. 79–101.

Jacobsen, T.W. and Farrand, J. (1987). *Franchthi Cave and Paralia: Maps, Plans, and Sections*, Excavations at Franchthi Cave, Greece 1, Indiana University Press, Bloomington.

Jones, R.E. (1986). *Greek and Cypriot Pottery. A Review of Scientific Studies*, Fitch Laboratory Occasional Paper 1, The British School at Athens, Athens.

Katzenberg, M.A. and S.R. Saunders (2000) (Eds.). *Biological Anthropology of the Human Skeleton*, Wiley-Liss, John Wiley & Sons, New York.

Kent, S. (1999). The archaeological visibility of storage: delineating storage from trash areas. *American Antiquity* 64:79–94.

Kolodny, A. (1974). *La populaton des Iles de la Gréce essai de géographies insulaire en Méditerrané orientale*, Centre National de la Recherche Scientifique, Aix–de–Provence.

Kosmopoulos, L.W. (1948). *The Prehistoric Inhabitation of Corinth, Vol. 1*, München Verlag Bisher F. Bruckmann, Munich.

Kotjabopoulo, E. and Trantalidou, K. (1993). Faunal analysis of the Skoteni Cave. In Sampson, A., *Skoteni, Tharrounia: the cave, the settlement and the cemetery*, Athens, pp. 392–434.

Kotsakis, K. (1983). *Kerameiki technologia kai kerameiki diaforopoiisi. Provlimata tis graptis kerameikis tis mesis epohis tou Sesklou*, Didaktoriki Diatrivi, Thessaloniki.

Kottack, C. (1974). *Anthropology: The Exploration of Human Diversity*, Random House, New York.

Kroeber, A. L. (1927): Disposal of the dead. *American Anthropologist* 29:308–315.

Lambert, N. (1972). Grotte d'Alépotrypa (Magne). *Bulletin de Correspondance Hellénique* 96:845–871.

_____(Ed.) (1981). *La Grotte Préhistorique de Kitsos (Attique), missions 1968–1978*, ADPF–Ecole Français d'Athèns, Paris.

Larje, R. (1987). Animal bones. In Helström, P., *Paradeisos. A Late Neolithic Settlement in Aegean Thrace*, Medelhavsmuseet, Memoir 7, Stockholm, pp 89–118.

Larsen, C.S. (1995). Biological changes in human populations with agriculture. *Annual Review of Anthropology* **24**: 185–213.

Leach, E. (1982). *Social Anthropology*, Oxford University Press, New York/Oxford.

Lemonnier, P. (1986). The study of material culture today: Toward an anthropology of technical systems. *Journal of Anthropological Archaeology* **5**: 147–186.

_____(1992). *Elements for an Anthropology of Technology*, Anthropological Papers, Museum of Anthropology 88, University of Michigan, Ann Arbor.

Little, B.J., Lanphear, K.M., and Owsley, D.W. (1992). Mortuary display and status in a Nineteenth Century Anglo-American cemetery in Manassas, Virginia. *American Antiquity* **57**: 397–418.

McGeehan–Liritzis, V. and Gale, H.H. (1988). Chemical and lead isotope analyses of Greek Late Neolithic and Early Bronze Age metals. *Archaeometry* **30**:199–255.

McGrew, W.W. (1985): *Land and Reunification in Modern Greece, 1800–1881: The Transition of the Tenure and Exploitation of Land from Ottoman Rule to Independence*, Kent State University Press, Kent, OH.

McGuire, R.H. (1992). *Death, Society, and Ideology in a Hohokam Community*, Westview Press, Boulder, CO.

McIntosh, R. (1989). Middle Niger terracottas before the Symplegades Gateway. *African Arts* **22**:74–83.

McIntosh, S.K. (Ed.). (1999a). *Beyond Chiefdoms: Pathways to Complexity in Africa*, Cambridge University Press, Cambridge.

McIntosh, S.K. (1999b). Pathways to complexity: An African perspective. In: McIntosh, S.K. (Ed.), *Beyond Chiefdoms: Pathways to Complexity in Africa*, Cambridge University Press, Cambridge, pp. 1–30.

McNeill, William H. (1978), *The Metamorphosis of Greece since World War II*, University of Chicago Press, Chicago/London.

Maniatis, Y. and M.S. Tite (1981). Technological examination of Neolithic–Bronze Age pottery from Central and Southeast Europe and from the Near East. *Journal of Archaeological Science* **8**: 59–76.

Mauss, M. (1935). Les techniques due corps. *Journal du Psychologie* **32**: 271–293.

Meiklejohn, C., and Zvelebil, M. (1991). Health status of European population at the agricultural transition and the implications for the adoption of farming. In Bush, H., and Zvelebil, M. (Eds.), *Health in Past Societies: Biocultural Interpretations of Human Skeletal Remains in Archaeological Contexts*, BAR Publishing, BAR International Series 567, pp. 129–145.

Merrifield, R. (1987). *The Archaeology of Ritual and Magic*, B.T. Batsford Ltd, London.

Miller, M. 1995. The production of personal ornaments and craft specialization in the Greek Neolithic. *American Journal of Archaeology* **93**:333 [Abstract].

Milojĉić, V.J. (1955). Vorbericht über die Ausgrabungen auf der Otzaki-Magula 1954. *Archäologischer Anzieger* **70**: 157–182.

Milojĉić, V.J., Boessneck, J., and Hopf, M. (1962). *Die deutschen Ausgrabungen auf der Argissa–Magula in Thessalien, I. Das präkeramische Neolithikum sowie die Tier– und Pflanzenresete*, Beiträge zur ur– und frühgeschichtlichen Archäologie des Mittelmeer–Kulturraumes 2, Rudolf Habelt, Bonn.

Milojĉić, V.J., von den Driesch, A., Enderle, K., Milojĉić-v. Zumbusch, J., and Kilian, K. (1976). *Die deutschen Ausgrabungen auf Magulen um Larisa in Thessalien 1966. Argissa–Magula, Karagyös Magula, Bunar Baschi*, Beiträge zur ur– und frühgeschichtlichen Archäologie des Mittelmeer–Kulturraumes 15, Rudolf Habelt, Bonn.

Morris, I. (1997). An archaeology of equalities? The Greek city-states. In Nichols, D.L., and Charlton, T.H. (Eds.), *The Archaeology of City-States*, Smithsonian Institution Press, Washington D.C., pp. 91–106.

Mottier, Y. (1981). *Die deutschen Ausgrabungen auf der Otzaki–Magulain Thessalien, I: Das Mittlere Neolithikum*, Beiträge zur ur– und frühgeschichtlichen Archäologie des Mittelmeer–Kulturraumes 15, Rudolf Habelt, Bonn.

Moundrea–Agrafioti, H.A. (1980). Palaioethnologika simperasmata apo ti meleti ton lithinou kai osteïnon ergaleion tou neolithikou oikismou Prodromou Karditsas. Praktika apo to A'synedrio thessalikon spoudon. *Thessalika Chronika* **13**: 489–497.

_____(1981). *La Thessalie du sud–est au Néolithique: outillage lithique et osseux*. Unpublished doctoral dissertation, Department of Ethnology, University of Paris, Paris.

_____(1987). Problémes d'emmanchement dans le Neolithique grec: les gaines et manches en bois de cervidé. In Stordeur, D. (ed.), *Le Main et l'outil. Manches et emmanchements préhistriquies*, Maison de L'Orient, Lyon, pp. 247–256.

Morphy, H. (1994). The interpretation of ritual: Reflections from film on anthropological practice. *Mar* (N.S.) **29**:117–146.

Murphy, R.F. (1989). *Cultural and Social Anthropology: An Overture*, Third Edition, Prentice-Hall, Englewood Cliffs, N.J.

Myrick, D.C., and Watucki, A. (1971). *How Greece Developed its Agriculture*, Foreign Agricultural Economic Report No. 67, Economic Research Service, U.S. Department of Agriculture, Washington D.C.

Nanaglou, S. (2001). Social and monumental space in Neolithic Thessaly, Greece. *European Journal of Archaeology* **4**:303–322.

Nelson, B. (1994) (Ed.) *The Ancient Southwest Community*, University of New Mexico Press, Albuquerque.

Netting, R. (1972). Sacred power and centralization: Aspects of political adaptation in Africa. In Spooner, B., (Ed.), *Population Growth: Anthropological Implications*, MIT Press, Cambridge, pp. 219–244.

O'Shea, J.M. (1981). Social configurations and the archaeological study of mortuary practices: A case study. In Chapman, R., Kinnes, I., and Randsborg, K. (Eds.), *The Archaeology of Death*, Cambridge University Press, Cambridge, pp. 39–52.

_____(1984). *Mortuary Variability: An Archaeological Investigation*, Academic Press, New York.

Orphian dis-Georgiadis, L. (1981). *Les pratiques funéraires à l'époque néolithique en Grèce et en Anatolie*, Ph.D. dissertation, Université de Sorbonne, Paris.

Ortner, D.J., and Putschar, W.G.J. (1981). Indentification of pathological conditions in human skeletal remains. *Smithsonian Contribution to Anthropology* **28**: 1–54.

Otto, B. 1985. *Die verzierte Keramik der Sesklo– und Diminikultur Thessaliens*, Philipp von Zabern, Mainz.

Owsley, D.W., Berryman, H.E., and Bass, W.M. (1977). Demographic and osteological evidence for warfare at the Larson site, South Dakota. *Plains Anthropologist Memoir* **13**: 22–78 (Part 1), 119–132 (Part 2).

Papathanasopoulos, G.A. (1971). Archailogika Chronika. Spilaia Dirou, 1971. *Athens Annals of Archaeology* **4**:289–304.

Pappa, M. and Besios, M. (1999a). The Makriyalos Project: Rescue excavations at the Neolithic site of Makriyalos, Pieria, Northern Greece. In Halstead, P. (Ed.), *Neolithic Society in Greece*, Sheffield Studies in Archaeology 2, Sheffield Academic Press, Sheffield pp. 108–120.

Pappa, M. and Besios, M. (1999b). The Neolithic settlement at Makriyalos, Northern Greece: Preliminary report on the 1993-1995 excavations. *Journal of Field Archaeology* **26**:177–195.

Parker Pearson, M. (1982). Mortuary practices, society and ideology: an ethnoarchaeological study. In Hodder, I. (Ed.), *Symbolic and Structural Archaeology*, Cambridge University Press, Cambridge, pp. 99–113.

_____(1984). Economic and ideological change: Cyclical growth iun the pre-state societies of Jutland. In Miller D., and Tilley, C. (Eds.), *Ideology, Power, and Prehistory*, Cambridge University Press, Cambridge, pp. 69–72.

Peebles, C., and S. Kus (1977). Some archaeological correlates of ranked societies. *American Antiquity* **42**:421–448.

Pelapsis, A.A., and Thompson, K. (1960). Agriculture in a restrictive environment: The case of Greece. *Economic Geography* **36**:145–157.

Penney, D. (1985). Continuities of imagery and symbolism in the art of the Woodlands. In Brose, D., Brown, J.A., and D.W. Penney (Eds), *Ancient Art of the American Woodland Indians*, Harry Abrams, New York, pp. 147–198.

Perlès, C. (1990). *Les industries lithiques taillées de Franchthi (Argolide, Grèce) II: les industries du mésolithique et du néolithique initial*, Excavations at Franchthi Cave. Greece 5, Indiana University Press, Bloomington.

_____(1992). Systems of exchange and organization of production in Neolithic Greece. *Journal of Mediterranean Archaeology* **5**:115–164.

Perlès, C., and Vaughan, P. (1983). Pièces lustrées, travail des plantes et moissons à Franchthi (Xème–IVème mill. B.C.). In Cauvin, M.–C. (Ed.), *Traces d'utilisation sur les outils néolithiques du Proche–Orient*, Maison de L'Orient, Lyon, pp. 209–229.

Perlès, C., and Vitelli, K.D. (1999). Craft specialization in the Neolithic of Greece. In Halstead, P. (Ed.), *Neolithic Society in Greece*, Sheffield Studies in Archaeology 2, Sheffield Academic Press, Sheffield, pp. 96–107.

Phelps, W.W. (1975). *The Neolithic Pottery Sequence in Southern Greece*. Doctoral dissertation, Institute of Archaeology, London.

_____(1981–1982). Three Peloponnesian Neolithic problems. In *Praktika B' Diethnouse synedriou peloponnisiakon spoudon*, Athens, pp. 363–372.

Pilali-Papasterio, A., and Papaevthimiou-Papanthimou, E. (1989). Nees anaskafikez erevnes sto Mandalo D. Makedonia. *Egnatia* **1**:17–27.

116

Price, T.D., Schoeninger, M.J., and Armelagos, G.J. (1985). Bone chemistry and past behaviour: An overview. *Journal of Human Evolution* **14**: 419–447.

Pullen, D. 1985. Social Organization in Early Bronze Age Greece: A Multi–dimensional Approach. Doctoral dissertation, Indiana University, University Microfilms (8516653).

Ravesloot, J.C. (1988). *Mortuary Practices and Social Differentiation at Casas Grandes, Chihuahua, Mexico*, University of Arizona Anthropological Papers 49. University of Arizona Press, Tempe.

Renfrew, Colin (1972). *The Emergence of Civilization: The Cyclades and the Aegean in the Third Millennium B.C.*, Methuen and Co., Ltd, London.

_____(1973). Trade and craft specialization. In Theocharis, D.R., *Neolithic Greece*, National Bank of Greece, Athens, pp. 179–191.

_____(1984). Trade as action at a distance. In Renfrew, C. (ed.), *Approaches to Social Archaeology*, Harvard University Press, Cambridge, pp. 86–134.

Renfrew, C., Gimbutas, M., and Elster, e. (Eds.) (1986). *Excavations at Sitigroi. A Prehistoric Village in Northeast Greece, Vol. 1*, Institute of Archaeology, Monumenta Archaeologica 13, UCLA, Lost Angeles.

Ridley, C. and Wardel, K.A. (1979). Rescue excavations at Servia 1971–1973: A preliminary report. *Annual of the British School at Athens* **74**: 185–226.

Rodden, R.J. (1962). Excavations at the Early Neolithic site at Nea Nikomedia, Greek Macedonia (1961 season). *Proceedings of the Prehistoric Society* **28**:267–288.

_____(1964). Recent discoveries from prehistoric Macedonia: an interim report. *Balkan Studies* **5**:109–124.

_____(1965). An Early Neolithic village in Greece. *Scientific American* **212**(4):82–88.

Rondiri, V. (1985). Epifaneiaki kerameiki neolithikon theson tis Thessalias: katanomi sto choro. *Anthropologika* **8**:53–74.

Runnels, C.N. (1983). Trade and communication in prehistoric Greece. *Ekistics* **302**:417–420.

Runnels, C.N., and Hansen, J.M. (1986). The olive in the prehistoric Aegean: The evidence for domestication in the Early Bronze Age. *Oxford Journal of Archaeology* **5**:299–308.

Runnels, C.N, and van Andel, T.H. (1987). The evolution of settlement in the southern Argolid, Greece. An economic explanation. *Hesperia* **56**:303–334.

Rutter, J.B. (1993). Review of Aegean Prehistory II: The prepalatial Bronze Age of the Southern and Central Greek Mainland. *American Journal of Archaeology* **97**:745–797.

Sampson, A. (1981). *I Neolithiki kai I Protoelladiki I stin Euboia*, Arheion Euboïkon Meleton, Supplement 24, Athens.

_____(1989). Some chronological problems of the end of the Neolithic and Early Bronze Age. In Maniatis, Y. (ed.), *Archaeometry*, Amersterdam, Elsevier, pp. 709–718.

_____(1992). Late Neolithic remains at Tharrounia, Euboea: A model for the seasonal uses of settlement and caves. *Annual of the British School at Athens* **87**:61–101.

_____(1993). *Skoteni, Tharrounia: The Cave, The Settlement and The Cemetery*, Athens.

Saxe, A. (1970). *Social Dimensions of Mortuary Practices*. Doctoral dissertation, Department of Anthropology, University of Michigan, Ann Arbor.

_____(1971). Social dimensions of mortuary practices in a Mesolithic population from Wadi Halfa, Sudan. In Brown, J.A. (Ed.), *Approaches to the Social Dimensions of Mortuary Practices*, Memoirs of the Society for American Archaeology 25, Washington, D.C., pp. 39–57.

Schachermeyr, F. (1976). *Die agaische Frühzeit. 1: die vormykenischen Perioden*, Austrian Academy of Sciences, Vienna.

Schmidt P. (1997). *Iron Technology in East Africa: Symbolism, Science and Archaeology*, Indiana University Press, Bloomington/Indianapolis.

Schultz, M. (2001). Paleohistopathology of bone: A new approach to the study of ancient diseases. *Yearbook of Physical Anthropology* **44**:106–147.

Sears, W. H. 1961. The study of social and religious systems in North American archaeology. *Current Anthropology* **2**:223–246.

Seeman, M.F. (1979). The Hopewell interaction sphere: The evidence for interregional trde nd structural complexity. *Indiana Historical Society, Prehistoric Research Series* **5**: 235–438.

_____(1988). Ohio Hopewell trophy-skull artefacts as evidence for competition in Middle Woodland societies, Circa 50 B.C.-A.D. 350. *American Antiquity* **53**:565–577.

Séfériadès, M. 1992. L'outillage: le métal. In. Treuil, R. (Ed.), *Dikili Tash. Village préhistorique de Macédoine orientale. Fouilles de Jean Deshayes (1961–1975), Supplement XXVI du Bulletin du Correspondance du Hellenique*, Ecole Française d'Athènes, Athènes, pp. 113–119.

Shackleton, J.C. (1988). *Marine Molluscan Remains from Franchthi Cave*. Excavations at Francthi Cave, Greece 4, Indiana University Press, Bloomington.

Shanks, M., and Tilley, C. (1982). Ideology, symbolic power, and ritual communication: A reinterpretation of Neolithic mortuary practices. In Hodder, I. (Ed.), *Symbolic and Structural Archaeology*, Cambridge University Press, Cambridge, pp. 129–154.

Shaw, C.T. (1970). *Igbo-Ukwu: An Account of Archaeological Discoveries in Eastern Nigeria*, Faber, London.

Sherratt, A.G. (1981). Plough and pastoralism: aspects of the secondary products revolution. In, Hodder, I., Isaac, G., and Hammond, N., (Eds.), *Patterns of the Past: Studies in Honour of David E. Clarke*, Cambridge University Press, Cambridge, pp. 261–305.

_____(1983). The secondary exploitation of animals in the Old World. *World Archaeology* 15:90–104.

Sprague, R. (1968). A suggested terminology and classification for burial description. *American Antiquity* 33:479–485.

Sterner, J. (1992). Sacred pots and 'symbolic reservoirs' in the Mandara Highlands of Northern Cameroon. In David, N., and Sterner, J., (Eds.), *An African Commitment. Papers in Honour of Peter Lew Shirmie*, University of Calgary Press, Calgary, pp. 171–179.

Stickel, E.G. (1969). Status differentiation at the Rincon site. *Archaeological Survey Annual Report* 10:209–261.

Stone, E.C. (1997). City-states and their centres: The Mesopotamian example. In Nichols, D.L., and Charlton, T.H., (Eds.), *The Archaeology of City-States*, Smithsonian Institution Press, Washington, D.C., pp. 15–26.

Stos–Gale, Z.A. and C.F. Macdonald (1991). Sources of metal and trade in the Bronze Age Aegean. In Gale, N.H. (Ed.), *Bronze Age Trade in the Mediterranean*, Studies in Mediterranean Archaeology 90, Jonsered, pp. 249–288.

Stravopodi, E. (1993). An anthropological assessment of the human findings from the cave and the cemetery. In Sampson, A., *Skoteini, Tharrounia: The Cave, the Settlement and the Cemetery*, Athens, pp. 378–391.

Stuart–Macadam, P. (1987a). A radiographic study of porotic hyperostosis. *American Journal of Physical Anthropology* 74:511–520.

_____(1987b). Porotic hyperostosis: New evidence to support the anemia theory. *American Journal of Physical Anthropology* 74:521–526.

Sugiyama, S. (1992). World view materialized at Teotihuaca, Mexico. *Latin American Antiquity* 4:103–129.

Sutton, S.B. (1991). Population, economy, and settlement in post–revolutionary Keos: a cultural anthropological study. In Cherry, J.F., Davis, J.L., and Mantzourani, E. (Eds.), *Landscape Archaeology as Long–Term History: Northern Keos in the Cycladic Islands from Earliest Settlement until Modern Times*, UCLA Institute of Archaeology Press, Los Angeles, pp. 383–402.

_____(1994). Settlement patterns, settlement perceptions: Rethinking the Greek village, In Kardulis, N. (Ed.), *Beyond the Site: Regional Studies in the Aegean Area*, University Press of America, New York, pp. 313–335.

Tainter, J. (1975a). Social inference and mortuary practices: An experiment in numerical classification. *World Archaeology* 7: 1–15.

_____(1975b). *The Archaeological Study of Social Change: Woodland systems in West–central Illinois*. Doctoral dissertation, Northwestern University, University Microfilms, Ann Arbor.

_____(1977). Modeling change in prehistoric social systems. In Binford, L. (Ed.), *For Theory Building in Archaeology*, Academic Press, New York, pp. 327–351.

_____(1978). Mortuary practices and the study of prehistoric social systems. *Advances in Archaeological Methods and Theory* 1: 105–141.

_____(1989). *The Collapse of Complex Societies*, Cambridge University Press, Cambridge.

Tainter, J., and Cordy, R. (1977). An archaeological analysis of social ranking and residence groups in prehistoric Hawaii. *World Archaeology* 9:94–112.

Talalay, L.E. (1987). Rethinking the function of clay figurine legs from Neolithic Greece: an argument by analogy. *American Journal of Archaeology* 91:161–169.

_____(1991). Body imagery of the Ancient Aegean. *Archaeology* 44(4):46–49.

_____(1993). *Deities, dolls, and devices: Neolithic figurines from Franchthi Cave, Greece*, Excavations at Franchthi Cave. Greece 9, Indiana University Press, Bloomington.

Taylor, W. (1969). *A Study of Archaeology*, Southern Illinois University Press, Carbondale.

Thass-Thienemann, T. (1973). *The Interpretation of Language* (2 Vols.), Jason Aronson, New York.

Theochares, D.R. (1958). Ek tis prokeramikis Thessalias. *Thessalika* 1:70–86.

_____(1960). Ek tis prokeramikis Thessalias. *Archaeologika Deltion (Chronika)* 4: 63–83.

_____(1968). Anaskafai en Sesklo. *Praktika Arhaiologikis Etairias* 1968: 24–30.

_____(1973). *Neolithic Greece*. National Bank of Greece, Athens.

Treuil, R., Darcque, P., Poursat, J.-CL., and Touchais, G. (1989). *Les civilisations égéennes du Néolithique et de l'Age due Bronze*, Presses Universitaires de France, Novelle Clio, Paris.

Tsountas, C. (1908). *Ai proïstorikai akropoleis diminiou kai Seskou*, Sakellariou, Athens.

Tsuneki, A. (1989). The manufacture of *Spondylus* shell objects at Neolithic Dimini, Greece. *Orient* **25**:1–21.

Ubelaker, D. (1989). *Human Skeletal Remains: Excavation, Analysis, Interpretation*, Taraxacum, Washington, D.C.

Ucko, P. 1969: Ethnography and archaeological interpretation of funerary remains. *World Archaeology* **1**:262–280.

Van Andel, T.H., Runnels, C.N., and Pope, K.O. (1986). Five thousand years of land use and abuse in the Southern Argolid, Greece. *Hesperia* **55**:103–128.

Van Andel, T.H., and Sutton, S.B. (1987). *Landscape and people of the Franchthi Region*, Excavations at Francthi Cave. Greece 2, Indiana University Press, Bloomington.

Van Andel, T.H., Zangger, E., and Demitrack, A. (1990). Land use and soil erosion in prehistoric and historical Greece. *Journal of Field Archaeology* **17**:379–396.

Van Andel, T.H., and Runnels, C.N. (1987). *Beyond the Acropolis. A Rural Greek Past*, Standord University Press, Stanford.

_____(1995). The earliest farmers in Europe. *Antiquity* **69**:481–500.

Van Gennep, A. (1960). *The Rites of Passage*, The University of Chicago Press, Chicago.

Vehik, S.C. (1975). *Sociocultural Implications of Central European Early Bronze Age Mortuary Practices*. Unpublished Doctoral dissertation, Department of Anthropology, University of Missouri, Columbia.

Vermeule, E. (1964). *Greece in the Bronze Age*, The University of Chicago Press, Chicago.

Vitelli, K.D. (1974). *The Greek Neolithic Patterned Urfinis Ware from the Franchthi Cave and Lerna*, Doctoral dissertation, University Pennsylvania, Philadelphia.

_____(1984). Greek Neolithic pottery by experiment. In Rice, M.P. (Ed.), *Pots and Potters: Current Approaches in Ceramic Archaeology*, UCLA Institute of Archaeology, Monograph 24, Los Angeles, pp. 113–131.

_____(1989). Were pots first made for foods? Doubts from Franchthi Cave. *World Archaeology* **21**: 17–29.

_____(1991). The possible uses of plant extracts by prehistoric potters. Paper presented at the 1991 SAA meeting, New Orleans, LA.

_____(1993). *Franchthi Neolithic Pottery: Classification and Ceramic Phases 1 and 2*, Excavations at Franchthi Cave. Greece 8, Indiana University Press, Bloomington.

_____(1999). 'Looking up' at early ceramics in Greece. In Skibo, J.M., and Feinman, G.M. (Eds.), *Pottery and People: A Dynamic Interaction*, The University of Utah Press, Salt Lake City, pp. 184–198.

Von den Driesch, A. and K. Enderle 1976. Die Tierreste aus der Agio–Sofia Magula. In Milojĉić, V., von den Driesch, A., Enderle, K., Milojĉić–v.Zumbusch, J., and Kilian, K. (Eds.), *Die deutschen Asugrabungen auf Magulen um Larisa in Thessalien 1966. Agia Sofia–Magula. Karagyös–Magula. Bunar Basch*, Beiträge zur ur– und frühgeschichtlichen Archäologie des Mittelmeer–Kulturraumes 15, Rudolf Habelt, Bonn, pp. 15–54.

Wace, A.J., and Thompson, M.S. (1912). *Prehistoric Thessaly*, AMS Press, New York.

Wagstaff, M. (1968). Rural migration in Greece. *Geography* **5**:175–179.

Washburn, D.K. (1983). Symmetry analysis of ceramic design: Two tests of the methods on Neolithic material form Greece and the Aegean. In Washburn, D.K. (ed.), *Structure and Cognition in Art*, Cambridge University Press, Cambridge, pp. 138–164.

_____(1984). A study of the red on cream and cream on red designs on Early Neolithic ceramics from Nea Nikomedia. *American Journal of Anthropology* **88**: 305–324.

Wason, P.K. (1994). *The Archaeology of Rank*, Cambridge University Press, Cambridge.

Weinberg, S.S. (1962). Excavation at prehistoric Elateia, 1959. *Hesperia* **31**:158–209.

_____(1970). The Stone Age in the Aegean, in *Cambridge Ancient History 1, Part 1*, Cambridge University Press, Cambridge, pp. 557–672.

Wiessner, P. (1984). Reconsidering the behavioural basis for style: A case study among the Kalahari San. *Journal of Anthropological Archeology* **3**: 190–234.

Wickins, J. (1986). *The Archaeology and History of Cave Use in Attica, Greece, from Prehistoric through Late Roman Times*, Ph.D. dissertation, Indiana University, Bloomington.

Welbourn, A. (1984). Endo ceramics and power strategies. In Millder, D. and Tilley, C. (Eds.), *Ideology, Power, and Prehistory*, Cambridge University Press, Cambridge, pp. 17–24.

Wells, B., C.N. Runnels, and E. Zangger (1990). The Berbati–Limnes archaeological survey—the 1988 season. *Opuscula Atheniensia* **18**:207–238.

Whittle, A. (1996). *Europe in the Neolithic: The Creation of New Worlds*, Cambridge University Press, Cambridge.

Willey, G.R., and Sabloff, J.A. (1980). *A History of American Archaeology*, Thames and Hudson, London.

Winters, H.D. (1968). Value systems and trade cycles of the Late Archaic in the Midwest. In Binford, S.R., and Binford L.R. (Eds), *New Perspectives in Archaeology*, Aldine Press, Chicago, pp. 175–220.

Xirotiris, N.I. (1982). Apotelesmata ton anthropologike esetaseo ton kamenon osteon apo to Souphli Magoula and Platia Magoula Zarkou. In Gallis, G.A., *Kafseis Nekron apo tin Neolithiki Epochi sti Thessalia*, Athens, pp. 190–199.

Zachos, K. (1987). Ayios Dhimitrios, a Prehistoric Settlement in the Southwestern Peloponnesos: The Neolithic and Early Helladic Periods, Doctoral dissertation, Boston University, Boston.

———(1990). The Neolithic period in Naxos. In *Cycladic Culture. Naxos in the Third Millennium BC*, N.P. Goulandris Foundation, Museum of Cycladic Art, Athens, pp. 29-38.

———(1996a). Metallourgia. In Papathanasopoulos, G. (Ed.), *O Neolithikos Politismos stin Ellada*, Goulandris Foundation, Athens, pp. 140–143.

———(1996b). Kosminmata—Metallina. In Papathanasopoulos, G. (Ed.), *O Neolithikos Politismos stin Ellada*, Goulandris Foundation, Athens, pp. 166–167.

Zangger, E. (1991). Prehistoric coastal environments in Greece: The vanished landscapes of Dimini Bay and Lake Lerna. *Journal of Field Archaeology* **18**:1–15.

www.ingramcontent.com/pod-product-compliance
Lightning Source LLC
Chambersburg PA
CBHW061001030426
42334CB00033B/3321